SALUTE TO THE
ARMED FORCES
WORD SEARCH

SALUTE TO THE ARMED FORCES WORD SEARCH

THUNDER BAY
P·R·E·S·S

San Diego, California

Thunder Bay Press
An imprint of Printers Row Publishing Group
9717 Pacific Heights Blvd, San Diego, CA 92121
www.thunderbaybooks.com • mail@thunderbaybooks.com

Copyright © 2025 Printers Row Publishing Group

All rights reserved. No part of this publication may be reproduced, distributed, or transmitted in any form or by any means, including photocopying, recording, or other electronic or mechanical methods, without the prior written permission of the publisher, except in the case of brief quotations embodied in critical reviews and certain other noncommercial uses permitted by copyright law.

Printers Row Publishing Group is a division of Readerlink Distribution Services, LLC.
Thunder Bay Press is a registered trademark of Readerlink Distribution Services, LLC.

Correspondence regarding the content of this book should be sent to Thunder Bay Press, Editorial Department, at the above address.

Publisher: Peter Norton • Associate Publisher: Ana Parker
Editorial Director: April Graham
Art Director: Charles McStravick
Editor: Traci Douglas
Production Team: Beno Chan, Julie Greene

Cover image credit: MariaArefyeva via iStock/Getty Images Plus

ISBN: 978-1-6672-0869-5

Printed in Dongguan, China

29 28 27 26 25   1 2 3 4 5

INTRODUCTION

There are more than 18 million Americans alive today who have served in the United States military, and tens of millions more service members who answered the call to duty throughout the nation's history, in peacetime and in war.

Within the pages of this book, you'll find a tribute to American veterans and active-duty service members, past and present. There is plenty of trivia, facts and figures, historical accounts, and tales of heroism to help you learn about—and honor—the Soldiers, Sailors, Marines, Airmen, Guardians, and Coast Guardsmen who protect and defend the country we call home. An accompanying puzzle for each article tests your knowledge and trains your brain while you discover more about our military.

Join us in a salute to the men and women of America's Armed Forces!

SALUTE TO THE ARMED FORCES!

Air Force
Army
Coast Guard
Commitment
Courage
Dedication

Defend
Discipline
Duty
Enlisted
Fight
Freedom

History
Honor
Marine Corps
Navy
Officer
Sacrifice

Service
Space Force
Tradition
Troops
Valor
Veteran

ARE YOU QUALIFIED?

*Not everyone interested in joining the Armed Forces is qualified.
Different jobs and branches have different requirements.
Below are the basic requirements for joining the U.S. Army
as an enlisted Soldier or as an officer.
Do you meet the qualifications?*

ENLISTED

Enlisted Soldiers perform important day-to-day operations and must ensure the success of their units' missions. The basic requirements for joining are:

- Be between 17 and 35 years old.
- Be medically and physically fit.
- Be a U.S. citizen or permanent resident with a valid Green Card.
- Have a high school diploma or the equivalent.
- Earn a minimum score on the Army's entrance test.

OFFICER

Officers lead missions, make important decisions, and ensure the safety of the Soldiers under their command. The requirements to join the Army as an officer include:

- Be at least 17 but under 31 in the year of commissioning as an officer, or under 27 if you commission from the U.S. Military Academy at West Point.
- Be medically and physically fit.
- Be a U.S. citizen by the time you commission as an officer.
- Be a college graduate by the time you're commissioned as an officer.
- Complete a background check, questionnaire, and interview.
- Provide the required documentation for a security clearance.

ARE YOU QUALIFIED?

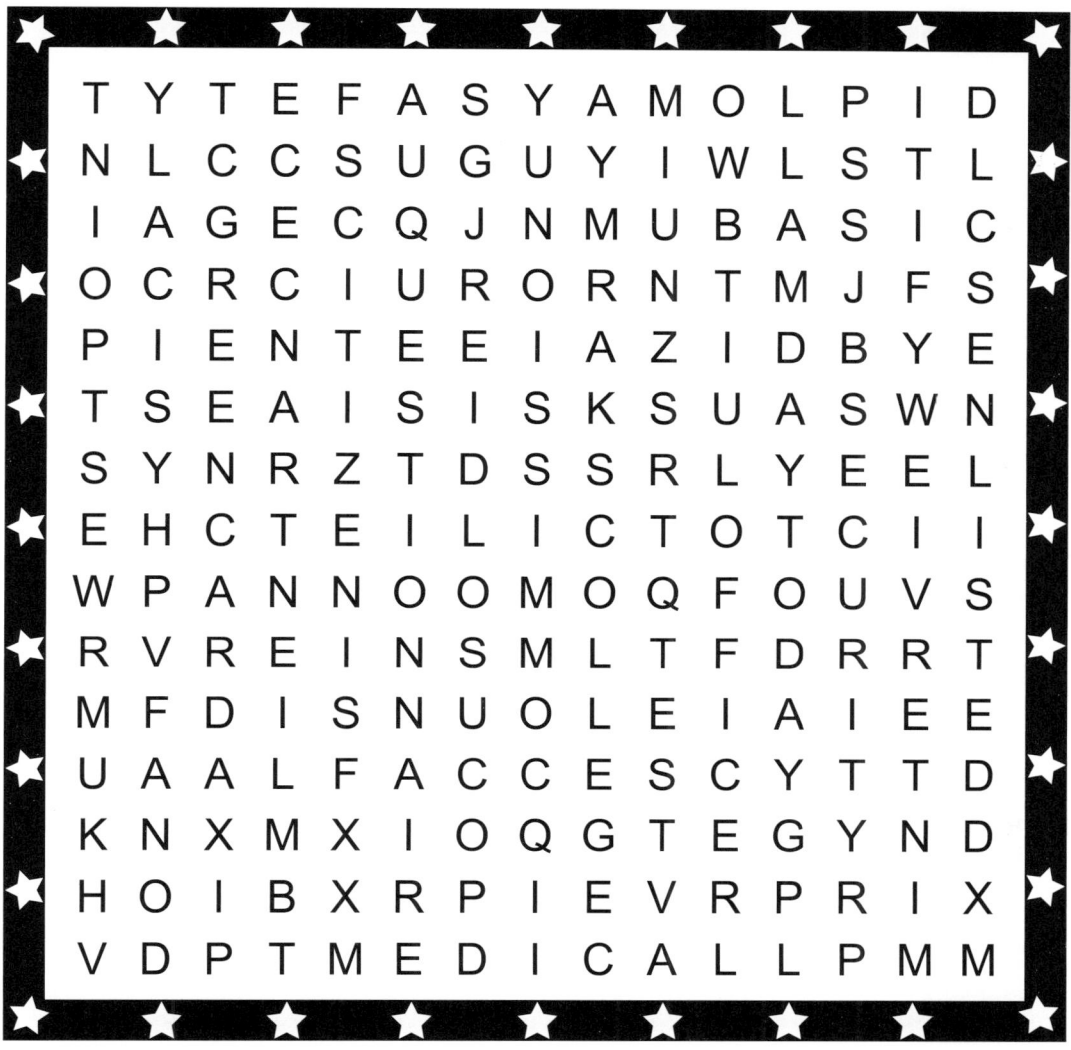

Army
Basic
Citizen
College
Commission
Day-to-day

Diploma
Enlisted
Entrance
Fit
Green card
Interview

Medical
Missions
Officer
Physical
Questionnaire
Safety

Security
Soldier
Success
Test
Unit
West Point

FUN FACTS

*Learn more about our Armed Forces
with these bits of trivia.*

★ The Department of Defense (DOD) is the nation's largest employer. There are nearly 1.29 million personnel on active duty and another 1.1 million National Guard and Reserve personnel.

★ The majority of active-duty service members—more than one-third—are under age 25. There are more than 100,000 over the age of 40, the smallest age group. The branch with the oldest members is the Space Force, where the average age of a Guardian is 31.4 years. The youngest branch is the Marine Corps: the average Marine is 25.3 years old, and 63 percent of all Marines are under age 25.

★ The U.S. Army is the largest branch, with more than 450,000 Soldiers on active duty. The smallest branch is the Space Force, with just under 9,000.

★ Active-duty troop levels peaked at more than 3 million during the Vietnam War and have declined since; numbers have remained relatively stable, at around 1.5 million, since the late 1990s.

★ Women make up about 17.5 percent of active-duty forces. The Navy and Air Force are the two branches with the most women, each with 21 percent of active-duty personnel being female.

★ The DOD owns nearly 30 million acres of land worldwide, and is the largest consumer of energy in the United States.

★ Because a high school diploma or GED is a requirement of joining, 99 percent of the U.S. military has a high school education. Only 60 percent of the general population has the same.

★ In 2022, the United States spent $877 billion on the military, making it the world's leader in military spending.

★ Think a uniform is a uniform? The Army, Air Force, and Space Force all share the same camouflage pattern, but the Navy has its own distinct pattern, and the Marine Corps has two (desert and woodland). Each branch also has other uniforms, including service uniforms and dress uniforms; in some branches, these vary by season and by rank.

FUN FACTS

```
S M N S P A C E F O R C E N P
E E A F Y Y D Y P H L W E A X
N D T J V I L M G J Q W C I S
I I I K A A P V S R J V I D S
R P O D N A L Q E S E E V R E
A L N F P J P E A K B N R A R
M O A G V D R L S X Y O E U D
U M L R I N E M O W L F S G A
T A G V E Q F S N D N J P F L
R D U Y T D S P E N D I N G H
E R A H N N A S A R P W U C R
S A R R A U T E E E C F N Z U
E N D P M Z N B L W E A B M A
D K W E A Y R E S E R V E U G
U N I F O R M F T B C I Y J Y
```

Acres	Energy	Navy	Service
Army	Guardian	Oldest	Space Force
Branch	Land	Peak	Spending
Desert	Leader	Rank	Uniform
Diploma	Marines	Reserve	Vietnam
Dress	National Guard	Season	Women

IN THE ARMY NOW

★ ★ ★ ★ ★ ★ ★ ★ ★ ★ ★ ★ ★

If you were a male under the age of 40 in 1942, you had to carry a Selective Service card. Then the local draft board could send you a letter of induction beginning with the word* Greetings *and indicating the date and time you were expected to report to your local draft board for transportation to the induction center. Joining the military has changed since then!

Inductions took place in a single day, often beginning in the predawn darkness. First, men filed into a long assembly line for a physical examination, with about 25 men passing through the process per hour. They came into the examination area in just their briefs, with an identifying number marked on the back of their hands. A few hours later, they emerged from the end of the building, either accepted or rejected.

The strange, intimidating atmosphere accelerated heartbeats and contributed to dysfunctional behavior—some men couldn't urinate into a cup; others did so on the floor. Most inductees found it uncomfortable to answer the numerous personal questions; many men with ailments tried to conceal them. To check for mental infirmities, a psychiatrist might ask, "Why does the sun rise in the morning and set at night?" for which even people of average intelligence and education struggled for the right answer.

Those who wanted to avoid service used various techniques like doping themselves with aspirin to elevate their heartbeat or ingesting substances to increase their blood pressure. Fainting could happen—sometimes genuine and sometimes faked—but doctors and sergeants kept the line moving. Unless a man was morbidly obese, had a significant physical disability, or was afflicted with a medical condition such as epilepsy, venereal disease, or flat feet, he would be fingerprinted and checked against FBI files. Those who passed the screenings were interviewed briefly and asked what branch of service they preferred.

The new draftees signed their induction papers and received a serial number with instructions to memorize it. Then the officer in charge assembled the men, ordered them to raise their right hand, and administered the Selective Service's oath of allegiance. The inductees received a two-week furlough and were sent home to settle their personal affairs with the reminder, "You're in the Army now."

Those who failed the physical exam went home with their new classifications—and occasionally with regrets or mixed emotions. Some of the "misdiagnosed" promptly enlisted in another branch of the service.

IN THE ARMY NOW

```
Q S E R J A S P I R I N P H K
Z M C O B H L A N O S R E P P
N S C R T D R A C J E L K R E
P E X A E D W A T D L J E S P
S R O P C E R L A X R B F D O
Y V R H R T N W A R M Y I R D
C I E Y E P N I Q U W S N A S
H C C S J E Q H N V E G G F E
I E I I E C Q A V G I N E T T
A B F C C C H C X D V I R B A
T R F A T A Y N X Q R T P O N
R A O L E S V F O B E E R A I
I N Z I D Y B O O T T E I R R
S C S T N E M L I A N R N D U
T H G U O L R U F D I G T O K
```

Accepted	Card	Interview	Predawn
Ailments	Dope	Number	Psychiatrist
Army	Draft board	Oath	Rejected
Aspirin	Fingerprint	Officer	Screening
Avoid	Furlough	Personal	Service branch
Briefs	Greetings	Physical	Urinate

DOG TAGGED

★ ★ ★ ★ ★ ★ ★ ★ ★ ★ ★ ★

Learn about the history of military identification tags.

Only 58 percent of the soldiers killed in action during the American Civil War were positively identified. Fighters had a legitimate concern that if they were killed, their families would never know what happened to them—other than that they were missing in action. Soldiers started writing their names on a piece of paper or a handkerchief and pinning it to their clothing before going into battle. Some carved their names into small wooden disks, then hanging the disks from their necks with a piece of string. Others made their own ID tags by grinding off one side of a coin and etching their name on it.

Eventually, retail merchants started producing and selling metal disks to soldiers. During the Civil War, *Harper's Weekly* magazine advertised "soldier's pins" made of silver or gold and etched with a soldier's name and unit. These were similar to the identification tags worn by dogs, so it wasn't long before soldiers began referring to their own ID tags as "dog tags."

By the 1890s, the U.S. Army and Navy were experimenting with metal identification tags for recruits. ID tags were first officially issued to U.S. Army troops in 1906. During World War I, French soldiers wore a bracelet with a metal disk called a *plaque d'identité* engraved with their name, rank, and formation. When America entered the war in 1917, all U.S. Soldiers were issued two aluminum tags stamped by hand with their name, rank, serial number, unit, and religion. The tags were suspended from their necks by cord or tape.

By World War II, dog tags were rectangular with rounded ends, and stamped by machine. The tags were first made of brass and later of a corrosion-resistant alloy of nickel and copper. By the end of the war, all tags were made of stainless steel. They were suspended from the neck by a rope, a beaded chain, or a stainless-steel wire with a plastic cover.

During the Vietnam War, Soldiers started taping their tags together so that they wouldn't make any noise and give away their position. By the end of the war, rubber covers were issued to keep the tags silent. A soldier often put one tag in his boot, in case his body was dismembered and normal means of identification were no longer possible. That method remains in place today.

DOG TAGGED

```
Z W E A T Y T I R T J U Y S N
S V M K L N I A H C W B Q N I
B V A E B S N O I G I L E R O
U M N P N H U J R A N K J B C
L N X V M G Z I Y R O P E A H
D P S T I U R C E R T B U K W
Y L F N E T N A W C A E S O G
Q R O G I L L I V I P M O M A
R S R G Q P E I M E E D Z I T
U P M L N B K C Q U D B S S G
B A A B W R C E A I L I I S O
B P T W I A I Y S R L A D I D
E E I O P S N K F V B N T N O
R R O U N S Q M E M S T A G R
M Y N U U I H R S X S Y G S R
```

Aluminum · Engraved · Nickel · Rope
Bracelet · Formation · Paper · Rubber
Brass · Gold · Pins · Silver
Chain · ID tag · Rank · Tape
Coin · Missing · Recruits · Unit
Dog tag · Name · Religion · Wood disk

U.S. AIR FORCE BASES

*The U.S. Air Force has numerous stateside bases and installations.
Is there one located near you?*

ALABAMA
Maxwell Air Force Base

ALASKA
Eielson Air Force Base
Elmendorf Air Force Base

ARIZONA
Davis-Monthan Air Force Base
Luke Air Force Base

ARKANSAS
Little Rock Air Force Base

CALIFORNIA
Beale Air Force Base
Edwards Air Force Base
Travis Air Force Base
Vandenberg Air Force Base

DELAWARE
Dover Air Force Base

FLORIDA
Eglin Air Force Base
Hurlburt Field
MacDill Air Force Base
Tyndall Air Force Base

GEORGIA
Moody Air Force Base
Robins Air Force Base

HAWAII
Hickam Air Force Base

IDAHO
Mountain Home Air Force Base

ILLINOIS
Scott Air Force Base

KANSAS
McConnell Air Force Base

LOUISIANA
Barksdale Air Force Base

MASSACHUSETTS
Hanscom Air Force Base

MISSISSIPPI
Columbus Air Force Base
Keesler Air Force Base

MISSOURI
Whiteman Air Force Base

MONTANA
Malmstrom Air Force Base

NEBRASKA
Offutt Air Force Base

NEVADA
Creech Air Force Base
Nellis Air Force Base

NEW MEXICO
Cannon Air Force Base
Holloman Air Force Base
Kirtland Air Force Base

NORTH CAROLINA
Pope Army Airfield
Seymour Johnson Air Force Base

NORTH DAKOTA
Grand Forks Air Force Base
Minot Air Force Base

OHIO
Wright-Patterson Air Force Base

OKLAHOMA
Altus Air Force Base
Tinker Air Force Base
Vance Air Force Base

SOUTH CAROLINA
Shaw Air Force Base

SOUTH DAKOTA
Ellsworth Air Force Base

TEXAS
Dyess Air Force Base
Goodfellow Air Force Base
Lackland Air Force Base
Laughlin Air Force Base
Randolph Air Force Base
Sheppard Air Force Base

UTAH
Hill Air Force Base

WASHINGTON
Fairchild Air Force Base
McChord Field

WYOMING
F. E. Warren Air Force Base

U.S. AIR FORCE BASES

```
W Q E D W A R D S S X N V R G
M O C S N A H U B D K A A E O
F S Z I M I X F F N C H N V O
H P L O D N A R S S O T D O D
J G O R Y H D C N S R N E D F
E D N V I R O I Y B E O N E E
Y Q Z L O T B A E A L M B L L
X T U H T O J A L R T S E L L
V K C S R T L T A H T I R S O
E C R S Y E U Z U I I V G W W
M E I E L S O N G C L A M O B
T S W Y H C B D H K G D V R M
M A C D I L L L A D N Y T D
L O A B U R I U I M Z J P H E
E M O H N I A T N U O M H L H
```

Altus	Eglin	Laughlin	Mountain Home
Beale	Eielson	Little Rock	Randolph
Davis-Monthan	Ellsworth	Luke	Robins
Dover	Goodfellow	MacDill	Scott
Dyess	Hanscom	McChord	Tyndall
Edwards	Hickam	Moody	Vandenberg

SPACE FORCE FAST FACTS

★ ★ ★ ★ ★ ★ ★ ★ ★ ★ ★ ★ ★

Here are six facts about America's sixth—and newest—branch of the Armed Forces.

1. The Space Force was officially instituted on December 20, 2019, through signing of legislation by President Donald Trump. It previously existed as the Air Force Space Command, instituted in 1982. The purpose of the institution isn't to fight in space, but to protect the nation's assets (such as satellites) in orbit, to detect missile launches, and to provide GPS targeting for missiles. Another purpose was to consolidate military space activities from across the Department of Defense.

2. The branch's motto is *Semper Supra*, meaning "always above." Their official song is also called "Semper Supra" and was released in 2022.

3. The service chief for the United States Space Force is the Chief of Space Operations. The first Chief was General John W. Raymond, who was also the first Guardian sworn in as the inaugural official member of the Force. The position is currently held by General B. Chance Saltzman. The Chief Master Sergeant of the Space Force—the most senior enlisted member of the organization—is John F. Bentivegna, who has been in the position since 2023.

4. In September 2020, about 2,400 troops transferring into the Space Force were sworn in during a virtual mass ceremony. In December of that year, the first seven people to directly enlist in the branch graduated from basic training at Texas's Joint Base San Antonio–Lackland.

5. Space Force's first combat operations took place in January 2020, when it provided U.S. troops at Al Asad Airbase in Iraq with early warning of Iranian Islamic Revolutionary Guard Corps missile strikes.

6. The current uniforms were a cost-saving measure: they're modeled on current Army and Air Force uniforms. But Guardians (members of the Space Force) are set to get their own service dress uniform in 2025.

SPACE FORCE FAST FACTS

```
K R C E R E M O N Y J P E S U
Z E J W G O I N O T N A N A S
E F L N E W E S T L R A Q T F
S S S T C O N S O L I D A T E
E N X T R R W L Y R A L O F K
M A Y B L O V W F S A U G L V
P R I X R S A O M S L G N A F
E T V N T R R A E W N D C Q
R V I R N C O D A L S I N K H
S N U I E F X D I I P T O L C
U M N N I K O E R S G E M A U
P G E N L I S T B S L G Y N H
R U U E O L K E A I F R A D C
A H V O X E V C S M M A R M Y
S A T E L L I T E S X T K E S
```

Air Force	Detect	Missiles	Semper supra
Airbase	Early warning	Newest	Sworn in
Al Asad	Enlist	Orbit	Targeting
Army	GPS	Raymond	Transfer
Ceremony	Lackland	San Antonio	Trump
Consolidate	Launch	Satellites	Uniforms

GOT WHAT IT TAKES? U.S. MARINE FORCES SPECIAL OPERATIONS COMMAND

★ ★ ★ ★ ★ ★ ★ ★ ★ ★ ★ ★

To be eligible for an elite unit in the Armed Forces, candidates must meet or exceed fitness standards, then go through rigorous training. Learn what it takes to be a member of the United States Marine Forces Special Operations Command.

Known as MARSOC, the Marines' program is the newest component of the U.S. Special Operations Command, having been activated in 2006. These Marines are responsible for conducting direct action, foreign internal defense, special reconnaissance, unconventional warfare, and counterterrorism in other nations. MARSOC emphasizes the ability to work seamlessly in a foreign environment by learning new languages and understanding different cultures.

To qualify for the MARSOC training, Marines need a score of 225 on the U.S. Marines physical fitness test, which requires:

- 15 pull-ups, no time limit (20 to be competitive);
- 75 sit-ups in 2 minutes (100 to be competitive);
- 3-mile run in 22:10 (under 18:00 to be competitive).
- In addition, candidates must pass a swimming test that involves a 25-meter underwater swim, rifle retrieval, tower jump, 30-minute water tread, 5-minute flotation with trousers, and a timed 500-meter swim. An aptitude test and psychological evaluation are also conducted.

Candidates who pass the initial screening are then subjected to an assessment course, a two-week program to determine whether a Marine has the maturity, intelligence, determination, and physical attributes necessary to be a member of MARSOC. From there, the selected Marines spend the next six months in courses to acquire new language, cultural, tactical, and technical skills. When they are assigned to their 14-member units, they receive even more specialized training based on their upcoming assignments.

GOT WHAT IT TAKES? U.S. MARINE FORCES SPECIAL OPERATIONS COMMAND

```
D I R E C T A C T I O N T D O
S E N I R A M A L R E T I L E
E R U T L U C D S P U L L U P
M P A R E T A W R E D N U W R
L U Y R I E V A L U A T I O N
A Z Z C R G M A T U R I T Y J
N E A T T R O U S E R S H S G
G L F G T R W R P M A R S O C
U M R G I A F L O T A T I O N
A O Y F R N O S P U T I S J H
G Z L F K T N E M S S E S S A
E E A P T I T U D E Q W Q U J
O R E C N E G I L L E T N I P
E D E T E R M I N A T I O N Q
G L A C I N H C E T T U S C V
```

- Aptitude
- Assessment
- Culture
- Determination
- Direct action
- Elite
- Evaluation
- Flotation
- Intelligence
- Language
- Marines
- MARSOC
- Maturity
- Pull-ups
- Rifle
- Rigorous
- Sit-ups
- Tactical
- Technical
- Tread
- Trousers
- Underwater
- Unit
- Warfare

UNITED STATES COAST GUARD (USCG) RANKS

Coast Guardsmen in the United States Coast Guard may be enlisted, warrant officers, or commissioned officers. Coast Guard ranks designate job responsibilities and utilize the below names. At the E9 level, different positions exist at the same pay grade; the title depends on the Guardsman's job. Warrant officers receive a commission upon promotion to chief warrant officer 2, but they remain specialists or experts in their area; commissioned officers are generalists.

GRADE	RANK	ABBREVIATION
E1	Seaman Recruit	SR
E2	Seaman Apprentice	SA
E3	Seaman	SN
E4	Petty Officer Third Class	PO3
E5	Petty Officer Second Class	PO2
E6	Petty Officer First Class	PO1
E7	Chief Petty Officer	CPO
E8	Senior Chief Petty Officer	SCPO
E9	Master Chief Petty Officer	MCPO
	Fleet/Command Master Chief Petty Officer	CMC
	Master Chief Petty Officer of the Coast Guard	MCPOCG
W2	Chief Warrant Officer 2	CWO2
W3	Chief Warrant Officer 3	CWO3
W4	Chief Warrant Officer 4	CWO4
O1	Ensign	ENS
O2	Lieutenant Junior Grade	LTJG
O3	Lieutenant	LT
O4	Lieutenant Commander	LCDR
O5	Commander	CDR
O6	Captain	CAPT
O7	Rear Admiral Lower Half	RDML
O8	Rear Admiral Upper Half	RADM
O9	Vice Admiral	VADM
O10	Admiral	ADM
	Fleet Admiral (reserved for wartime only)	FADM

UNITED STATES COAST GUARD (USCG) RANKS

```
T B L F C L I E U T E N A N T
E R N J O T H I R D C L A S S
X E A M M I L N E J W O T V V
P C M D M Q G N R E C R U I T
E I A U I I L E P A T T G N T
R F E H S I Z R P S S R C P W
T F S N S E O P I I E L H A A
T O E T I M R L L T E I I Y R
V L E D O E A A S V X S E G R
D D O T N R I A E U X I F R A
S V I T E C M L O H S E M A N
R O I N E S G F J Y T F X D T
N C E P E T T Y O F F I C E R
E G S C O M M A N D E R M I X
R F V I C E A D M I R A L B F
```

Apprentice	Expert	Officer	Senior
Chief	Generalist	Pay grade	Specialist
Commander	Level	Petty Officer	Third class
Commission	Lieutenant	Promotion	Title
Enlisted	Master	Recruit	Vice admiral
Ensign	Names	Seaman	Warrant

NOTABLE QUOTABLES: EXPRESSING GRATITUDE

★ ★ ★ ★ ★ ★ ★ ★ ★ ★ ★ ★ ★

- ★ "There is nothing stronger than the heart of a volunteer." —General James H. Doolittle

- ★ "No man is entitled to the blessings of freedom unless he be vigilant in its preservation." —General Douglas MacArthur

- ★ "This will remain the land of the free so long as it is the home of the brave." —Elmer Davis

- ★ "Word to the Nation: Guard zealously your right to serve in the Armed Forces, for without them, there will be no other rights to guard." —President John F. Kennedy

- ★ "America without her Soldiers would be like God without His angels." —Claudia Pemberton

- ★ "What counts is not necessarily the size of the dog in the fight—it's the size of the fight in the dog." —General Dwight D. Eisenhower

- ★ "The patriot's blood is the seed of freedom's tree." —Thomas Campbell

- ★ "I only regret that I have but one life to lose for my country." —Captain Nathan Hale

- ★ "The most precious commodity with which the Army deals is the individual soldier who is the heart and soul of our combat forces." —General J. Lawton Collins

- ★ "America is hope. It is compassion. It is excellence. It is valor." —Paul Tsongas

- ★ "These fallen heroes represent the character of a nation who has a long history of patriotism and honor—and a nation who has fought many battles to keep our country free from threats of terror." —Michael N. Castle

- ★ "True heroism is remarkably sober, very undramatic. It is not the urge to surpass all others at whatever cost, but the urge to serve others at whatever cost." —Arthur Ashe

- ★ "It is foolish and wrong to mourn the men who died. Rather, we should thank God that such men lived." —General George S. Patton

- ★ "Some people live an entire lifetime and wonder if they have ever made a difference in the world, but the Marines don't have that problem." —President Ronald Reagan

- ★ "We don't know them all, but we owe them all." —Unknown

NOTABLE QUOTABLES: EXPRESSING GRATITUDE

```
O U M G N O T T A P V J G U Y
D R A U G H P W M R I C O E J
M T B R A V E L C L G G P V U
S R P L H F V I N O I S A R S
I E E E S E C F Y F L N T E G
O E H L M S A E R D A L R S N
R T N S O B D R H M N I I Z I
E N W U A X E Q T O T Y O N S
H U L E D D T R S C P K T T S
S L V R J C C X T A O E J H E
I O R E A G A N U O G N D G L
V V U S K Z N E W J N N F I B
A S T Y M R K C B B F E O F K
D L T S D N C A O Y H D Q S J
E E I S E N H O W E R Y B O T
```

Ashe	Eisenhower	Hope	Reagan
Blessings	Fight	Kennedy	Serve
Brave	Guard	Life	Soul
Castle	Hale	Patriot	Tsongas
Collins	Heart	Patton	Vigilant
Davis	Heroism	Pemberton	Volunteer

ACRONYMS AND ABBREVIATIONS

★ ★ ★ ★ ★ ★ ★ ★ ★ ★ ★ ★ ★

FYI, the military has a lot of acronyms and abbreviations. Seasoned vets will recognize them, but civilians may need some help. Here are just a few of them.

AIT or "A school": Advanced individual training. This is the hands-on career training and instruction that service members engage in before being qualified to do their specific jobs. Each branch handles this in a different way.

ASVAB: Armed Services Vocational Aptitude Battery. This multiple-choice test is given to prospective recruits before they enlist to test their qualifications for enlisting and determine what jobs they might be suited for.

BAH: Basic allowance for housing. The additional compensation service members receive to pay for off-base housing if government quarters aren't available.

CO: Commanding officer, the individual in charge of a military unit.

CONUS/OCONUS: Continental United States, or CONUS, is the 48 contiguous states plus the District of Columbia; OCONUS is outside the continental U.S.

DOD: Department of Defense, the department of the federal government that oversees military operations.

FOB: Forward operating base. A secure temporary position from which a military unit can carry out operations.

LES: Leave and earnings statement. Similar to a civilian paycheck, recording pay, taxes, and withholdings, but also stating the service member's leave balance.

MEPS: Military Entrance Processing Station, where new service members take their ASVAB, get a physical, and swear in to their chosen branch.

NCO: Non-commissioned officer, an enlisted service member who has earned a position through promotion through the ranks rather than through commission.

OPSEC: Operational security. This is the process by which service members identify and protect sensitive information.

PCS: Permanent change of station. Active-duty service members may relocate from one duty station to another every few years.

PT: Physical training, key for helping service members meet and maintain required fitness standards.

ACRONYMS AND ABBREVIATIONS

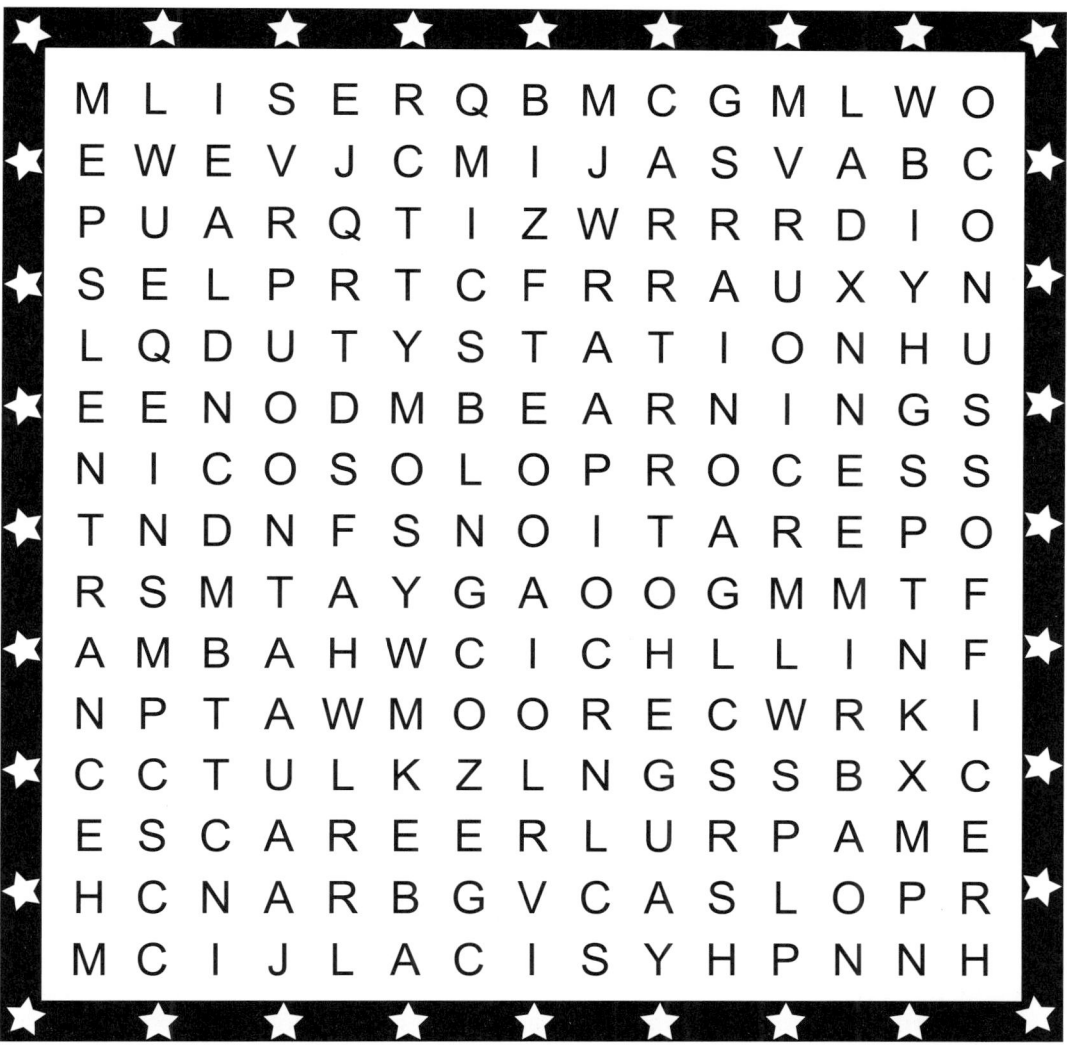

A School
Allowance
ASVAB
BAH
Branch
Career

CONUS
DOD
Duty station
Earnings
Entrance
FOB

Leave
LES
MEPS
NCO
OCONUS
Officer

Operations
OPSEC
PCS
Physical
Process
Unit

BATTLE OF ANTIETAM

★ ★ ★ ★ ★ ★ ★ ★ ★ ★ ★ ★ ★

September 17, 1862, was the deadliest single-day battle in American history, but was key to a Union victory in the Civil War.

Confederate General Robert E. Lee—eager to move the Civil War's fighting out of the South and into Union territory—pressed the full force of his army into battle when he invaded Maryland in September 1862. The Union Army saw a victory as the Battle of South Mountain and the Confederates countered with a victory at the Battle of Harpers Ferry, leading Lee to select an area near Antietam Creek as the best strategic position to make his last stand. He gathered his forces there on September 15. Union Major General George B. McClellan sent his forces in response on September 16. At dawn the next morning, McClellan attacked.

Union forces outnumbered the Confederates by nearly two to one, but the Confederates had an early advantage, with Lieutenant General Stonewall Jackson's men holding strategic ground and Union Soldiers forced to abandon another key defensive position. The Union's final assault in the afternoon, led by Major General Ambrose E. Burnside, pushed the Confederate forces over the bridge at Antietam Creek, but a Confederate division arriving after a 17-mile march from Harpers Ferry enabled the Confederates to drive back the Union assault.

The fierce fighting throughout the day ended with more than 22,0000 casualties on both sides, with especially high numbers of officers killed or wounded. Though the two sides continued to skirmish over the next two days, Lee withdrew from the battlefield and McClellan did not renew his attacks, leading the battle to be considered a tactical draw. Despite this—and inspired by the Confederates failing to push to the Federal capital—President Abraham Lincoln used the opportunity to issue his Emancipation Proclamation on September 22. The announcement promised to free all slaves from Southern states if the Confederates refused to lay down their arms by January 1, 1863. The Proclamation changed not only the course of the war, but of American history.

BATTLE OF ANTIETAM

Abandon	Casualties	Lee	Position
Antietam	Civil War	Lincoln	Skirmish
Assault	Creek	Maryland	Strategic
Battle	Deadliest	McClellan	Union
Bridge	Defensive	Morning	Victory
Burnside	Jackson	Officers	Withdraw

THE AIRMAN'S CREED

★ ★ ★ ★ ★ ★ ★ ★ ★ ★ ★ ★ ★

I am an American Airman.
I am a Warrior.
I have answered my Nation's call.

I am an American Airman.
My mission is to Fly, Fight, and Win.
I am faithful to a Proud Heritage,
A Tradition of Honor,
And a Legacy of Valor.

I am an American Airman.
Guardian of Freedom and Justice,
My Nation's Sword and Shield,
Its Sentry and Avenger.
I defend my Country with my Life.

I am an American Airman.
Wingman, Leader, Warrior.
I will never leave an Airman behind,
I will never falter,
And I will not fail.

The Airman's Creed was introduced by General T. Michael Moseley, Air Force Chief of Staff, in 2007; his purpose in introducing the creed was, in part, to "reinvigorate the warrior ethos in every Airman of our Total Force." The creed provides each member of the Air Force with a value structure and a tangible statement of the beliefs that govern their service.

"I am an American Airman" is repeated throughout the creed; so is the word "warrior." The creed emphasizes that Air Force members are defenders of the nation, called to fight for the United States, its freedoms, and the Constitution.

THE AIRMAN'S CREED

```
J Q S D S L E I X C F N X D L
F H E L E E N A M G N I W V U
T H U E G G V A K S T W G G F
Z S L I A A Y Y L X O E Z H H
S W A H T C I B U E F H B U T
E O V S I Y V R E A A L T Z I
R R L H R D M F M L X D Y E A
V D H O E D E E T A I E E M F
I A E Y H D R F X L N E O R F
C W L K H I E O E T L S F J R
E O U O C U T E R N E A P S E
F C W A R R I O R L D G C A E
G B N E P K V I E C X S Y T D
W K U V D P H Y J X F G H E O
S E N T R Y P L F W T P I E M
```

Airman	Ethos	Leader	Sword
American	Faithful	Legacy	Valor
Beliefs	Fight	Moseley	Values
Call	Fly	Sentry	Warrior
Creed	Freedom	Service	Win
Defend	Heritage	Shield	Wingman

WEAPONS OF WAR

★ ★ ★ ★ ★ ★ ★ ★ ★ ★ ★ ★ ★ ★

What is a Marine (or a Soldier, or a Sailor, or an Airman . . .) without a weapon?
These are just some of the individual weapons currently used by the U.S. Armed Forces.

BAYONETS AND KNIVES

Aircrew Survival Egress Knife (Marine Corps and Army aircrews)
M9 bayonet
M7 bayonet
M11 knife (explosive ordnance disposal)
OKC-3S bayonet (Marine Corps)
Ka-Bar combat knife
Gerber Mark II dagger
MK 3 knife (Navy SEALs)
Strider SMF (Marine Corps)
Tomahawk
Entrenching tool

GRENADES

M67 fragmentation grenade
AN/M14 thermite grenade
AN/M18 colored smoke grenade
M7A3 CS gas grenade
M47 riot control grenade

SIDEARMS

Beretta M9
SIG Sauer M11
SIG Sauer M17
SIG Sauer M18
Heckler & Koch P11 underwater pistol
Glock Mk 26 Mod 0 (Glock 26) (United States Special Operations Command)
M45A1 CQBP Close Quarters Battle Pistol (Marine Corps)

RIFLES

XM7 (Army)
M16A4 (Marine Corps and Army)
M16A3 (Navy SEALs and Seabees)
M27 IAR Infantry Automatic Rifle (Marine Corps Automatic Rifleman)
M38 SDMR Squad Designated Marksman Rifle (Marine Corps Designated Marksmen)
M39 Enhanced Marksman Rifle (Marine Corps Designated Marksmen/Scout Snipers)
SIG Sauer 716 G2 (Joint Special Operations Command)

CARBINES

M4A1
XM7 (Army)
GAU-5A ASDW Aircrew Self-Defense Weapon (Air Force)
Mk 16 Mod 0 (Army Rangers)
Heckler & Koch HK416 (Joint Special Operations Command)
SIG Sauer MCX Rattler Reduced Signature Assault Rifle (United States Special Operations Command)
Low Visibility Assault Weapon (United States Special Operations Command)

SHOTGUNS

Mossberg 500 pump-action 12 gauge
Mossberg 590 pump-action 12 gauge
Mossberg 590A1 pump-action 12 gauge
Saiga-12 (Coast Guard and U.S. Military Police)

SUBMACHINE GUNS

B&T APC9 Pro-K Sub Compact Weapon (SCW) (U.S. Military Police units and Air Force)
Heckler & Koch MP7A1 (Naval Special Warfare Development Group and Join Special Operations Command)
SIG Sauer MPX (Army and Joint Special Operations Command)
Colt RO635 SMG (Marine Corps)

SWORDS

Model 1840 Army Noncommissioned Officers' Sword
Model 1852 Navy Officers' Sword
Model 1860 Navy Chief Petty Officer Cutlass
Model 1902 Army Officers' Sword
Coast Guard Officers' Sword
Marine Noncommissioned Officers' Sword
Marine Officers' Mameluke Sword
Air Force Academy Cadets' Sword
West Point Cadets' Sword

WEAPONS OF WAR

```
Z S E W S H Z W M V K C N M U
L T C M G S K W G J K G O H C
O Y I Y D B E E S R S N F L I
R Q L D O E F R Z P E Z I U T
T R O R R R G C G F A N E F J
N M P L H E F R W E B C A O E
O A K K O T U I K S E U R D M
C R L C X T H A R M E T E R E
T K Q O P A S E S N S L L O S
O S X L F D G I R G Z A K W R
I M K G A N U F P M I S C S E
R A R G A E L F I R I S E D P
B N G R S T R I D E R T H H I
G E N T R E N C H R D D E L N
R L O V M Y Y R T N A F N I S
```

Aircrew	Entrench	Marksman	Seabees
Beretta	Glock	Pistol	SIG Sauer
Colt	Grenade	Police	Snipers
Cutlass	Heckler	Rangers	Strider
Dagger	Infantry	Rifle	Sword
Egress	Knife	Riot control	Thermite

THE NAVY'S SONG

★ ★ ★ ★ ★ ★ ★ ★ ★ ★ ★ ★ ★

The U.S. Navy's unofficial song, "Anchors Aweigh,"
had less to do with serving on the seven seas than as a fight song to
be sung at the annual Army-Navy football game in 1906.
However, the tune has evolved lyrically into more than a football call to arms.

Though "Anchors Aweigh" came into being in 1906, it was the culmination of a tradition that began with the selection of Navy Lieutenant Charles A. Zimmermann in 1887 as bandmaster at the Naval Academy. "Zimmy" was a graduate of the prestigious Peabody Conservatory in Baltimore. He became a beloved figure in 1892 when he began composing a march for every graduating class. To return the honor, the midshipmen presented him with a gold medal each year.

In November 1906, midshipman Alfred Hart Miles approached the bandmaster to request a new march. He wanted a fight song to inspire the Navy football team in its upcoming contest with Army in early December. So for the month of November, Zimmerman and Miles sat together at the Naval Academy Chapel organ as the bandmaster worked out the tune and Miles wrote the lyrics. Their song—"Anchors Aweigh"—was played by the Navy band as the entire midshipman brigade sang the lyrics. It helped inspire Navy to a 10–0 victory, their first win against Army in six years. Afterward, the song was dedicated to the Naval Academy's class of 1907. It was so popular that it was adopted as the unofficial song of the U.S. Navy.

Despite the tune's popularity, the Navy did not adopt it as its official song because the lyrics were so specific to the academy. In an attempt to change that, famed Hollywood lyricist George D. Lottman (who wrote the score for *An Officer and a Gentleman*) rewrote the first two verses to make it more acceptable. (With the inclusion of female students at the Academy since 1976, perhaps "Anchors Aweigh" will need yet another update before long. "Anchors Aweigh, my boys and girls" might be the future refrain.)

THE NAVY'S SONG

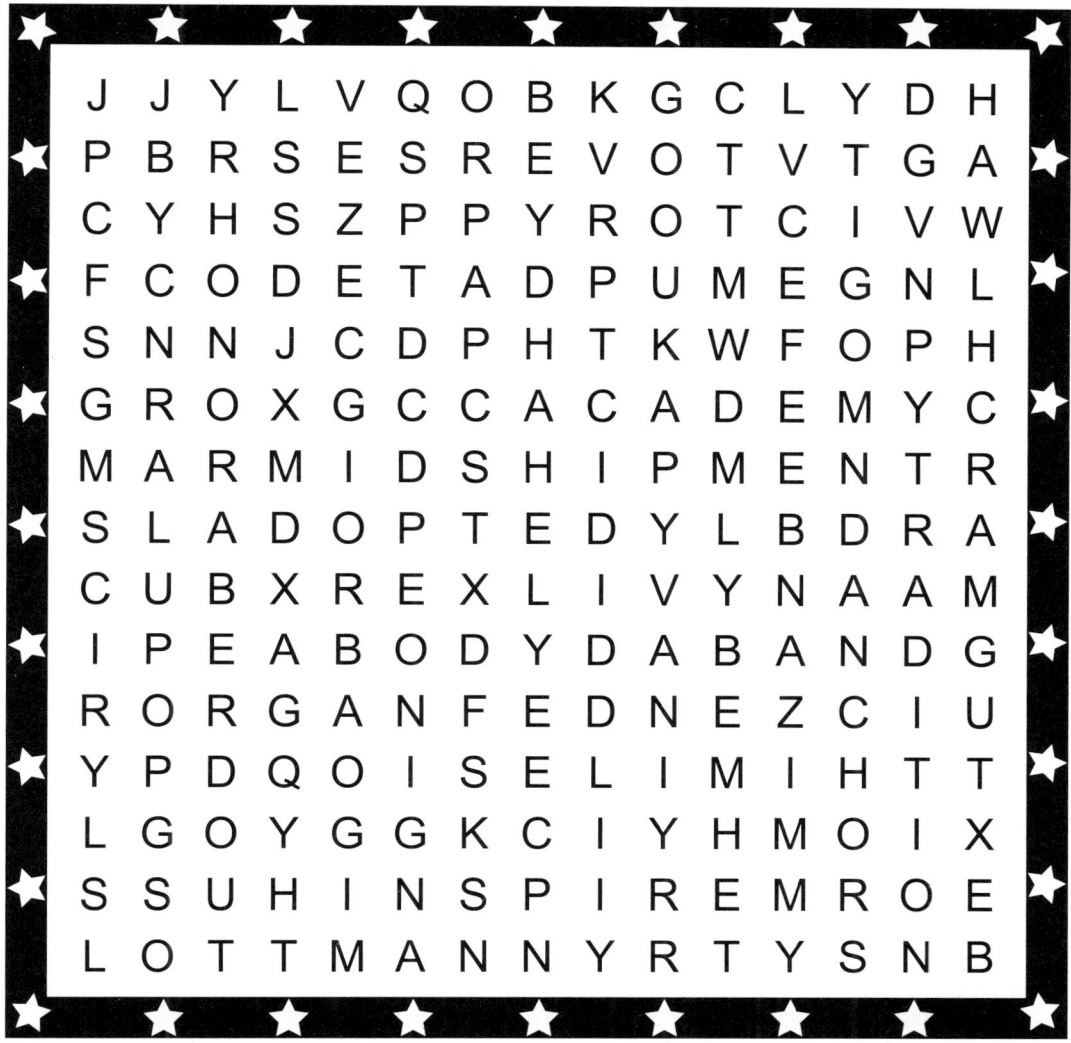

Academy	Fight	Midshipmen	Song
Adopted	Honor	Miles	Tradition
Anchors	Inspire	Navy	Updated
Aweigh	Lottman	Organ	Verses
Band	Lyrics	Peabody	Victory
Chapel	March	Popular	Zimmy

HISTORICAL DOGS OF WAR: SALLIE

★ ★ ★ ★ ★ ★ ★ ★ ★ ★ ★ ★ ★

The creation of the Army K-9 Corps in 1942 gave dogs an official role in the United States Military. But plenty of four-legged troops had already served in battle alongside human warfighters since the nation's earliest days. Here is just one of their stories.

Sallie Ann—a brindle Staffordshire bull terrier, named after a pretty local girl—was just a puppy in May 1861 when she found a home with the 11th Pennsylvania Infantry, who were training at Camp Wayne in West Chester. When the company headed south a year later, they marched toward the fighting with their mascot Sallie at the head of the regiment, trotting alongside the horse of its commander.

Sallie saw combat in each of her regiment's engagements, beginning with Cedar Mountain. She was singed by a bullet during the Battle of Antietam but refused to be sent to safety in the rear. On July 1, 1863, during a chaotic retreat from the fighting in Gettysburg, Sallie became separated from her regiment after she was overtaken by Confederate soldiers. She returned to her regiment's previous location on Oak Ridge, where she spent three days protecting the bodies of wounded and dead comrades before she was recovered.

Sallie survived being struck by a bullet in the neck in May 1864. Unfortunately, in February 1865, she was fatally struck in the head during fighting near Dabney's Mill: when two killed and two wounded soldiers were lifted from the pile into which they'd fallen, Sallie's lifeless body was discovered beneath them. Other members of the regiment braved heavy enemy fire in order to give her a burial on the spot.

In 1890, the veterans of the 11th Pennsylvania Infantry erected a monument at Gettysburg: a statue of a bronze soldier looking over the field. Fittingly, at the base of the monument is a statue of Sallie.

Turn to page 92 for the story of another four-legged soldier.

HISTORICAL DOGS OF WAR: SALLIE

```
S S I N F A N T R Y H T T S P
E S E G D I R K A O I A T Z K
D E Z N O R B Y Y N E R R K Q
A R E G I M E N T R H U P G U
R R I S W I W F T B Y N N S N
M N M S T H Y E I P O I J K P
O O S Y X A R U P G N O L R V
C M A S C O T U P I H N O V E
B H B R V Z P U A Q B T C V T
B U L L E T V R E I E P I L E
Z G R W S U T X H C R A M F R
A N T I E T A M T W Y O D O A
B A I N A V L Y S N N E P A N
H L U L O L N N A E I L L A S
M O N U M E N T W O U N D E D
```

Antietam	Fight	Pennsylvania	Sallie Ann
Army	Infantry	Pile	Statue
Bronze	March	Protect	Training
Bullet	Mascot	Puppy	Union
Burial	Monument	Regiment	Veterans
Comrades	Oak Ridge	Retreat	Wounded

A SUPERIOR ADMIRAL: CHESTER NIMITZ

★ ★ ★ ★ ★ ★ ★ ★ ★ ★ ★ ★ ★

*There have been innumerable excellent leaders
in the U.S. Navy through the years.
This is the story of one.*

Chester William Nimitz graduated from the U.S. Naval Academy in 1905 seventh in a class of 114. He spent the next 26 years working with submarines and expanding his education. In 1933, he moved to cruisers, and after promotion to rear admiral in 1938, he led a cruiser division and then a battleship division.

On December 31, 1941, following the Japanese attack on Pearl Harbor, Admiral Nimitz went to Honolulu, Hawaii, as commander in chief of the Pacific Fleet. In March 1942, the Joint Chiefs of Staff added all naval, sea, and air forces in the entire Pacific Ocean area to his responsibilities. Aided by Pearl Harbor code-breakers, Nimitz stopped a Japanese assault on Port Moresby, New Guinea, on May 7–8, 1942, which was the first carrier battle of the war. A month later, he sent the only three carriers in the Pacific to the Midway Atoll, where the ships repulsed four Japanese assault groups from June 2 to June 6. When he learned that four Japanese carriers had been sunk, Nimitz informed Washington, "Pearl Harbor has now been partially avenged."

Nimitz pressed forward in the Pacific, beginning with the amphibious assault by the 1st Marine Division on Guadalcanal on August 7, 1942. As more men and ships became available, he expanded operations in the Solomon Islands and provided naval support for General Douglas MacArthur's New Guinea operations.

In 1943, Nimitz began a major offensive in the Central Pacific called "the island-hopping campaign." Starting in the Caroline Islands at Tarawa Atoll in November 1943, he moved against the Marshall Islands and the Marianas in 1944. He left tactical control with commanders he could trust, putting Admiral William Halsey in the South Pacific and Admiral Raymond Spruance in the Central Pacific, with Rear Admiral Richmond Kelly Turner in charge of amphibious operations. In October 1944, Nimitz joined forces with General MacArthur for operations in the Philippines. Promoted to the new five-star rank of Fleet Admiral on December 5, 1944, Nimitz then formulated strategy for assaulting Iwo Jima and Okinawa.

Nimitz devised the strategy for winning the War in the Pacific and implemented it with the best officers and pilots in the Navy. After the official surrender of Japan in Tokyo Bay on September 2, 1945, Nimitz became Chief of Naval Operations on December 15.

A SUPERIOR ADMIRAL: CHESTER NIMITZ

```
P Y F I S F E I H C T N I O J
H M L M A R I A N A S P B T A
I E E A V E N G E D D O A L M
L D E E I M I S M T N R T U P
I A T N H F M P A E A T T A H
P C A I O I I R C W L M L S I
P A D U N H T U A C S O E S B
I M M G O U Z A R A I R S A I
N K I W L S T N T R N E H L O
E R R E U O U C H R O S I Y U
S E A N L U C E U I M B P V S
V N L L U C J T R E O Y Q A O
C R U I S E R S I R L M P N K
L U S Z H J A M I J O W I Y Z
S T R A T E G Y Y E S L A H W
```

Academy
Amphibious
Assault
Avenged
Battleship
Carrier

Cruisers
Fleet Admiral
Halsey
Honolulu
Iwo Jima
Joint Chiefs

MacArthur
Marianas
Navy
New Guinea
Nimitz
Philippines

Port Moresby
Solomon Islands
Spruance
Strategy
Tarawa Atoll
Turner

SEE THE HISTORIC SITES

★ ★ ★ ★ ★ ★ ★ ★ ★ ★ ★ ★ ★

*Not just anyone is qualified to join the Armed Forces,
but everybody can visit these historic locations, monuments,
and museums preserving our military heritage.*

Gettysburg National Military Park: This acreage in Pennsylvania was the location of one of the most important battles of the Civil War (and one of the most famous speeches by any American). Visitors can step into the same battlefield locations where Union and Confederate Soldiers fought, explore a museum steeped in history, visit the Soldiers National Cemetery, and see the house where Lincoln slept the night before he delivered the Gettysburg Address.

USS Midway Aircraft Carrier: The longest-serving aircraft carrier of the twentieth century was decommissioned in 1992 and opened as a museum in San Diego in 2004. Visitors can tour more than 60 locations throughout the ship, including sleeping quarters, the galley, the brig, pilot ready rooms, and the engine room. The flight deck has 26 restored naval aircraft on display, spanning from the Battle of Midway in 1942 to today, and more World War II–era aircraft are on display on the hangar deck.

Pearl Harbor National Memorial: Site of the devastating attack that launched the United States into World War II, this National Park Service location on Hawaii's island of Oahu shares the events of the December 7, 1941, attack and honors the service members who lost their lives during it. The main site is the USS *Arizona* Memorial, a floating bridge built across the hull of the sunken battleship and accessible only by a shuttle boat run by the Navy. The *Arizona* is visible beneath the water through an opening in the building's floor; the ship is the final resting place of 1,102 of the 1,177 Sailors and Marines killed on it during the attack, their names inscribed in marble at a shrine at the end of the memorial.

Concord's North Bridge: The "shot heard round the world" was fired on April 19, 1775, on a Massachusetts bridge. The battle between militia members and British soldiers marked the beginning of the American Revolution and was a pivotal moment in the Battles of Lexington and Concord. Though the original bridge is no longer in place (the current bridge was constructed in 1956), the surrounding Minute Man Historical Park contains an obelisk monument erected in 1836 and a "Minute Man" statue erected in 1875.

SEE THE HISTORIC SITES

```
K K Z R T S M J H Q C D L G S
S U R Q V U A B P W M R C L Q
I E U A E Y R H T T O O I Y Z
L X Z S P R I M F A N C V X Y
E S U I A E Z C S I U N I K N
B M H G T T O A H T M O L H O
O S Y K T E N R R I E C W I T
U H A O A M A R I L N K A S G
A T S A C E P I N I T W R T N
Q H T I K C N E E M E J K O I
X J U F T F A R C R I A I R X
A U M S S E R D D A D N H I E
G R U B S Y T T E G U Q W C L
P E A R L H A R B O R S P T Z
Y A W D I M M I N U T E M A N
```

Address	Civil War	Militia	Park
Aircraft	Concord	Minute Man	Pearl Harbor
Arizona	Gettysburg	Monument	Ship
Attack	Historic	Museum	Shrine
Carrier	Lexington	Oahu	Site
Cemetery	Midway	Obelisk	Union

OPERATION IRAQI FREEDOM MEDAL OF HONOR: MICHAEL MONSOOR

★ ★ ★ ★ ★ ★ ★ ★ ★ ★ ★ ★ ★

During the War on Terrorism, nine military personnel were awarded the Medal of Honor for valorous action in Iraq (six were awarded posthumously). Each recipient has an extraordinary story—this is just one.

Michael Monsoor was born in 1981 in Long Beach, California, the third of four children; his father, George, was a former Marine. As a child, Michael suffered from asthma, but improved his condition through swimming, and he later played high school football.

Monsoor enlisted in the Navy in 2001. After basic training, he enrolled in Basic Underwater Demolition/SEAL (BUD/S) training but voluntarily withdrew, then enrolled again two years later, in 2004. He graduated in September as one of the top performers in his class; after further training, he graduated from SEAL Qualification Training (SQT) in March 2005. He was then assigned to Delta Platoon, SEAL Team 3.

SEAL Team 3 was sent to Ramadi, Iraq, in April 2006 with an assignment of training Iraqi Army soldiers. Monsoor regularly took a lead position in his platoon during patrols, and the team frequently encountered insurgent fighters. During one incident in May, Monsoor rescued an injured comrade from the street while under continuous enemy fire, an action that earned him the Silver Star.

In September of that year, Monsoor was one of about 32 Navy SEALs fighting with Army, Marine Corps, and Iraqi troops to regain control of the insurgent-controlled city. While their role was to provide reconnaissance and cover for other troops as they fought in Ramadi, they were often attacked directly by the insurgents. On the afternoon of September 29, Monsoor was lying on a rooftop between two SEAL snipers. The three were providing cover to an Army patrol stringing concertina wire in the rail yard. The two snipers were lying prone, aiming their rifles through holes blasted in the wall, with Monsoor kneeling behind the low rooftop wall, when a grenade sailed onto the rooftop and hit Monsoor in the chest.

Monsoor was up on one knee, and he was the only man on the roof who could have dived away and escaped the grenade's blast. Instead, he dropped on the grenade and absorbed the blast with his body, thereby saving the lives of his two fellow SEALs.

Monsoor was still alive, but barely. Both the snipers on the roof were wounded, and one of them, Lieutenant John Seville, called a nearby SEAL team for assistance. That team was on a building 150 meters away, called for casualty evacuation, and fought their way through the streets to Monsoor's position, but it was too late for him—he died on the way to the hospital at Camp Ramadi.

For this action, "above and beyond the call of duty," 25-year-old Master-at-Arms Second Class Michael Monsoor was awarded the Medal of Honor on April 8, 2008.

OPERATION IRAQI FREEDOM MEDAL OF HONOR: MICHAEL MONSOOR

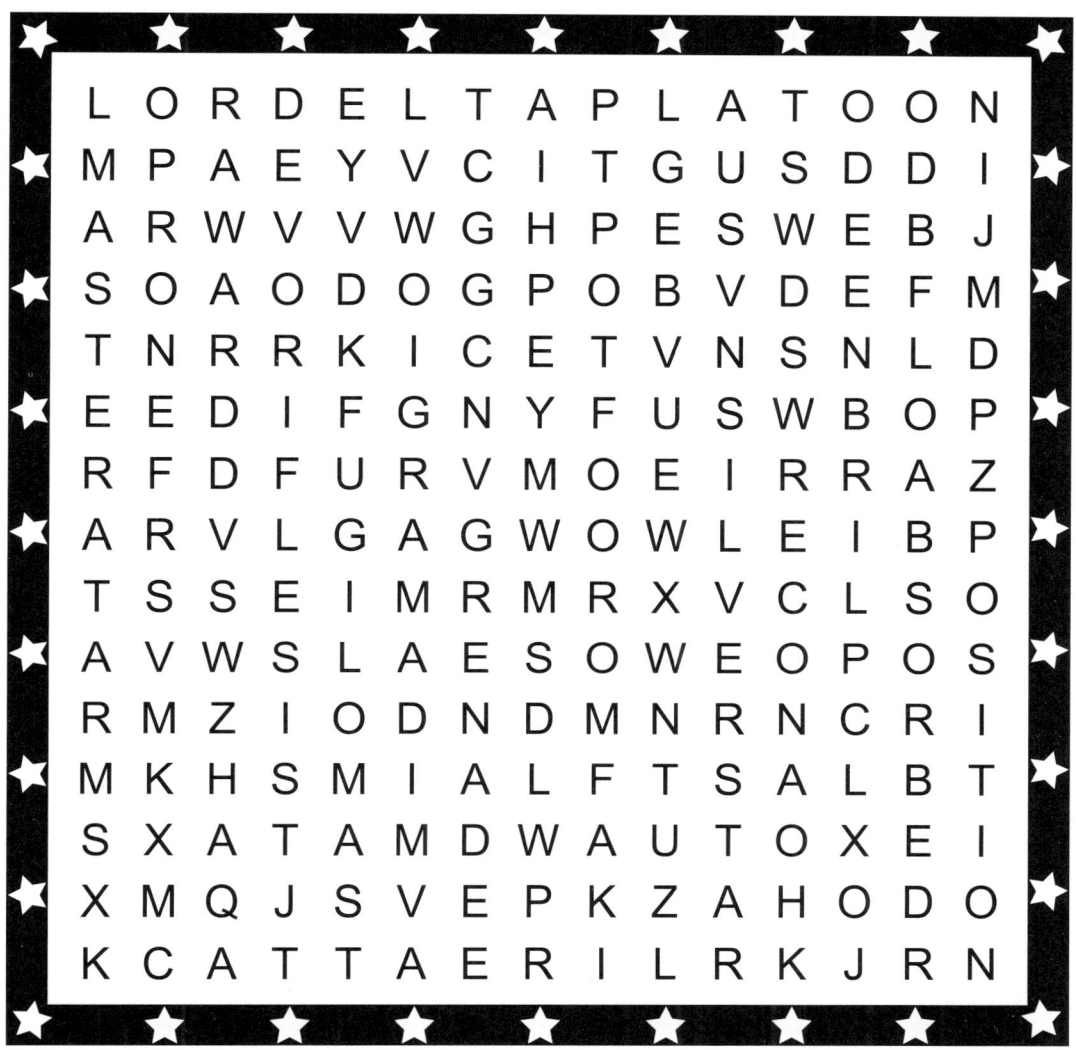

Absorbed	Delta Platoon	Patrol	Rooftop
Asthma	Fight	Position	Save
Attack	Grenade	Prone	SEAL
Award	Master-at-arms	Ramadi	Silver Star
Blast	Monsoor	Recon	Swimmer
Cover	Navy	Rifles	Wounded

HOW THE PENTAGON GOT ITS SHAPE

★ ★ ★ ★ ★ ★ ★ ★ ★ ★ ★ ★

The Pentagon, home of the Department of Defense, is the world's most iconic office building—but how did it get such an odd shape?

In the 1930s, the War Department facilities were scattered among 23 locations throughout Washington, D.C., Maryland, and Virginia. When World War II broke out in Europe in September 1939, the department proved just as inefficient as leaders had complained prior to the war. By April 1941, a newly built headquarters in the Foggy Bottom area of Washington, D.C., was already too small.

Brigadier General Brehon Somervell took command as the chief of the Army's Construction Division in December 1940. The following July, he declared that the War Department needed a new headquarters that would house more than 40,000 people. Somervell met with prominent architect George E. Bergstrom and Lieutenant Colonel Hugh "Pat" Casey, chief of design for the Construction Division. Somervell wanted four million square feet of air-conditioned office space, no more than four floors, and a horizontal construction that wouldn't obstruct the view of the nation's capital. And he wanted the plans on his desk in two business days.

Casey located an odd-shaped 67-acre tract east of Arlington Cemetery, perched on a hill over the Potomac. Bergstrom set a team of engineers to drafting irregularly shaped designs to fit the tract. The result wasn't pretty, but the pentagon shape they came up with fit the asymmetrical layout of the land. The War Department staff, the Secretary of War, and Congress all approved plans within a few days. Along with President Franklin D. Roosevelt, they moved quickly to approve funding for construction.

The Senate authorized construction on August 14, 1941. After hearing some opposition to the location (because it would obstruct the view between the Lincoln Memorial and Arlington Cemetery), Roosevelt directed the building to be moved three-quarters of a mile south. Although no longer destined for an odd-shaped tract, the project was moving too quickly to make any costly or time-consuming design changes to the structure; besides, Roosevelt liked the five-sided design. But the new location did allow architects to make the building more symmetrical.

Groundbreaking took place in September 1941; employees moved in seven months later. The whole construction was completed in 17 months, at an approximate cost of $83 million. The building's official title, the "New War Department Building in Arlington," was too much of a mouthful; Army officials and employees began using the name "Pentagon" informally, and it became the official name within a few months.

The Pentagon has three times more floor space than New York's Empire State Building. With 6,500,000 square feet of space that occupies 29 acres of land, the building has five floors aboveground plus two basement levels. Each floor has five "ring" corridors: from the innermost "A" ring to the fifth and outermost "E" ring. But even today, the Pentagon is regarded as one of the most efficient office buildings in the world. Although it has a total of 17.5 miles of corridors, it takes no more than seven minutes to walk between any two points in the building.

HOW THE PENTAGON GOT ITS SHAPE

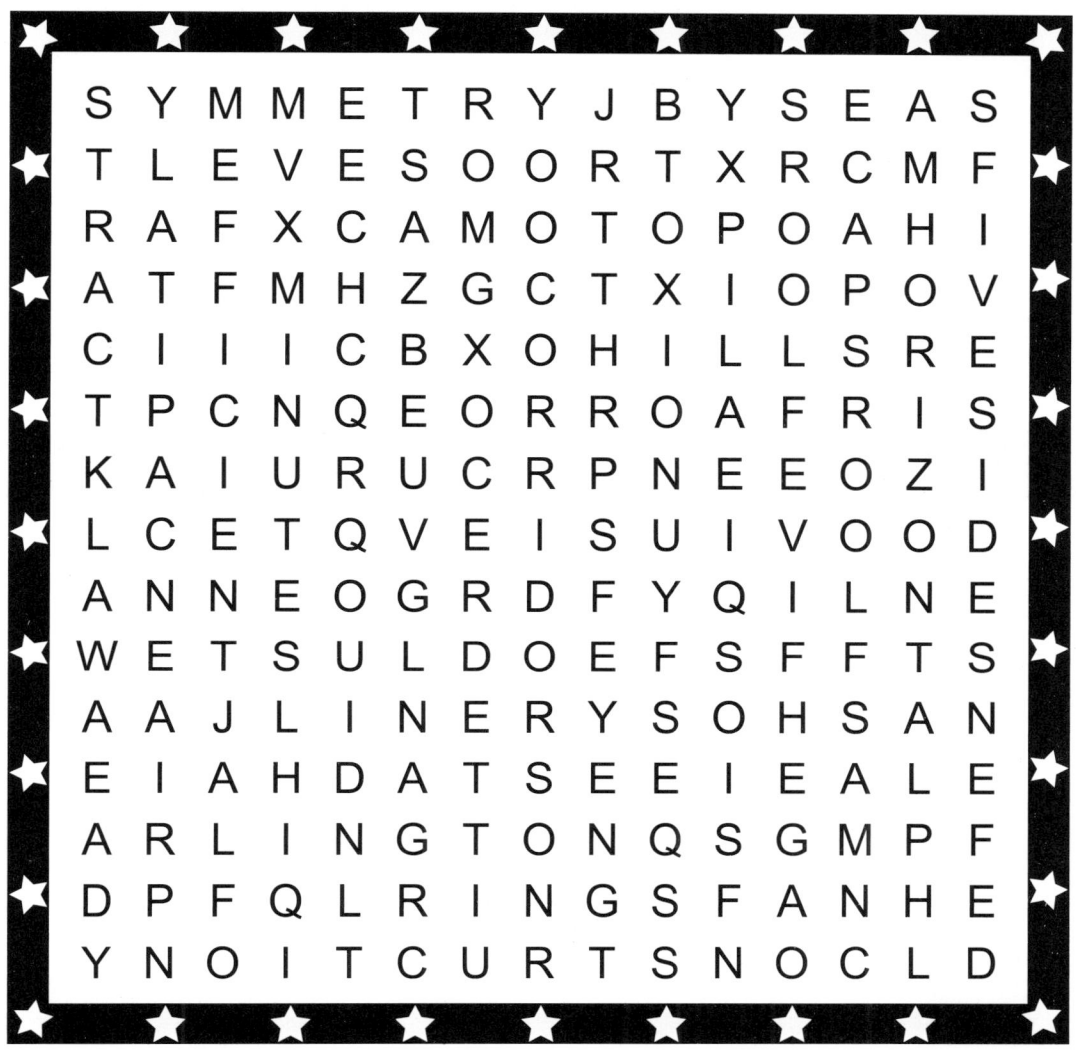

Arlington	Design	Horizontal	Rings
Capital	Efficient	Irregular	Roosevelt
Casey	Five floors	Minutes	Shape
Construction	Five sides	Office	Symmetry
Corridors	Floor space	Plans	Tract
Defense	Hill	Potomac	Walk

UNITED STATES MARINE CORPS (USMC) RANKS

★ ★ ★ ★ ★ ★ ★ ★ ★ ★ ★

Marines in the United States Marine Corps may be enlisted, warrant officers, or commissioned officers. Marine Corps ranks designate job responsibilities and utilize the below names. At the E8 and E9 levels, different positions exist at the same pay grade; the title depends on the Marine's job. Warrant officers receive a commission upon promotion to chief warrant officer 2, but they remain specialists or experts in their area; commissioned officers are generalists.

GRADE	RANK	ABBREVIATION
E1	Private	PVT
E2	Private First Class	PFC
E3	Lance Corporal	LCpl
E4	Corporal	Cpl
E5	Sergeant	Sgt
E6	Staff Sergeant	SSgt
E7	Gunnery Sergeant	GySgt
E8	Master Sergeant	MSgt
	First Sergeant	1stSgt
E9	Master Gunnery Sergeant	MGySgt
	Sergeant Major	SgtMaj
	Sergeant Major of the Marine Corps	SgtMajMC
W1	Warrant officer 1	WO
W2	Chief Warrant Officer 2	CWO2
W3	Chief Warrant Officer 3	CWO3
W4	Chief Warrant Officer 4	CWO4
W5	Chief Warrant Officer 5	CWO5
O1	Second Lieutenant	2ndLt
O2	First Lieutenant	1stLt
O3	Captain	Capt
O4	Major	Maj
O5	Lieutenant Colonel	LtCol
O6	Colonel	Col
O7	Brigadier General	BGen
O8	Major General	MajGen
O9	Lieutenant General	LtGen
O10	General	Gen

UNITED STATES MARINE CORPS (USMC) RANKS

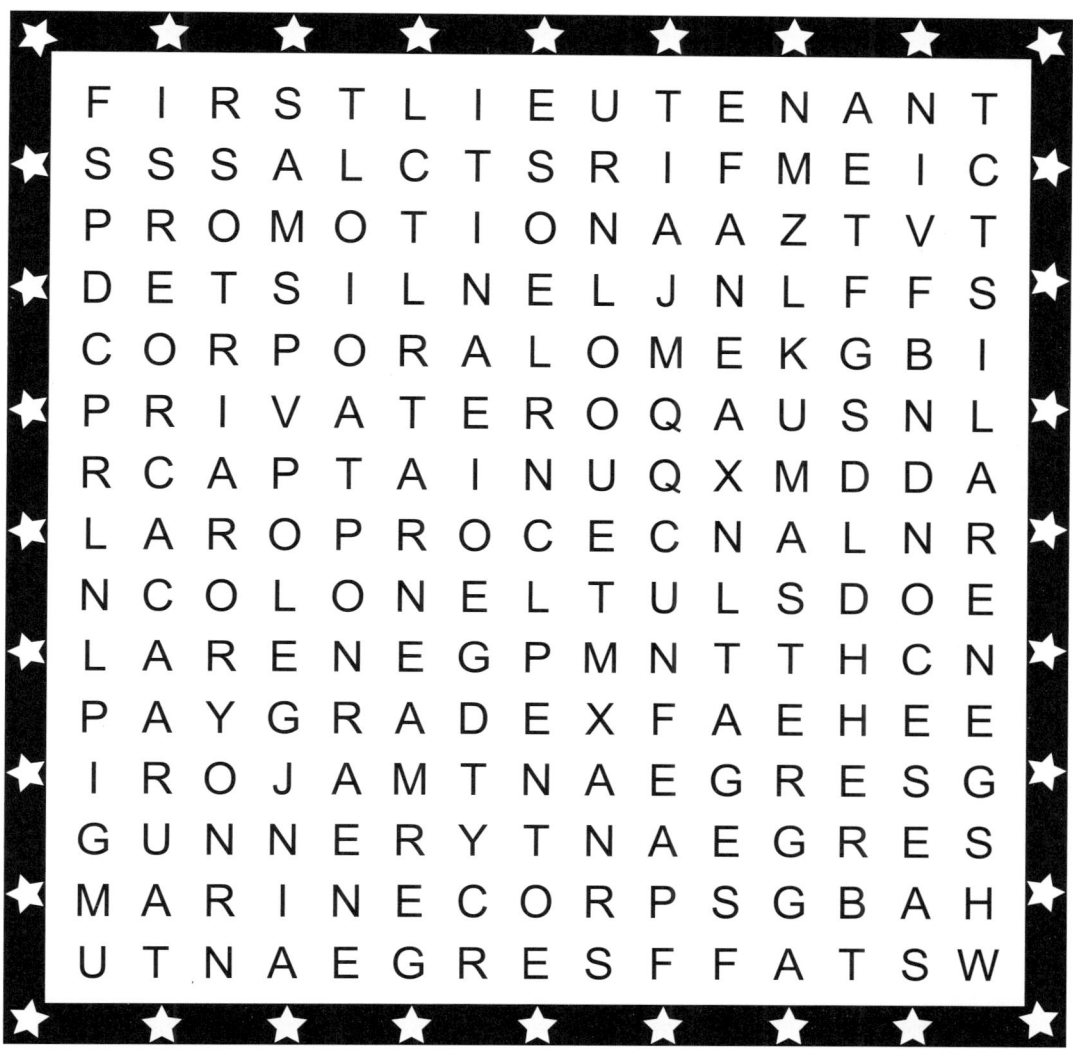

Captain	First Lieutenant	Marine Corps	Second
Colonel	General	Master	Sergeant
Corporal	Generalist	Pay grade	Sergeant Major
Enlisted	Gunnery	Private	Staff Sergeant
Expert	Lance Corporal	Promotion	Title
First class	Major	Ranks	Warrant

WORLD WAR II AIRCRAFT

★ ★ ★ ★ ★ ★ ★ ★ ★ ★ ★ ★ ★

The United States military employed more than 240 aircraft during World War II, and they played a crucial role in fighting—and winning—that war. Here are details about just a few of the planes put to use.

Boeing B-29 Superfortress: Introduced in 1942, one of the largest and most sophisticated aircraft used in the war was also the most expensive, with a cost of $3 billion (more than $50 billion today) to design and produce. The state-of-the-art plane—with a pressurized cabin and a computerized fire-control system—specialized in high-altitude strategic bombing. Famously, the *Enola Gay* and *Bockscar* were the B-29s used to drop atomic bombs on Hiroshima and Nagasaki, respectively.

Consolidated B-24 Liberator: With approximately 18,500 units rolling off assembly lines, this heavy bomber is the most-produced American military aircraft in history. Though aircrews preferred the Boeing B-17 Flying Fortress (precursor to the B-29 Superfortress), the B-24 was the dominant bomber used in the Pacific Theater, where its long-range, high-cruise speed, and ability to carry a heavy bomb load, made it superior for fighting in that region. It also played a key role in strategic bombing in Western Europe and was used by the U.S. Army Air Forces and Allied air forces in every theater.

Douglas C-47 Skytrain: Although this plane was unarmed, it was arguably one of the most important planes of the war thanks to its usefulness as a passenger carrier, paratroop transport, and cargo transport. Utilized by the Army Air Forces, Navy, and Marine Corps, C-47s transported 22 million tons of supplies and flew 67 million passenger miles before war's end. Notably, the C-47 was vital to the success of Allied campaigns in the Pacific; in Europe, the planes dropped more than 50,000 paratroopers during the first few days of the invasion of Normandy.

North American P-51D Mustang: Long before Tom Cruise flew this plane into America's collective consciousness in 2022's *Top Gun: Maverick*, the P-51 Mustang was a critical component of the Army Air Forces' air strategy at the end of World War II. Introduced in late 1943, the Mustang had a range of 1,650 miles, making it the first fighter plane capable of escorting heavy bombers round trip on their raids. Notably, Mustang pilots provided critical air support to bombers flying missions deep inside German borders, and they were involved in the D-Day offensive.

WORLD WAR II AIRCRAFT

Bockscar	Douglas	Normandy	Strategic
Boeing	Escort	Pacific Theater	Strategy
Bombing	Liberator	Raids	Supplies
Cargo	Long range	Range	Support
Carrier	Missions	Skytrain	Transport
D-Day	Mustang	State-of-the-art	Unarmed

TOYS FOR TOTS

★ ★ ★ ★ ★ ★ ★ ★ ★ ★ ★ ★ ★

*The Marine Corps Reserve holiday tradition all started with
a Raggedy Ann doll in 1947 Los Angeles.*

A CHARITABLE IMPULSE

Diane Hendricks handcrafted the doll and asked her husband, Bill, to give it to an organization delivering Christmas toys to needy children. To their surprise, there was no such group, so Diane informed Bill that he needed to start one. So Major Bill Hendricks, a member of the Marine Corps Reserves, duly enlisted his fellow reservists and collected and distributed 5,000 toys that year. They called their toy drive Toys for Tots.

Toys for Tots was so successful that the Marine Corps promptly adopted it as an official Marine charity, making it a national program in 1948. Every American city with a Marine Reserve Center sponsored campaigns with the announced goal to "bring the joy of Christmas to America's needy children."

Major Hendricks was a Marine Reservist on weekends, but his day job was director of public relations for Warner Bros. Studio, and he used his expertise and connections to advance the Toys for Tots program. In 1948, Walt Disney designed the logo still in use today. Nat King Cole, Peggy Lee, and Vic Damone recorded the Toys for Tots theme. Hollywood continued to help through the years, with John Wayne, Bob Hope, Frank Sinatra, Tim Allen, Garth Brooks, and Clint Eastwood on a long list of celebrities who've donated their time and talent to the program. First ladies Nancy Reagan, Barbara Bush, Michelle Obama, and Melania Trump have all served as the national spokesperson in various years.

A TOY UNDER EVERY TREE

In 1991, the Marine Corps established the Toys for Tots Foundation as a tax-deductible public charity, which enabled individuals and American corporations to donate even more money, toys, and time. In 2003, *Reader's Digest* named the Toys for Tots Foundation "America's Best Children's Charity." *Forbes* magazine also named the foundation one of the top 10 charities on its "Gold Star" list.

Since Diane Hendricks crafted that first doll, the Marine Corps Reservists have built a program that has procured more than 670 million toys for more than 300 million children. In 1995, the Secretary of Defense approved Toys for Tots as an official activity of the U.S. Marine Corps and an official mission of the U.S. Marine Corps Reserve.

In the last several years, the organization has expanded its service and outreach beyond providing toys during the holiday season. It now engages in year-round activities including distributing toys and school supplies to children in foster care and to Native American children, as well as providing literacy resources to economically disadvantaged children.

Former U.S. Marine Wilford Brimley summed up the reason behind the organization's efforts: "It's the right thing to do."

TOYS FOR TOTS

```
F T O Y S F O R T O T S L D D
G X L O S A N G E L E S M O B
F O U N D A T I O N N T A O G
U C H I L D R E N L H K R W O
X N S C S I D B N Y E B G Y H
B A J E A N T O S E M J O L E
R T B S I E G E N M E J R L R
I I P C E T R I R A H D P O D
M O M R H V I T A A T P Y H R
L N C H I A R R U P C I Y H I
E A G C K T R E B O M Y O R C
Y L E P K W G I S E F A O N K
L A I C I F F O T E L O C C S
C H R I S T M A S Y R E Z L U
W Z R A G G E D Y A N N C O N
```

Brimley	Donations	Logo	Program
Campaigns	Foundation	Los Angeles	Raggedy Ann
Celebrities	Hendricks	National	Reserves
Charity	Hollywood	Needy	Service
Children	Joy	Official	Theme
Christmas	Literacy	Outreach	Toys for Tots

ARLINGTON BY THE NUMBERS

★ ★ ★ ★ ★ ★ ★ ★ ★ ★ ★ ★

Arlington National Cemetery is one of the most famous cemeteries in the nation, if not the world. Learn more about the final resting place of so many of America's heroes.

30: The number of funerals that take place daily. Flags fly at half-staff from half an hour before the first daily funeral service until half an hour after the last. Funerals are conducted Monday through Friday.

38: The number of monuments and memorials present in the cemetery. These commemorate individuals, military units, wars, and battles. These include memorials in honor of the Battle of the Bulge during World War I, the terrorist bombing of the U.S. Marine Corps barracks in Beirut in 1983, the Nurses Memorial commemorating the 653 military nurses buried there, and 9/11 Pentagon Group Memorial, honoring the 184 victims of the September 11, 2001, attack on the Pentagon.

47: Highest number of funerals held in a single day, during the Vietnam War.

63: The number of authorized faith emblems that may be included on a grave marker to indicate the deceased's faith.

70: The number of sections into which the cemetery is divided. Notable sections include Section 60, the southeastern part of the cemetery, which is the burial ground of service members killed in the War on Terror since 2001. Section 27 contains the remains of 3,800 African Americans who lived in the Freedman's Village, a community established during the Civil War as a temporary settlement for formerly enslaved people.

639: The number of acres in the cemetery, located across the Potomac River from Washington, DC.

4,735: Number of unknowns buried in Arlington, most from the Civil War.

8,500: The approximate number of trees in the cemetery, across 300 different species.

$150,000: The amount of money the federal government paid for the land. After being occupied by the Union Army during the Civil War, the land was used to bury fallen Union soldiers when local cemeteries grew overcrowded. The Supreme Court ruled in 1882 that the federal government had illegally seized the land; instead of forcing the government to exhume the dead and move the graves, Custis Lee—the owner at the time—sold it to the government.

4,000,000: The number of annual visitors to the cemetery.

ARLINGTON BY THE NUMBERS

```
R S R B T A R L I N G T O N G
V E E H A L F S T A F F O Z F
I E C E H E L S E L T T A B C
S R A S G A L F F W S U C A U
I T L U N K N O W N S R I U R
T R P S P O T O M A C I V T E
O S G L H O N O R S Q E I Y K
R T N A Q I V S P N U B L S R
S N I R J Y P E O E T X W N A
O E T E I Y T G T O G M A O M
A M S N I Q A E S E Y O R I E
C U E U A T V Z R T R Y U T V
R N R F N T Y B U R I A L C A
E O C E M E T E R Y O N N E R
S M P P V I E T N A M R U S G
```

Acres	Civil War	Monuments	Trees
Arlington	Flags	Pentagon	Units
Battles	Funerals	Potomac	Unknowns
Beirut	Grave marker	Resting place	Veterans
Burial	Half-staff	Sections	Vietnam
Cemetery	Honor	Terror	Visitors

TWIST ME A DIZZY

Here are a few examples of colorful slang used by the armed forces during twentieth-century wartime operations.

Egg beater: helicopter (Korean War)

Give a dirty orb: to give a dirty look (World War II)

Ceiling work: high-altitude planes protecting airmen at lower levels (World War I)

Boom-boom girl: prostitute (Vietnam War)

Hot skinny: rumors about important things (Vietnam War)

Latrine telegram: a rumored report (World War II)

Plutonium wine: moonshine brewed on a nuclear submarine (Cold War)

Brain bucket: helmet (Korean War)

Bone jar: means "hello," a corruption of the French *bonjour* (World War I)

Messy bucket: "thank you," from the French *merci beaucoup,* meaning "many thanks" (World War II)

Agony wagon: ambulance (World War II)

Deep kimchi: in serious trouble (Korean War)

Dinky dau: crazy, from the Vietnamese *dien caid au,* meaning "ridiculous" (Vietnam War)

Behavior report: a love letter reply (World War II)

Smoke a thermometer: have your temperature taken (World War I)

Bottled sunshine: beer (World War II)

Bought guts: courage inspired by too much bottled sunshine (World War II)

Twist a dizzy: roll a cigarette (World War II)

Completely cheesed: extremely bored (World War II)

Applesauce enema: mild criticism of a subordinate so he or she feels less "chewed out" (Vietname War)

Big pickle: the atomic bomb (Korean War)

TWIST ME A DIZZY

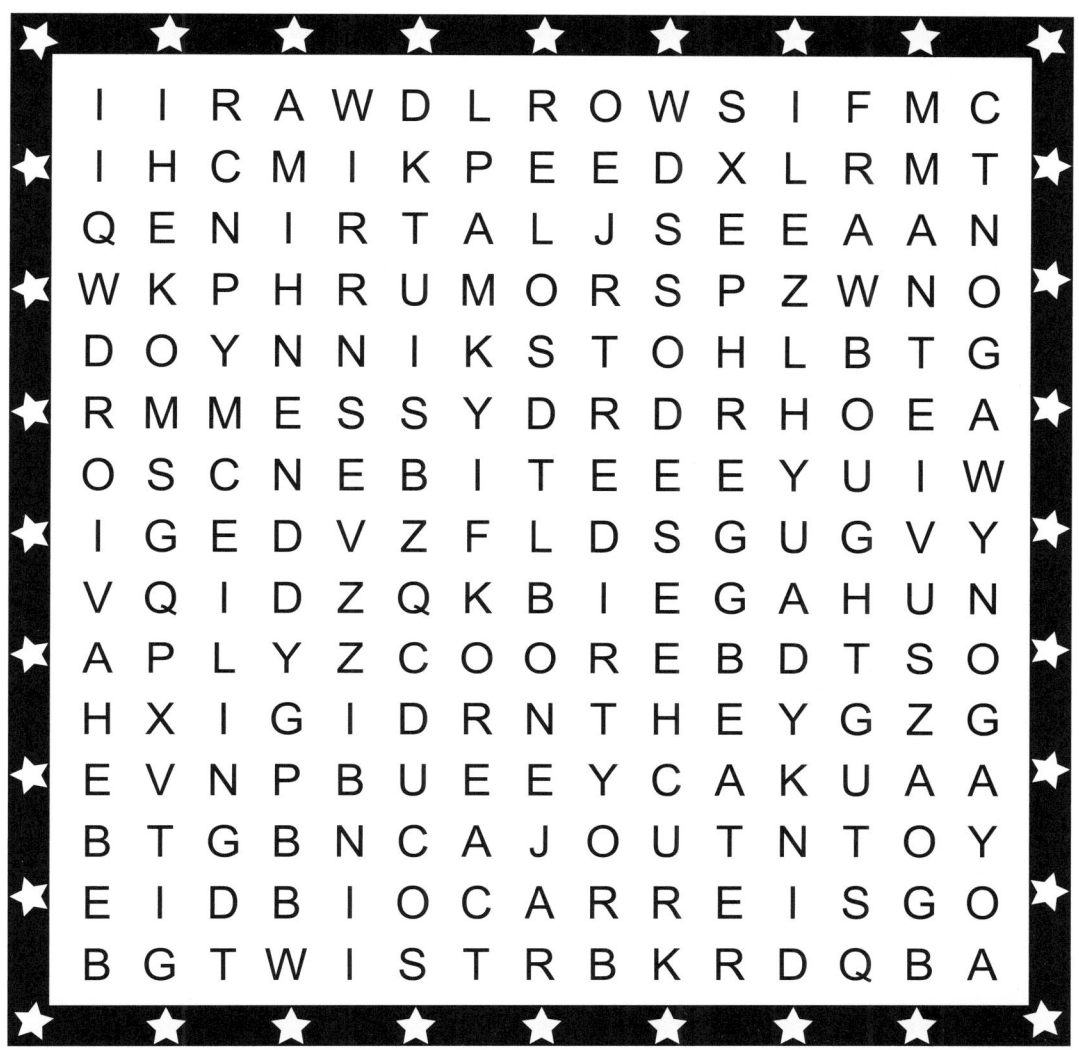

Agony wagon
Behavior
Big pickle
Bone jar
Bought guts
Ceiling

Cheesed
Deep kimchi
Dinky dau
Dirty orb
Dizzy
Egg beater

Hot skinny
Korea
Latrine
Messy
Report
Rumors

Slang
Smoke
Twist
Vietnam
War
World War II

AUDIE MURPHY: UNLIKELY HERO

★ ★ ★ ★ ★ ★ ★ ★ ★ ★ ★ ★ ★

The sharecroppers' son and future actor and singer was also the most decorated combat soldier of World War II—and possibly in history.

Born in 1925 in rural Texas, young Audie Murphy was the seventh of twelve children and left school in fifth grade to support his family by picking cotton. His mother died in 1941, and when the Japanese attacked Pearl Harbor in December of that year, sixteen-year-old Audie attempted to join the Army, the Navy, and the Marine Corps, but was rejected by all of them for being underage and underweight. His older sister helped him falsify his birth year (changing it to 1924), and he was finally accepted into the Army on June 30, 1942.

After completing basic training in Texas, Private Murphy was sent to French Morocco in February 1943 as part of Company B, 1st Battalion, 15th Infantry Regiment, 3rd Infantry Division. He went on to participate in campaigns in North Africa, Italy, France, and Germany, including participating in the Allied invasion of Sicily, the Battle of Anzio, the liberation of Rome, and the invasion of Southern France. He is credited with killing 241 enemy soldiers and his heroic actions earned him numerous military and civilian medals and decorations, including the Medal of Honor, two Silver Stars, the Legion of Merit, French Legion of Honor, the Belgian Croix de Guerre, and the Texas Legislative Medal of Honor (posthumous).

Murphy was discharged from the Army in 1945 with the rank of First Lieutenant. When the Korean War broke out in 1950, he was commissioned a Captain in the Texas National Guard. He was never sent to Korea, but he spent another 19 years actively serving with the Guard, and then with the Army Reserve, retiring with the rank of Major.

Turn the page to find out more about Murphy's postwar life.

AUDIE MURPHY: UNLIKELY HERO

Army	Enemy	Italy	Retire
Battle of Anzio	Falsify	Major	Rome
Captain	France	Medals	Sicily
Cotton	Germany	Morocco	Texas
Decorations	Hero	Murphy	Underage
Discharged	Invasion	Reserve	Unlikely

AUDIE MURPHY: HIS LEGACY

★ ★ ★ ★ ★ ★ ★ ★ ★ ★ ★ ★ ★

The most decorated combat soldier of World War II was also a hero off the battlefield.

In 1945, actor and producer James Cagney spotted an article about Audie Murphy in *Life* magazine and brought Murphy to Hollywood. Murphy had his first bit part in 1948 and his first leading role, in the film *Bad Boy*, in 1949. He made more than 40 feature films and a television series before the end of his acting career in 1969. Though he found steady work in Westerns, he is perhaps best remembered for his performance in 1955's *To Hell and Back*, in which Murphy played himself in the film adaptation of his 1949 war memoir.

Audie Murphy is remembered today for his work on behalf of fellow veterans. Since the end of World War II, Murphy had experienced insomnia, depression, and other symptoms of post-traumatic stress disorder. Few World War II service members knew how to address what was known as "battle fatigue" or "shell shock" at the time; plagued by nightmares, in addition to guilt and grief over his wartime experiences, Murphy turned to sleeping pills and slept with a loaded gun under his pillow. In an effort to help military personnel returning from the Korean and Vietnam Wars, he campaigned for the government to conduct more studies into the psychological effects of combat and to expand health-care benefits for war veterans.

Murphy's efforts resulted in the Audie L. Murphy Memorial VA Hospital being dedicated to him in 1973. Numerous units of the U.S. Army have also established chapters of the Sergeant Audie Murphy Club (SAMC), which honor noncommissioned officers who "exemplify leadership characterized by personal concern for the needs, training, development, and welfare of Soldiers and concern for families of Soldiers."

Audie Murphy sadly was killed in a plane crash in 1971, just days before he turned 46. He was buried with full military honors at Arlington National Cemetery, and his grave remains one of the cemetery's most visited.

AUDIE MURPHY: HIS LEGACY

```
N O T G N I L R A W S G U M F
H K I X T R G U H S N N L A A
I C Y V X K D S M B R I M N M
Z A G B L I R L U Q E T E T I
E B E Y E L I O R P T C M E L
R D E R A F L E W A S A O I I
A N N O I S I V E L E T I V E
C A M P A I G N Y D W R R B S
H L M K L H O L L Y W O O D L
T L A T I P S O H P T S D K B
L E W U W X H M Z C A B L H A
A H W F Y U O A K B M I B T D
E O T R A I N I N G F A Y C B
H T H I Q W O R Z E L T S W O
R W G T N C R I Q C A G N E Y
```

Acting
Arlington
Audie
Bad Boy
Cagney
Campaign

Families
Films
Health care
Hollywood
Honor
Hospital

Korea
Life
Memoir
PTSD
SAMC
Television

To Hell and Back
Training
Vietnam
Welfare
Westerns
Work

THE HIGHEST HONORS

★ ★ ★ ★ ★ ★ ★ ★ ★ ★ ★ ★ ★

While the U.S. military is full of heroes, some individuals distinguish themselves through extreme acts of gallantry and sacrifice deserving of the highest recognition. Learn more about the top awards for valor given to our service members.

THE DETAILS

The two highest awards are branch-specific, while the Silver Star may be awarded to a member of any branch. What they all have in common is that the service member deserving of the award must have engaged in extraordinary heroism:

- While engaged in action against an enemy of the United States;
- While engaged in military operations involving conflict with an opposing foreign force; or
- While serving with friendly foreign forces engaged in an armed conflict against an opposing armed force in which the United States is not a belligerent party.

MEDAL OF HONOR

This is the highest U.S. military decoration that may be bestowed on a member of the Armed Forces. There are three distinct versions of the medal, each with a slightly different design: one for the Army, one for the Air Force, and one for the Navy, Marine Corps, and Coast Guard. Presented by the president, in the name of Congress, it is given to service members "who distinguish themselves through conspicuous gallantry and intrepidity at the risk of life above and beyond the call of duty" during armed conflict. Since the first Medal of Honor was bestowed in 1861, 3,538 medals have been awarded to 3,519 recipients (19 of which were double recipients). It is the only medal worn around the neck instead of pinned to a uniform.

SERVICE CROSS

The second highest military decoration is the Distinguished Service Cross (for the Army), the Navy Cross (for the Navy, Marine Corps, and Coast Guard when operating under the authority of the Department of the Navy), and the Air Force Cross. These medals are awarded for extraordinary heroism during armed conflict, consisting of heroic actions above and beyond those required for any other combat decorations but not meriting the Medal of Honor.

SILVER STAR

The third highest combat decoration awarded to members of the Armed Forces can be given to members of any branch. It is awarded for gallantry in action during armed conflict that is above and beyond that required for other combat decorations but not meriting the Medal of Honor or a Service Cross.

THE HIGHEST HONORS

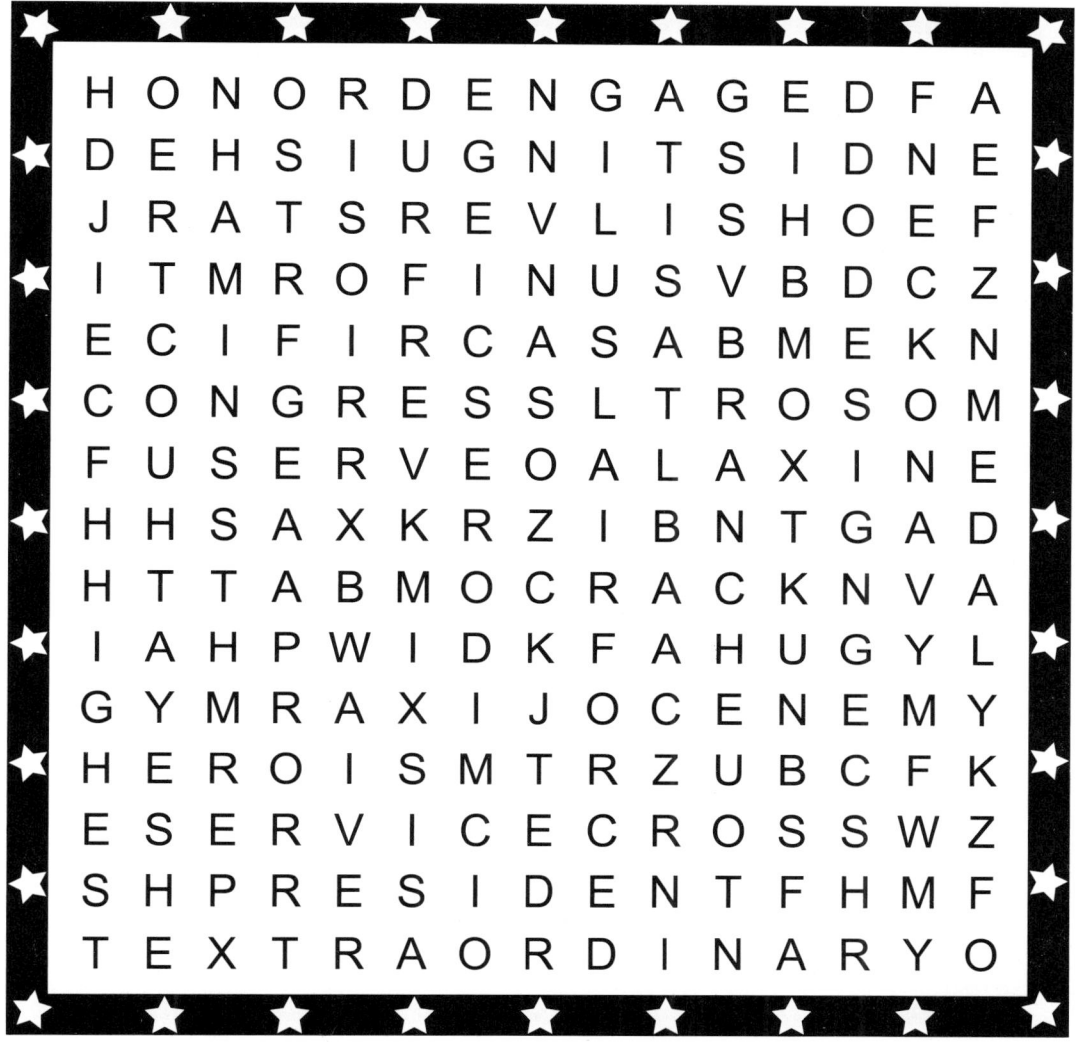

Action	Design	Highest	Sacrifice
Air Force	Distinguished	Honor	Serve
Army	Enemy	Medal	Service Cross
Branch	Engaged	Navy	Silver Star
Combat	Extraordinary	Neck	Uniform
Congress	Heroism	President	Valor

THE HUEY

★ ★ ★ ★ ★ ★ ★ ★ ★ ★ ★ ★ ★

The Vietnam War was known as the "helicopter war" because of how heavily each branch of the U.S. military relied on these aircraft. Nearly 12,000 helicopters were used for transporting troops and equipment, scouting, search and rescue, and providing air support for troops on the ground. Learn more about the most-utilized model.

The Bell UH-1 Iroquois was so pervasive in the Vietnam War that it has become a symbol for the conflict itself. The original designation was HU-1, which earned it the nickname the "Huey"; the moniker stuck even after its designation changed to UH-1 in 1962. Development of the Huey started in the 1950s to address the U.S. Army's need for a helicopter capable of performing medevac duties, but it quickly expanded well beyond this role, eventually being relied on to do "anything a horse could do."

The helicopters used during the Korean War had been powered by internal combustion engines. The Huey was the first new kind of helicopter powered by a turboshaft engine, meaning it had jet turbines powering the rotors, making it a faster, lighter, and more powerful aircraft. These qualities inspired the Army to develop innovative ways of utilizing its new weapon.

Helicopters began to see combat in 1961 with the Army and Marines, initially with heavy losses. Beginning in early 1963, an experimental Army unit at Fort Benning, Georgia, began developing a new tactical concept that combined light infantry with transport and air support from the Huey and similar helicopters: the air assault. With this tactic, a squadron of helicopters would transport troops directly into remote locations, often behind enemy lines, with additional helicopters providing gun support.

Later Hueys, known as "Slicks," were much larger than the originals and were intended for troop transport; attack-style Hueys, with joystick-guided missiles and heavy machine guns, were also developed. The combination of specialized troop-transport Hueys and Huey gunships enabled the military to engage in combat almost anywhere in the hilly jungle landscape of Vietnam, along with transporting ammunition and rapidly providing medical attention to troops in difficult terrain.

Bell produced more than 16,000 Hueys between 1955 and 1976, with more than 7,000 of them seeing action in Vietnam. Hueys came to be used by every branch of the U.S. military and have also been used in civilian roles for firefighting, search-and-rescue operations, and more. While the U.S. Army has retired the last of its Hueys, this iconic aircraft is still in use today by the Marine Corps in its latest iteration, the UH-1Y Venom.

THE HUEY

Air assault
Army
Bell
Combat
Fort Benning
Helicopter

Horse
Huey
Infantry
Iroquois
Marines
Medevac

Missile
Remote
Rescue
Rotors
Slick
Support

Symbol
Tactic
Transport
Troop
Venom
Vietnam

HELLO GIRLS AND WASPS

★ ★ ★ ★ ★ ★ ★ ★ ★ ★ ★ ★

Women weren't allowed to become permanent members of the U.S. Armed Forces until 1948, but many had served their country in other ways since the Revolutionary War. The two World Wars in the twentieth century saw women filling the ranks in unprecedented numbers for the first time.

NURSES, HELLO GIRLS, AND YEOMANETTES

The Army established the U.S. Army Nurse Corps (ANC) in 1901 as a permanent way for women to serve in the Army in a medical capacity. When the United States entered World War I in 1917, the ANC had just over 400 nurses on active duty; that number swelled to the thousands within a year. Nurses served in military hospitals, near the front lines, and in ambulance companies. Women also served in the U.S. Army Signal Corps as telephone and switchboard operators; these "Hello Girls" were stationed near the front lines in France. And with large numbers of sailors being sent overseas, the U.S. Navy also enlisted about 12,000 "yeomanettes," women who served in noncombat and non-commissioned officer roles.

WAVES, WACS, AND WASPS

More than 16 million Americans—mostly men—served on the front lines during World War II. That left numerous noncombat roles open in every branch of the military. Almost 350,000 women donned a uniform and served in the same clerical and nursing roles they'd filled during World War I, but also took on duties as varied and as dangerous as cryptography and aerial cargo transport.

The Women's Army Corps (WAC), initially formed as an auxiliary arm of the U.S. Army, was officially integrated into the Army in 1943; the 100,000 enlisted and 6,000 officer WACs were initially trained as switchboard operators, bakers, or mechanics, but were later able to serve overseas in a variety of roles. WAVES, or Women Accepted for Voluntary Emergency Service, were considered U.S. Navy Reservists, though they were not allowed to serve on naval ships; nearly 90,000 WAVES performed jobs including parachute rigging, intelligence gathering, and aeronautics in 900 locations on shore. The Marine Corps and Coast Guard also implemented women's reserve forces to fill roles vacated by men sent overseas. And 1,100 women joined the Women's Airforce Service Pilots (WASPs) program as licensed pilots transporting cargo and testing aircraft (though they were federal employees, not associated with any specific branch despite working with the U.S. Army Air Forces).

AFTER THE WAR

By the end of World War II, 432 women had been killed, 16 wounded and awarded Purple Hearts, and 88 taken prisoner during the conflict. Most branches cut back on the number of women in service to make room for the men returning to their positions from overseas. The status of women in the Armed Forces was up in the air until President Harry Truman signed the Women's Armed Services Integration Act in 1948. The act recognized women as full members of the military, eligible for the same benefits as their male counterparts.

HELLO GIRLS AND WASPS

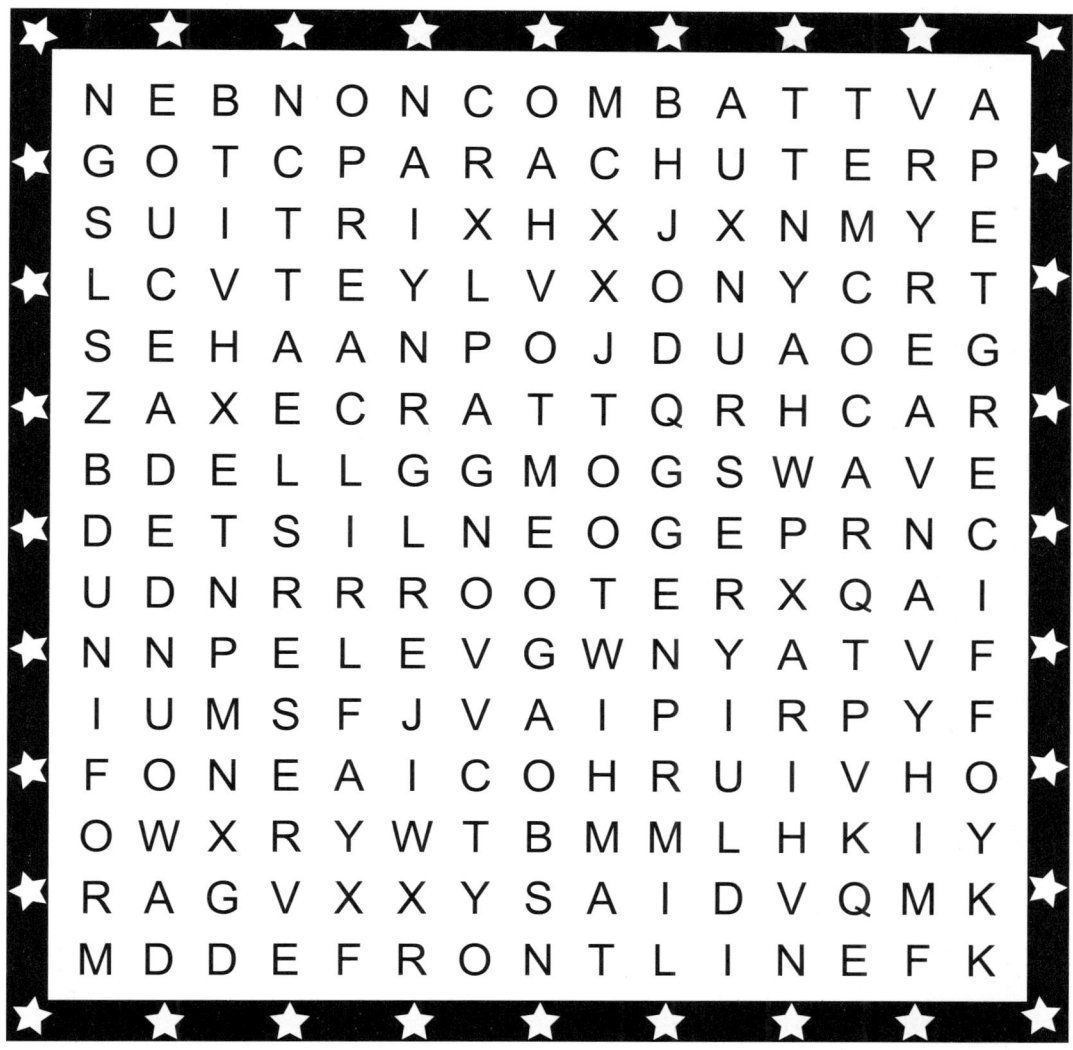

Army
Benefits
Cargo
Cryptography
Enlisted
Front line

Hello Girl
Integration
Navy
Noncombat
Nurse
Officer

Overseas
Parachute
Pilot
Reserve
Shore
Truman

Uniform
WAC
WASP
WAVE
Wounded
Yeomanette

JOKING AROUND

★ ★ ★ ★ ★ ★ ★ ★ ★ ★ ★ ★

Ask any veteran: one trait critical for military success is a sense of humor!

TARGET PRACTICE

The General had just arrived at the front lines when a sniper's bullet whizzed past his ear. He threw himself to the ground. When the rest of the men stood around doing nothing, the General yelled, "Isn't somebody going to kill that sniper?"

The Sergeant looked over and said, "No way, General. If we shoot him, they'll replace him with someone who's a better shot."

THE "F" WORD

A grandfather who'd been a pilot in World War II was telling his adolescent grandkids about his adventures in the war. "German pilots were a force to be reckoned with. One day, I was on a strafing mission when these Fokkers appeared out of nowhere." The kids looked at each other and giggled. Granddad went on: "I shot down one of them, but then I saw another Fokker coming at me." More giggles. Their mother, who'd been listening in, said, "You silly kids, 'Fokker' was the name of the German-Dutch aircraft company." "Right," said Granddad, "but these Fokkers were flying Messerschmitts."

RADIO POETS

Two patrols in the jungle were checking in with each other. The first radioed: "Eeny, meeny, miney, mo, how do you read my radio?"

Not wanting to be outdone, the receiving operator replied: "Fe, fi, fo, fum, loud and clear with a little hum."

PRIVATE JOKE

A group of Soldiers were standing in formation at an Army base. The Drill Sergeant said, "All right! All you idiots fall out."

The squad wandered away, but one Soldier remained at attention.

The Drill Sergeant walked over to him and raised an eyebrow. The Soldier said, "Sure were a lot of 'em, huh, Sergeant?"

JOKING AROUND

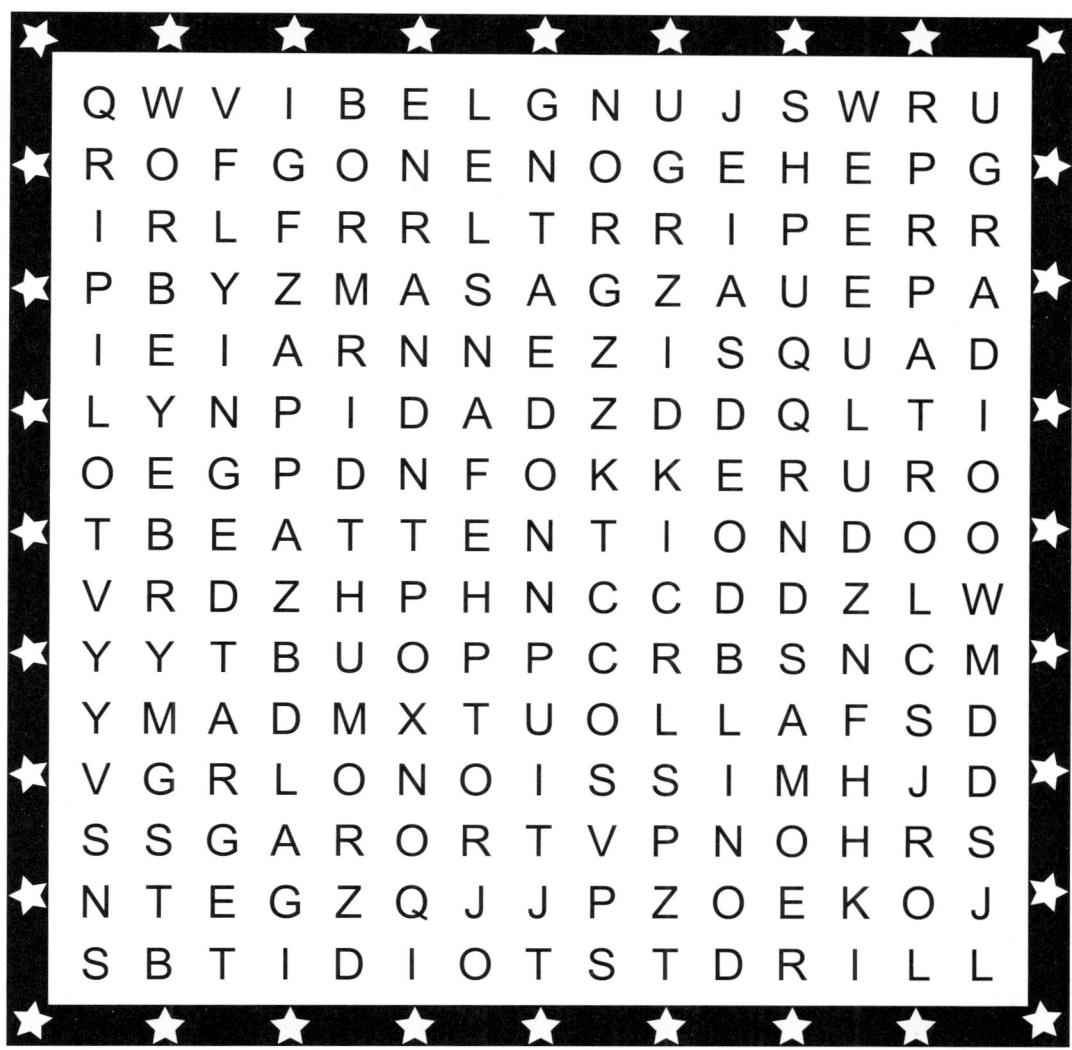

Army	Fokker	Joke	Sergeant
Attention	German	Jungle	Shoot
Drill	Granddad	Mission	Sniper
Eyebrow	Grandkids	Patrol	Squad
Fall out	Humor	Pilot	Target
Flying	Idiots	Radio	Whizz

KOREAN WAR MEDAL OF HONOR: HIROSHI MIYAMURA

★ ★ ★ ★ ★ ★ ★ ★ ★ ★ ★ ★ ★

During the Korean War, 146 military personnel were awarded the Medal of Honor for valorous action (103 were awarded posthumously). Each recipient has an extraordinary story—this is just one.

Hiroshi "Hershey" Miyamura was born in Gallup, New Mexico, in 1925. He was a Nisei, a first-generation Japanese American. In 1944, when many Japanese Americans were still being held in internment camps, Hershey entered the U.S. Army to serve with the famous 442nd Infantry Regiment—a group that was highly decorated for their brave service in World War II. However, the war was over soon after he enlisted. Miyamura returned home, married, and worked as an auto mechanic. Later, as an Army Reservist, Miyamura was sent to Korea as a machine-gun squad leader in Company H, 7th Infantry Regiment, 3rd Infantry Division.

On April 22, 1951, UN forces in Korea were overwhelmed by waves of Chinese soldiers and began retreating. Colonel Miyamura's squad defended a hill near Taejon-ni to slow the advance. On the night of April 24, a Chinese attack on Taejon-ni decimated the defense on the hill. Miyamura fought off the Chinese with his bayonet in hand-to-hand combat, killing at least 10 of them, before he tried to give first aid to his men and help them evacuate from the hill. When the next attack came, Miyamura held off the enemy with machine-gun fire and grenades. After his ammunition was gone, Miyamura destroyed his machine gun so it couldn't be captured by the enemy, then made his way to another gun emplacement, where he ordered the last of the defenders to evacuate while he provided covering fire.

Miyamura killed more than 50 Chinese before he retreated. Wounded, he collapsed from exhaustion. He was captured the next morning and marched to a North Korean prison camp, where he lost 50 pounds from starvation and dysentery during the 28 months he was held as prisoner. During most of that time, his family didn't know whether he was alive.

On August 20, 1953, Miyamura was released with other prisoners. When they arrived in Freedom Village, South Korea, Miyamura was led out to meet reporters. Brigadier General Ralph M. Osborne made an announcement that stunned him: "It is my pleasure to inform you that you have been awarded the Medal of Honor."

The medal had been awarded on December 21, 1951, but was kept secret because the Army didn't want to risk Miyamura being tortured by his captors as punishment. On October 27, 1953, at a White House ceremony, President Dwight D. Eisenhower presented the Medal to Miyamura. He was the second Japanese American to earn the award, and he continued to speak at memorial services until his death in 2022.

KOREAN WAR MEDAL OF HONOR: HIROSHI MIYAMURA

```
E T A U C A V E M A U B Y Y W
W F E M A G L N D A U Q S M D
Q S S O P K X I N F A N T R Y
B Q N D T L F T N K U H R A S
A K E E O W T N U Q O N E I E
Y T F E R U E E G D M R S L N
O Z E R S P R M E D A L E E T
N T D F R E C E Y O C D R A E
E V C I T Z E C O N H N V D R
T W S R B N S A R J I E I E Y
I O E J G I M L T H N F S R Z
N A E I F S P P S F E E T Z C
T G J C O E P M E P G D D N U
A Z L W Q I D E D N U O W O H
N F L P U N O I T I N U M M A
```

Ammunition	Destroy	Infantry	Prison
Army	Dysentery	Korea	Reservist
Bayonet	Emplacement	Leader	Retreat
Captors	Evacuate	Machine gun	Secret
Defend	Freedom	Medal	Squad
Defense	Gun	Nisei	Wounded

UNITED STATES NAVY (USN) RANKS

★ ★ ★ ★ ★ ★ ★ ★ ★ ★ ★ ★

Sailors in the United States Navy may be enlisted, warrant officers, or commissioned officers. Navy ranks designate job responsibilities and utilize the below names. At the E9 level, different positions exist at the same pay grade; the title depends on the Sailor's job. Warrant officers receive a commission upon promotion to chief warrant officer 2, but they remain specialists or experts in their area; commissioned officers are generalists.

GRADE	RANK	ABBREVIATION
E1	Seaman Recruit	SR
E2	Seaman Apprentice	SA
E3	Seaman	SN
E4	Petty Officer Third Class	PO3
E5	Petty Officer Second Class	PO2
E6	Petty Officer First Class	PO1
E7	Chief Petty Officer	CPO
E8	Senior Chief Petty Officer	SCPO
E9	Master Chief Petty Officer	MCPO
	Fleet/Command Master Chief Petty Officer	CMC
	Master Chief Petty Officer of the Navy	MCPON
W1	USN Warrant Officer 1	WO1
W2	USN Chief Warrant Officer 2	CWO2
W3	USN Chief Warrant Officer 3	CWO3
W4	USN Chief Warrant Officer 4	CWO4
W5	USN Chief Warrant Officer 5	CWO5
O1	Ensign	ENS
O2	Lieutenant Junior Grade	LTJG
O3	Lieutenant	LT
O4	Lieutenant Commander	LCDR
O5	Commander	CDR
O6	Captain	CAPT
O7	Rear Admiral Lower Half	RDML
O8	Rear Admiral Upper Half	RADM
O9	Vice Admiral	VADM
O10	Admiral	ADM
	Fleet Admiral (reserved for wartime only)	FADM

UNITED STATES NAVY (USN) RANKS

```
A P P R E N T I C E L T I T T
B F P Y J U N I O R G R A D E
T L L Y O C Q E K S I E T O N
S E F E R E C I F F O P N S S
I E D E T S I L N E Y X A C I
L T N O I T O M O R P E N T G
A A O R F H R E T S A M E I N
R D S S A L C T S R I F T U P
E M S E N I O R Z R K V U R A
N I I W A R R A N T F R E C Y
E R C O M M I S S I O N I E G
G A V I C E A D M I R A L R R
B L C O M M A N D E R H V P A
V S P E C I A L I S T Y W B D
P E T T Y O F F I C E R B R E
```

Apprentice	Expert	Master	Seaman
Chief	First class	Officer	Senior
Commander	Fleet Admiral	Pay grade	Specialist
Commission	Generalist	Petty Officer	Title
Enlisted	Junior grade	Promotion	Vice Admiral
Ensign	Lieutenant	Recruit	Warrant

BATTLE OF BELLEAU WOOD

★ ★ ★ ★ ★ ★ ★ ★ ★ ★ ★ ★

This key victory of World War I is entrenched in Marine Corps lore—for good reason.

The June 1918 fighting in Belleau Wood is a defining event in Marine Corps history: it was their first large-scale engagement and the deadliest in the Corps' history until that time. The U.S. 2nd and 3rd Divisions were fighting the German army alongside French and British forces in a hunting preserve near the Marne River. On June 1, the Germans infiltrated the French lines, forcing the Americans to fill in the gap they created on the road toward Paris, a mere 39 miles away; on June 2, the Germans advanced through the Wood.

The French ordered the Americans to dig trenches at the rear—an order Marine Captain Lloyd W. Williams ignored, famously stating "Retreat? Hell, we just got here!" Despite being heavily outnumbered, the Marines went on the offensive, attacking the Germans as they approached and forcing them into a retreat. Over the course of the next three weeks, the Marines continued their offensive, engaging in relentless hand-to-hand combat in the dense forest with difficult terrain. After six attacks, in which both sides incurred heavy casualties, the Germans were finally expelled from the Wood on June 26 by the 3rd Battalion, 5th Marines. The message that was sent to American Expeditionary Forces headquarters: "Woods now U.S. Marine Corps entirely."

The Marines' victory was a morale booster for the Allies, and it also helped prevent the Germans from taking Paris. In gratitude, the French renamed Belleau Wood the *Bois de la Brigade de Marine*, or "Wood of the Marine Brigade." And the Germans—who had severely underestimated the determination of their American opponents—dubbed the Marines *teufel hunden*, or "devil dogs" . . . a nickname the Marines embrace to this day.

BATTLE OF BELLEAU WOOD

```
R F U H C N E R F A O P Z X K
P R E V E N T W I L L I A M S
K R X M M A I E X P E L L E D
R X H C E C A P T A I N R E E
E R Q R I L O R E D C M A M T
V G T P A R I S O W O D G P E
I E D T S E R O F R L J R T R
R L D O T B W R A I Y F A E M
E B L C B E L L E A U L T R I
N R L A R G E S C A L E I R N
R I X L A F T C O M B A T A A
A T T A C K E Z V A V H U I T
M I V S E H C N E R T J D N I
Z S T E U F E L H U N D E N O
Z H E V I S N E F F O B O T N
```

Attack	Determination	Lore	Retreat
Belleau	Expelled	Marne River	Terrain
British	Forest	Morale	Teufel hunden
Captain	French	Offensive	Trenches
Combat	Gratitude	Paris	Williams
Deadliest	Large-scale	Prevent	Wood

MATHEW BRADY BY THE NUMBERS

★ ★ ★ ★ ★ ★ ★ ★ ★ ★ ★ ★

Before the American Civil War, images of soldiers and battles were mainly pen-and-ink drawings sketched by war correspondents. All that changed with the development of the camera—and the images captured by the war's best-known photographer, Mathew Brady.

0: Photographs Brady took of Lee's surrender to Grant. He didn't get the news until after the surrender had happened. When he arrived at Appomattox, he could only photograph the outside of the building and the empty room inside; Soldiers hunting for souvenirs had stripped the room of everything from pillow cushions to inkwells.

1: Number of photographs taken of an actual battle. The forgettable photo, taken at Sharpsburg, shows a man looking down on a smoky field. To the far right and far left you can make out horses facing the unseen battle. Technology didn't allow for action shots, so Brady's battlefield photos were limited to the aftermath of combat—gripping scenes of the carnage of war.

2: Photographic wagons complete with traveling darkrooms that Brady took to the battlefield. Because they looked so odd, Soldiers nicknamed them "whatsit" wagons, as in "What is it?"

2: Countries (France and Britain) that wanted to buy Brady's Civil War photos, which he called "War Views." Brady didn't want to sell them to a foreign nation, but the United States wasn't interested. The New York Historical Society wanted them, but they didn't have the money.

3: Minutes a subject had to pose motionless; otherwise, they'd appear as a ghostly, transparent image—or not at all.

6: The number of visiting card-sized photographs that Soldiers could get for $1.50 when they came to Brady's studios in New York City or Washington, D.C. These studio portraits, known as *cartes des vistes*, funded Brady's project to record the war.

38: Brady's age when the Civil War started and he decided to become the historical photographer of the war.

1844: Year that Brady opened his first studio at the corner of Broadway and Fulton Street in New York City. Before the war, the rich and famous all came to be photographed by "Brady of Broadway."

5,000: Number of photographers active during the Civil War.

8,000: Images in Brady's "War Views." When the U.S. government declined to purchase them, Brady put them in storage. In 1871, when he couldn't pay the $2,840 storage bill, the photos became the property of the storage company and were finally purchased by the government at auction. Four years later, the government awarded $25,000 to the destitute Brady for all rights to the photos.

$100,000: What Brady estimated his "War Views" were worth. Coincidentally, this was the same amount as the debt he'd accrued after spending four years taking the photographs.

MATHEW BRADY BY THE NUMBERS

Aftermath
Appomattox
Auction
Battle
Brady
Britain

Broadway
Camera
Carnage
Civil War
Combat
Darkrooms

Debt
Destitute
France
Grant
Images
Photographer

Sharpsburg
Still
Storage
Studio
Surrender
War Views

THE BLUE ANGELS

★ ★ ★ ★ ★ ★ ★ ★ ★ ★ ★ ★ ★

About 11 million spectators come out each year to watch the Naval Flight Demonstration Squadron, the brainstorm of Chief of Naval Operations Admiral Chester W. Nimitz to encourage recruitment.

Yes, their planes are blue, but their nickname doesn't come from their heavenly flights. The team's members noticed an ad for the Blue Angel, a New York City nightclub, in the *New Yorker* magazine and thought it would be the perfect nickname for the team.

Since 1946, more than 260 Navy and Marine Corps pilots have served with the Blue Angels squadron of 16 officers. The Blue Angels have always flown the most advanced planes, beginning with the Grumman F6F Hellcat and flying the F/A-18 Super Hornet today. The Super Hornet can reach a maximum speed of Mach 1.60. During shows, the Blue Angels' speeds range from 120 to 700 mph.

Without "Fat Albert," there would be no Angels. Fat Albert Airlines is the nickname for the Lockheed-Martin C-130T Hercules that carries 40 maintenance personnel, spare parts, and communication equipment to Blue Angels shows. The Fat Albert is staffed by an all-Marine crew of three officers and five enlisted personnel. The Hercules cargo plane is a far cry from the sleek Super Hornets, but it has its own characteristics that make it an asset in combat. Although it flies at speeds of only up to 360 mph, it can take off using runways as short as 2,500 feet. It can also perform a jet-assisted takeoff (JATO) by using eight solid fuel rocket bottles to thrust the Hercules into the air. With JATO the huge aircraft can take off within 1,500 feet by climbing at a 45-degree angle and rising 1,000 feet in 15 seconds.

THE BLUE ANGELS

```
O Q W H R L F P O D T T I F J
T C R G E F S X S G E E N M S
A O F T O R L A B W R E S K Q
J M A E S E C N A V D A P S U
E B K S G S N U M D Q G C S A
P A I Q P L H I L Y B R O T D
T T O N Z E B S C E F U W O R
S M A Q L G C U I K S M U L O
Z V I L K N T T L B N M N I N
Y C C E N A X H A C W A S P Z
W A E D X E H L G T T N M J T
T L T H R U S T X I O H F E I
S K A I R L I N E S L R G E M
B X T R E B L A T A F F S I I
R E C R U I T M E N T S S V N
```

Advances	Fat Albert	Navy	Sleek
Airlines	Flight	Nickname	Spectators
Asset	Grumman	Nightclub	Speed
Blue Angels	Hellcat	Nimitz	Squadron
Cargo	Hercules	Pilots	Takeoff
Combat	JATO	Recruitment	Thrust

NATIONAL MUSEUM OF THE UNITED STATES AIR FORCE

★ ★ ★ ★ ★ ★ ★ ★ ★ ★ ★ ★ ★

Located in Dayton, Ohio, is the world's largest and oldest military aviation museum.

In their hometown bicycle shop in Dayton, Wilbur and Orville Wright conceived and built the world's first power-driven, heavier-than-air machine capable of free, controlled, and sustained flight. And it was at the nearby Huffman Prairie Flying Field that the Wrights perfected their invention in the early 1900s. It is fitting that this is also the location of the world's largest and most complete collection of U.S. Air Force aircraft and artifacts.

Since the 1920s, artifacts related to Army aviation were collected and displayed in a variety of locations, usually on air bases. In order to preserve and protect these priceless and important pieces of American service history for future generations, the National Museum of the U.S. Air Force was established in 1922 and opened in 1923.

Located adjacent to Wright-Patterson Air Force Base in a complex of hangarlike buildings are housed more than 75,000 small items, including flight suits, G-suits, and space suits; trophies and memorabilia; technical equipment; and more than 360 aircraft and missiles. On display are balloons and aircraft dating from the early 1900s made of wire, wood, and fabric. Nearby are many of today's most modern aircraft, molded of composite materials formed to reflect radar energy—some piloted, some not. Creative displays invite visitors to imagine the challenges faced by pilots and support troops throughout the Air Force's history. A whimsical yet familiar life-size exhibit of an early military training aircraft transports anyone who has ever flown or maintained training aircraft back to a moment immediately following a minor "ground looping" accident. Mannequins represent the angry instructor pilot, the dejected student, the irritated maintenance chief, and the dumbfounded apprentice—all reacting to the nosed-over propeller-driven plane.

Every piece of hardware in the museum is accompanied by stories about its creation, construction, and utilization. Visitors can wander through acres of some of the most rare and iconic aircraft ever flown by American Airmen. The museum is the world's largest and oldest military aviation museum and today is charged with portraying the heritage and traditions of the Air Force. It is a treasure trove of Air Force history for those seeking to understand the evolution of American military airpower.

But the NMUSAF is far more than just a museum. As a large part of the Office of Air Force History, the museum staff provides technical and professional guidance to the U.S. Air Force History and Museums Program. This extensive program includes numerous field museums in addition to domestic and international heritage sites. The staff is accountable for more than 6,000 historical artifacts and aircraft and spacecraft on loan to 450 civilian museums, cities, municipalities, and veterans' organizations throughout the world.

NATIONAL MUSEUM OF THE UNITED STATES AIR FORCE

```
G U I D A N C E E Q I B O T I
Y R O T S I H R C N K T X N Q
B S I T E S A W A A I R M E N
Z U O F O R J X P E T O R M E
E X H I B I T S S B H P E P R
S N O I T I D A R T G H T I A
Q H Z D Y X S I L N I I I U W
A I R P O W E R O K R E U Q D
R E V O L U T I O N W S S E R
I O T I U S T H G I L F G T A
S R A G N A H N O T Y A D U H
E R G W I C O N I C L H C I S
H Q D V T A I V M U S E U M X
S P A C E C R A F T E P U M K
F A S U M N H E R I T A G E H
```

Airmen	Exhibits	Heritage	Sites
Airpower	Flight suit	History	Space
Aviation	G-suit	Iconic	Spacecraft
Dayton	Guidance	Museum	Traditions
Equipment	Hangars	NMUSAF	Trophies
Evolution	Hardware	Rare	Wright

BIG WEEK, PART I

★ ★ ★ ★ ★ ★ ★ ★ ★ ★ ★ ★ ★

"Big Week," the events that transpired from February 20 to February 25 in 1944, signaled a transformation in the American air campaign in Europe and the beginning of the end of the war for Germany.

"I could see the omen of the war's end when I lay in my sickbed and watched the bombers of the American Fifteenth Air Force fly across the Alps from their Italian bases to bomb German industrial targets and there wasn't a German fighter plane anywhere in sight."

—Albert Speer, Germany's Minister of Armaments

AIR SUPREMACY

If D-day was going to be a success, the Allies had to gain operational air supremacy over the Luftwaffe beforehand. The plan—later known as Big Week but officially called Operation Argument—was to lure the Luftwaffe into the skies by targeting German aircraft plants. Killing German pilots in the process would make aircraft production irrelevant: Germany would not be able to train new pilots at a fast enough rate to replace those killed. It would be the first time that Luftwaffe planes and pilots were targeted as the number-one priority, as opposed to using Allied aircraft for defensive purposes.

WAITING FOR WEATHER

By February 1944, there were enough bombers and escort fighters to begin the massive raids against Germany that General Henry H. "Hap" Arnold, commander of the Army Air Forces (AAF), had requested. But the weather over Europe wasn't right for sustained combat missions until Sunday, February 20, when Army meteorologists finally delivered a favorable forecast: an extended period of clear weather that would be perfect for visual bombardment.

PLANS INTO ACTION

General Carl "Tooey" Spaatz, the American air commander of the European theater, personally issued the order to begin the raids. Lieutenant General Jimmy Doolittle's 8th Air Force contributed the majority of the attack forces on this first mission, which consisted of more than 1,000 bombers. It was the first time that the AAF had launched that many bombers on a single raid. (Technically, only 971 of the bombers received mission credit, but more than 1,000 were launched.) Accompanying the bombers would be more than 900 long-range American fighter planes. In all, 16 bomber wings, 17 fighter groups, and 16 Royal Air Force (RAF) fighter squadrons from the U.K. darkened the skies over Europe.

Turn the page to find out what happened next.

BIG WEEK, PART I

```
X X Z S T L Y E W C L E A R L
Q U K S R A Y C O M B A T T C
X D A M K I D R A B M O B G D
B O M B E R S N Q M R A I D S
T A R G E T N F O R E C A S T
W J E M F S W O L R Z R E A T
Z R H A B U N P I R D R P W P
K T T J W D T E I T U A H U Z
C E A K U N M F F L A H U I S
A A E A D I N I A F O R R Q E
T L W W P J L G S R O T E B S
T L C I G S Y H C S C D S P C
A I E R H I Q T Y D I R P X O
V E K T O M B E S D E O I J R
C S N D L O N R A W P G N A T
```

Aircraft	Bombers	Industrial	Raids
Allies	Clear	Lure	Spaatz
Arnold	Combat	Mission	Squadron
Attack	Escort	Offense	Supremacy
Big Week	Fighter	Operation	Target
Bombard	Forecast	Pilots	Weather

BIG WEEK, PART II

★ ★ ★ ★ ★ ★ ★ ★ ★ ★ ★

"Big Week," the events that transpired from February 20 to February 25 in 1944, signaled a transformation in the American air campaign in Europe and the beginning of the end of the war for Germany. See the article on the previous page to find out what led up to it.

BIG PLANS FOR BIG WEEK

The attack plans for Big Week were complex. Six of the bomber wings flew a diversionary attack—without fighters—to Poland on a northern route, hoping to draw some of the German fighters away from the main bomber force. The rest of the bombers attacked aircraft-industry targets around Leipzig and Brunswick in central Germany. The damage was heavy, though unfortunately machine tools used in aircraft construction escaped significant destruction.

This daylight raid on February 20 had been preceded by an RAF night attack on Leipzig and would be followed each night by coordinated RAF nighttime bombing raids on targets that would be attacked again by American bombers each following day.

THE REST OF THE WEEK

The raids flown on February 21 and 22 were less successful; on February 23, the entire 8th Air Force was grounded due to low clouds and icing conditions, while the 15th Air Force, launching from bases in Italy, flew only 102 bombers against some ball-bearing factories in Austria. On February 24, the clouds broke and more massive attacks were launched on Germany. More than 800 bombers of the 8th and 15th Air Forces attacked Augsburg, Stuttgart, Schweinfurt, and Regensburg under clear skies. On February 25, more than 1,300 bombers and 1,000 fighters struck airplane factories in Germany. The 8th had dropped 10,000 tons of bombs—equaling the total tonnage dropped during the entire first year of its operation. Overall, Allied losses were relatively light and damage inflicted during these raids was severe—largely the result of a precision visual attack. When the participants in these last missions landed, Big Week officially came to an end.

SOMETHING LOST, SOMETHING GAINED

Roughly 2,600 airmen were killed, wounded, or captured during the operation. Of the 3,800 8th and 15th Air Force bombers that flew that week, losses totaled 6 percent—less than predicted by American commanders. RAF attacks against five German cities were equally massive: more than 2,300 bombers dropped nearly 10,000 tons of bombs. And the RAF suffered similar losses.

The effects on German industry were difficult to assess, but of greater impact was the damage done to the Luftwaffe, which lost a third of its single-engine fighters and 20 percent of its pilots. German losses continued into March, and by April the Luftwaffe was unable to effectively defend against the Allied air offensive. Big Week signaled a transformation in the air campaign against Germany.

BIG WEEK, PART II

Airmen
Attack
Augsburg
Austria
Bombs
Brunswick

Clouds
Damage
Daylight
Diversion
Force
Germany

Grounded
Icing
Impact
Italy
Leipzig
Losses

Pilots
Poland
Precision
Regensburg
Route
Tonnage

PRESIDENTS WHO SERVED

★ ★ ★ ★ ★ ★ ★ ★ ★ ★ ★ ★

The President may serve as Commander in Chief of the Armed Forces, but not all of them have spent time in the service. These are the ones who have.

U.S. ARMY/NATIONAL GUARD

George Washington
Thomas Jefferson (Virginia militia)
James Madison (Virginia militia)
James Monroe (Virginia militia)
Andrew Jackson
William Henry Harrison
John Tyler (Virginia militia)
James K. Polk (Tennessee militia)
Zachary Taylor
Millard Fillmore (New York militia)
Franklin Pierce
James Buchanan (Pennsylvania militia)
Abraham Lincoln (Illinois militia)
Andrew Johnson
Ulysses S. Grant
Rutherford B. Hayes
James Garfield
Chester A. Arthur (New York militia)
Benjamin Harrison
William McKinley
Theodore Roosevelt
Harry S. Truman
Dwight D. Eisenhower
Ronald Reagan

U.S. NAVY

John F. Kennedy
Lyndon B. Johnson
Richard Nixon
Gerald Ford
Jimmy Carter
George H. W. Bush

U.S. AIR FORCE

George W. Bush (Texas Air National Guard)

(No presidents have been members of the U.S. Coast Guard, U.S. Marine Corps, or U.S. Space Force.)

PRESIDENTS WHO SERVED

Arthur	Ford	Kennedy	Reagan
Buchanan	Grant	McKinley	Roosevelt
Bush	Harrison	Monroe	Taylor
Carter	Hayes	Nixon	Truman
Eisenhower	Jackson	Pierce	Tyler
Fillmore	Johnson	Polk	Washington

U.S. ARMY BASES

★ ★ ★ ★ ★ ★ ★ ★ ★ ★ ★ ★

The U.S. Army has numerous stateside bases and installations; these are just some of them. Is there one located near you?

ALABAMA
Fort Novosel
Redstone Arsenal

ALASKA
Fort Richardson
Fort Wainwright

ARIZONA
Fort Huachuca
Yuma Proving Ground

CALIFORNIA
Fort Irwin National Training Center
Presidio of Monterey

COLORADO
Fort Carson

GEORGIA
Fort Eisenhower
Fort Moore
Fort Stewart-Hunter Army Airfield

HAWAII
Fort Shafter
Schofield Barracks
Tripler Army Medical Center

KANSAS
Fort Leavenworth
Fort Riley

KENTUCKY
Fort Campbell
Fort Knox

LOUISIANA
Fort Johnson

MARYLAND
Aberdeen Proving Ground
Fort Detrick
Fort George G. Meade

MASSACHUSETTS
Fort Devens

MISSOURI
Fort Leonard Wood

NEW YORK
Fort Drum
Fort Hamilton

NORTH CAROLINA
Fort Liberty

OKLAHOMA
Fort Sill

PENNSYLVANIA
Carlisle Barracks

PUERTO RICO
Fort Buchanan

SOUTH CAROLINA
Fort Jackson

TEXAS
Fort Bliss
Fort Cavazos

UTAH
Dugway Proving Ground

VIRGINIA
Fort Belvoir
Fort Eustis
Fort Gregg-Adams
Fort Story

WASHINGTON
Fort Lewis

WISCONSIN
Fort McCoy

U.S. ARMY BASES

Bliss	Eustis	Lewis	Schofield
Buchanan	Hamilton	McCoy	Shafter
Campbell	Jackson	Moore	Stewart-Hunter
Carson	Johnson	Novosel	Story
Cavazos	Knox	Redstone	Tripler
Eisenhower	Leavenworth	Riley	Yuma

NOTABLE QUOTABLES: LEADERSHIP

★ ★ ★ ★ ★ ★ ★ ★ ★ ★ ★ ★ ★

- ★ "Do what is right, not what you think the high headquarters wants or what you think will make you look good." —General Norman Schwarzkopf

- ★ "Leadership is the art of getting someone else to do something you want done because he wants to do it." —General Dwight D. Eisenhower

- ★ "Lead me, follow me, or get the hell out of my way." —General George S. Patton, Jr.

- ★ "Discipline is the soul of an army. It makes small numbers formidable, procures success to the weak, and esteem to all." —Lieutenant General George Washington

- ★ "The art of war is simple enough. Find out where your enemy is. Get at him as soon as you can. Strike at him as hard as you can and as often as you can, and keep moving on." —General Ulysses S. Grant

- ★ "War's legitimate object is more perfect peace." —General William Tecumseh Sherman

- ★ "A competent leader can get efficient service from poor troops, while on the contrary an incapable leader can demoralize the best of troops." —General John J. Pershing

- ★ "Men think as their leaders think." —General Charles P. Summerall

- ★ "You can have all the material in the world, but without morale it is largely ineffective." —General George C. Marshall

- ★ "Leadership in a democratic Army means firmness, not harshness; understanding, not weakness; justice, not license; humaneness, not intolerance; generosity, not selfishness; pride, not egotism." —General Omar N. Bradley

- ★ "There is far more to professional fitness and skill in the techniques and tools of war. These the officer must have, but the final test of his ability is not in what he knows but in what he is. There is no substitute for those innate qualities which we generally refer to as character." —General Matthew B. Ridgway

- ★ "Never tell people how to do things. Tell them what to do and they will surprise you with their ingenuity." —General George S. Patton, Jr.

- ★ "Once you pick up the burden of leadership, you can never put it down again as long as you live. Sergeant or general, we all carry the same load." —General Winston B. Palmer

NOTABLE QUOTABLES: LEADERSHIP

```
B R A D L E Y P A L M E R S N
G U P P F O L L O W K A R T I
P U T A K E C A B I L I T Y Z
G R A N T O F H E C V A U N I
M B I M U T P B A S V N P N A
Q H W O H Q O F I R M N E S S
T U A R B C K N N B A N N U P
O Y S A G U Z I A T A C R F M
O A H L L A R E M M U S T W A
L W I E T L A D R R E D A E L
S G N H S J W I E E S A S F R
U D G K L J H R H N F E I G Z
L I T C K Y C P S E L P M I S
R R O D E I S E N H O W E R U
Q U N D E R S T A N D I N G A
```

Ability	Firmness	Patton	Simple
Art	Follow	Pride	Summerall
Bradley	Grant	Ridgway	Think
Burden	Leader	Right	Tools
Character	Morale	Schwarzkopf	Understanding
Eisenhower	Palmer	Sherman	Washington

ANGEL IN FATIGUES

★ ★ ★ ★ ★ ★ ★ ★ ★ ★ ★ ★ ★

The Army's most decorated nurse, and only the third woman to be promoted to the rank of Colonel, spent World War II providing medical assistance in a prisoner of war camp. Learn more about Ruby Bradley, the "angel in fatigues."

Ruby Bradley was born in 1907 on a farm in West Virginia. She taught school before becoming a nurse in 1933; a year later, she joined the Army Nurse Corps as a surgical nurse. When the Japanese attacked Pearl Harbor on December 7, 1941, Bradley was serving as hospital administrator at Camp John Hay on Luzon Island in the Philippines. The Japanese took over the site on December 23, and Bradley, along with a doctor and another nurse, hid in the nearby hills, but the trio was forced to surrender five days later. They were sent back to their former post, now a POW camp.

Despite the risks, Bradley and a doctor who was also a POW helped set up a dispensary and smuggled drugs and surgical instruments from the camp hospital in order to provide medical assistance to their fellow POWs. The first surgery they performed was an appendectomy, and Bradley later assisted a woman in labor by anesthetizing her with ether using gauze and a tea strainer.

Bradley was transferred to Santo Tomas Internment Camp in Manila in September 1943, and she remained there until it was liberated in February 1945. At Santo Tomas, Bradley shared her meager rations (half a cup of rice twice a day) with children in the camp, and stole as much extra food as she could to distribute to the children; as she lost weight and her uniform grew larger on her already-slender frame, she used the extra room to smuggle surgical equipment. During her time in captivity, Bradley assisted with 230 major operations and helped deliver 13 babies, earning the nickname "Angel in Fatigues" from her fellow prisoners.

After the war, Bradley stayed in the Army and earned a bachelor's degree in nursing through an Army training program. When the Korean War broke out in 1950, Bradley went to work as a combat nurse evacuating hospitals. In November of that year, during a counter-offensive during which nearly 100,000 enemy soldiers overran American troops, she helped to evacuate the sick and wounded onto a plane in Pyongyang—she was the last to board the plane, making it aboard just before her ambulance was destroyed by an enemy shell. When Ruby Bradley left Korea in 1953, she was given a full-dress honor guard ceremony—the first time in history a woman had received a national or international guard salute.

Bradley was promoted to the rank of Colonel in 1958. When she retired in 1963, she had earned 34 medals, including two Legion of Merit, two Bronze Stars, and the International Red Cross's Florence Nightingale Medal. She spent another 17 years working in the nursing field back home in West Virginia and passed away in 2002; she is buried in Arlington National Cemetery.

ANGEL IN FATIGUES

```
G N A Y G N O Y P Y M R W F Y
B M Y M U F S L Y R Q V I H O
R Z M R C Y A D L E G N A C S
O S S T R N L R S G Y J B G E
N E N S E U U A M R E Y U E N
Z O Q D Q C T U U U L R C T Q
E H O L Z U E G G S D A H A L
S T A B M O C R G M A S I U A
T V A E R O K O L J R N L C T
A M V C O L O N E L B E D A I
R S A N T O T O M A S P R V P
I E W N L E Z H A K J S E E S
T D E L I V E R Y D F I N T O
M J W J M L M A W L Q D I A H
S E U G I T A F S N O I T A R
```

Angel
Bradley
Bronze Star
Children
Colonel
Combat

Delivery
Dispensary
Drugs
Evacuate
Fatigues
Honor Guard

Hospital
Korea
Manila
Nurse
Plane
Pyongyang

Rations
Rice
Salute
Santo Tomas
Smuggle
Surgery

TRIPOLI TO MONTEZUMA, PART I

★ ★ ★ ★ ★ ★ ★ ★ ★ ★ ★ ★

"From the halls of Montezuma / to the shores of Tripoli; / We fight our country's battles / in the air, on land, and sea." Ever wondered what the "shores of" the capital of Libya and the "halls of" the last king of the Aztecs are doing in the "Marines' Hymn"?

THE SHORES OF TRIPOLI

Following the 1783 peace treaty with Great Britain, the Continental Congress sold off all the Navy's ships. Now without a navy, the new country was forced to pay tribute to the Barbary pirates who operated along the North African cost in order to protect its commercial interests in the area. Three of the Barbary areas—Morocco, Tunis, and Tripoli—kept their demands within reason, but the pasha of Algiers raised his fees so high that Congress established the United States Navy in 1794 and an independent United States Marine Corps in 1798.

In May 1801, the pasha of Tripoli, Yussif Karamanli, decided the U.S. wasn't paying him enough, and he declared war. America responded by sending Navy ships to blockade the port city. After a daring but lengthy naval campaign, President Thomas Jefferson sought a faster way to end the war. Marine Corps First Lieutenant Presley O'Bannon, along with Consul General William Eaton, led an army of about 400 mercenaries, along with seven Marines, and marched west 600 miles from Alexandria, Egypt, to Tripoli. After seven weeks, they arrived at the border city of Derna.

While three ships of the Navy's Mediterranean Squadron bombarded Derna by sea, mercenaries attacked from the south, and O'Bannon, his Marines, and additional mercenaries attacked from the east. In 30 minutes, O'Bannon and Eaton controlled Derna, and within the month Karamanli signed a peace treaty with the United States. (The elegant Mameluke sword gifted to O'Bannon by Prince Hamet, Ottoman viceroy, was adopted by the Marine Corps in 1825 as standard issue.)

Turn the page to find out about the "halls of Montezuma."

TRIPOLI TO MONTEZUMA, PART I

```
F Q N N Y Y T N E G L S M M Z
Y U B M R V K A S A O E O A G
S R Q Y M C A K L N R R N M M
Y K D H A U A N A I T O T E Z
T O T T R L W I Z V N H E L B
A B T T C F A K T I O S Z U A
E A R R H V L I E C C K U K R
R N I O E P X S C E V A M E B
T N B P D A Q T S R E R A D A
E O U D R U S X U O E A L O R
C N T K A W H V P Y Y M T Q Y
A Z E D O A N R E D T A M O L
E A R R S A H S A P Q N D O N
P O D P I R A T E S M L T M C
N M F M S E N I R A M I J H R
```

Attack	Eaton	Montezuma	Port
Aztecs	Hymn	Navy	Shores
Barbary	Karamanli	O'Bannon	Squadron
Commercial	Mameluke	Pasha	Sword
Control	Marched	Peace treaty	Tribute
Derna	Marines	Pirates	Viceroy

TRIPOLI TO MONTEZUMA, PART II

"From the halls of Montezuma / to the shores of Tripoli; / We fight our country's battles / in the air, on land, and sea." You learned about the "shores of" Tripoli on the previous page; now find out about the rest of the famous opening lines.

THE HALLS OF MONTEZUMA

By 1845, President James Polk's expansionist policies had led to a war with Mexico. After expelling the Mexican army from California, Sailors and Marines attacked Mexico's Pacific coastal cities and captured Monterrey. By September 1847, American forces had fought their way to Chapultepec Castle outside Mexico City. Home of the Mexican military academy, the stone-walled castle sat atop a 200-foot-high volcanic hill and was defended by approximately 800 soldiers, including some 100 military academy cadets.

While American artillery bombarded the castle, the Marines advanced, but they were halted by cannon fire 250 yards from the castle and took cover in a ditch. Other Marine and Army units flanked the castle and broke through its defenses. As the defenders turned to face them, the Marines rose, scaled the walls, and joined the melee, forcing the Mexican troops to surrender.

The next morning, a joint Marine and Army company attacked the Mexican capital. Closing on the San Cosmé Gate, they took heavy fire from entrenched artillery and infantry firing from the rooftops. As the Army troops returned fire from behind the walls of a garden, the leathernecks charged the gate.

When the triumphant Marines returned to Washington, they were presented with a flag featuring an eagle and an anchor, inscribed with their new motto: "From the halls of Montezuma to the shores of Tripoli."

TRIPOLI TO MONTEZUMA, PART II

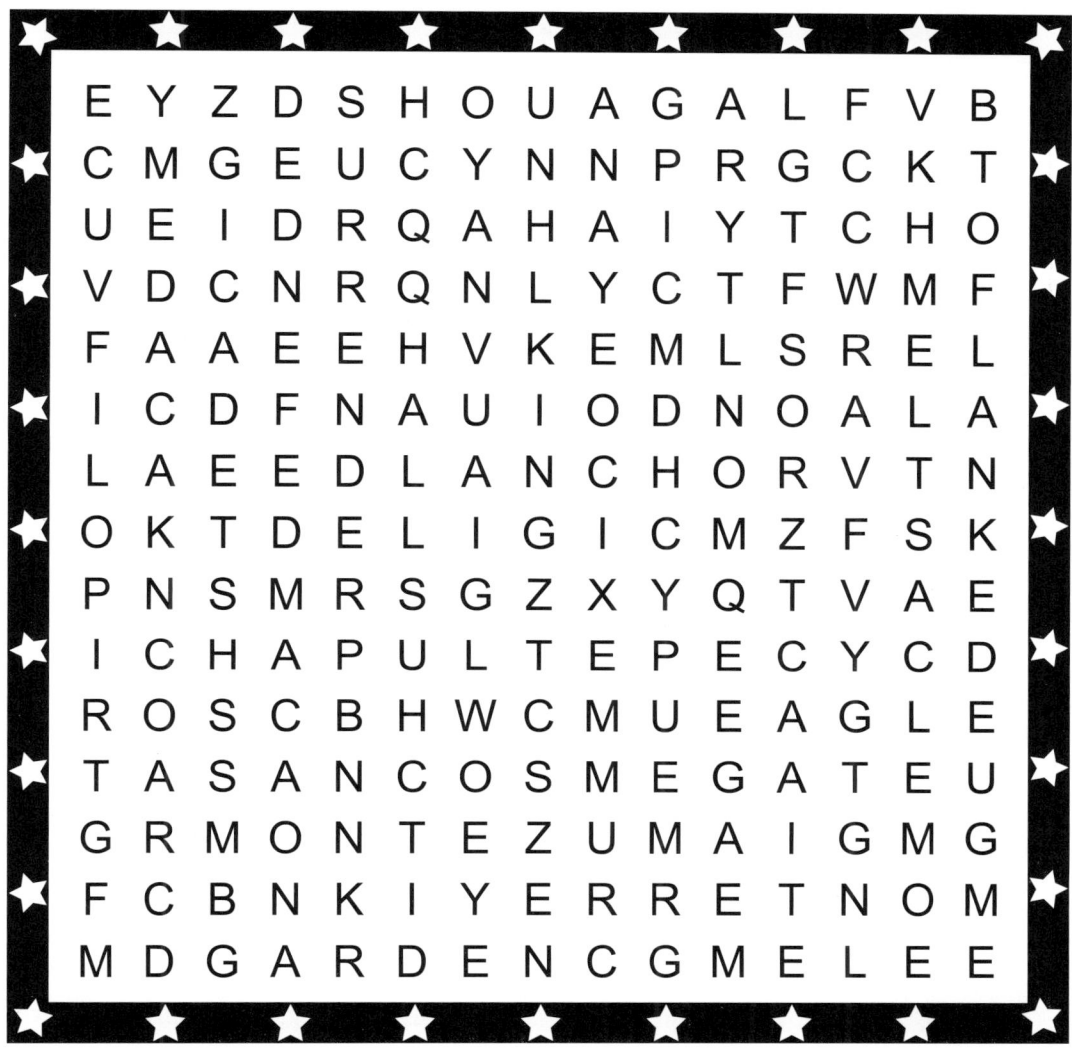

Academy
Anchor
Army
Cadets
Castle
Chapultepec
Defended
Ditch
Eagle
Flag
Flanked
Garden
Halls
Hymn
Melee
Mexico
Monterrey
Montezuma
San Cosmé Gate
Scaled
Surrender
Tripoli
Units
Volcano

HISTORICAL DOGS OF WAR: SERGEANT STUBBY

★ ★ ★ ★ ★ ★ ★ ★ ★ ★ ★ ★ ★

The creation of the Army K-9 Corps in 1942 gave dogs an official role in the United States Military. But plenty of four-legged troops had already served in battle alongside human warfighters since the nation's earliest days. One of their stories was on page 32; here is another.

The most decorated dog of World War I is also the only canine to be promoted to sergeant through combat. Stubby, a stray, inadvertently volunteered for service in July 1917 by wandering onto the Yale University campus where the 102nd Infantry Regiment was training. After developing a fondness for the bull terrier mix, Corporal James Robert Conroy smuggled him aboard the troop ship when the unit was sent to France.

Stubby served for 18 months, participating in four offenses and 17 battles, suffering from two separate injuries and a mustard gas attack (after which he was outfitted with his own custom gas mask). In addition to aiding his fellow soldiers by warning them of gas attacks and incoming artillery shells, and by locating missing soldiers, Stubby also single-handedly captured a German spy . . . by securely holding onto the enemy's posterior with his teeth.

Corporal Conroy smuggled Stubby back home at war's end, and Stubby quickly became a national celebrity. He was presented with a gold medal from the Humane Education Society by General John G. Pershing himself. When Stubby died in his sleep in 1926, Conroy had a taxidermy of the dog created, which houses his cremains. Conroy donated Stubby to the Smithsonian Institute in 1956, and the dog is still on display today—in full uniform—at the National Museum of American History.

HISTORICAL DOGS OF WAR: SERGEANT STUBBY

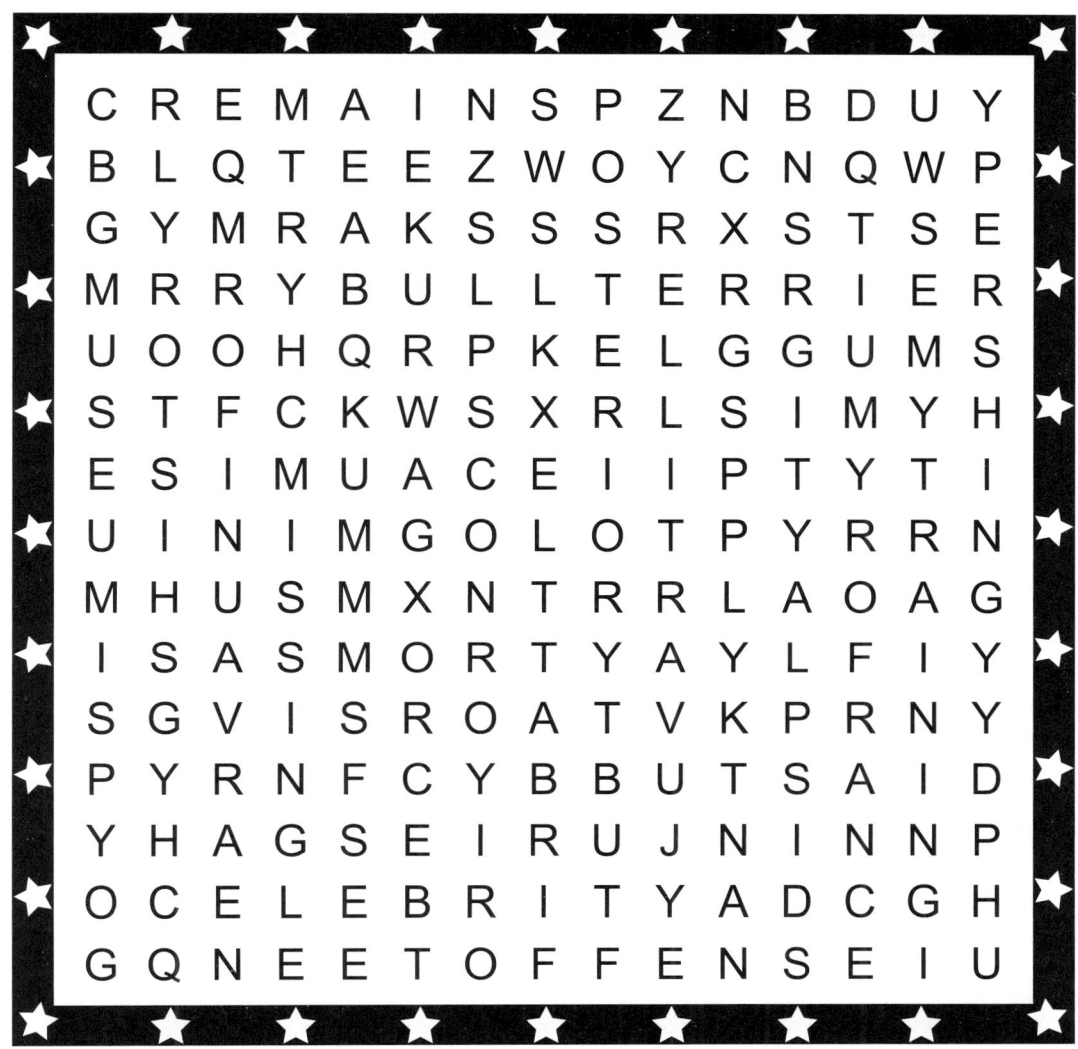

Army	Cremains	Missing	Spy
Artillery	Display	Museum	Stray
Battle	France	Offense	Stubby
Bull terrier	Gas mask	Pershing	Training
Celebrity	History	Posterior	Uniform
Conroy	Injuries	Smuggle	Yale

TOP U.S. COAST GUARD RESCUES

★ ★ ★ ★ ★ ★ ★ ★ ★ ★ ★ ★ ★

Here are the details of just a few of the most daring rescues carried out by the Coast Guard.

Rescue: Overland Expedition
When: 1897–98
Where: Near Point Barrow, Alaska
Lives saved: 260
The Coast Guard cutter *Bear* was sent on an expedition to rescue eight whaling ships trapped in the Arctic ice near Point Barrow, Alaska. Unable to navigate the ice, Lieutenant David H. Jarvis led a party of five other men, along with sled dogs and reindeer, on an overland expedition of 1,500 miles to rescue the stranded whaling crews.

Rescue: U.S. Army transport ship *Dorchester*
When: February 3, 1943
Where: Off the coast of Greenland
Lives saved: 230
The Coast Guard cutters *Comanche* and *Escanaba* responded to the torpedoing of the *Dorchester* in the frigid North Atlantic. Knowing that the survivors had only minutes to live in the icy waters, the crew of the *Escanaba* used what was then the new "retriever" rescue technique: rescue swimmers in wetsuits swam to victims and secured a line to them so they could be hauled onto the ship. The *Escanaba* saved 133 men (one of whom died later) and the *Comanche* saved 97.

Rescue: Hurricane Katrina
When: August 29, 2005
Where: New Orleans and the Mississippi Gulf Coast
Lives saved: 33,545
More than 5,000 Coast Guardsmen served in Katrina operations. Seventy-six Coast Guard and Coast Guard Auxiliary aircraft took part in the search-and-rescue operations that saved 24,135 lives from danger, mostly the people on the roofs of their homes. Coast Guardsmen also evacuated 9,409 patients from local hospitals. Flying 1,817 sorties, the aircrews saved more than 12,000 lives; 42 cutters and 131 small boats rescued more than 21,000. *Time* magazine noted: "The Coast Guard was saving lives before any other federal agency—despite the fact that almost half the local Coast Guard personnel lost their own homes in the hurricane."

TOP U.S. COAST GUARD RESCUES

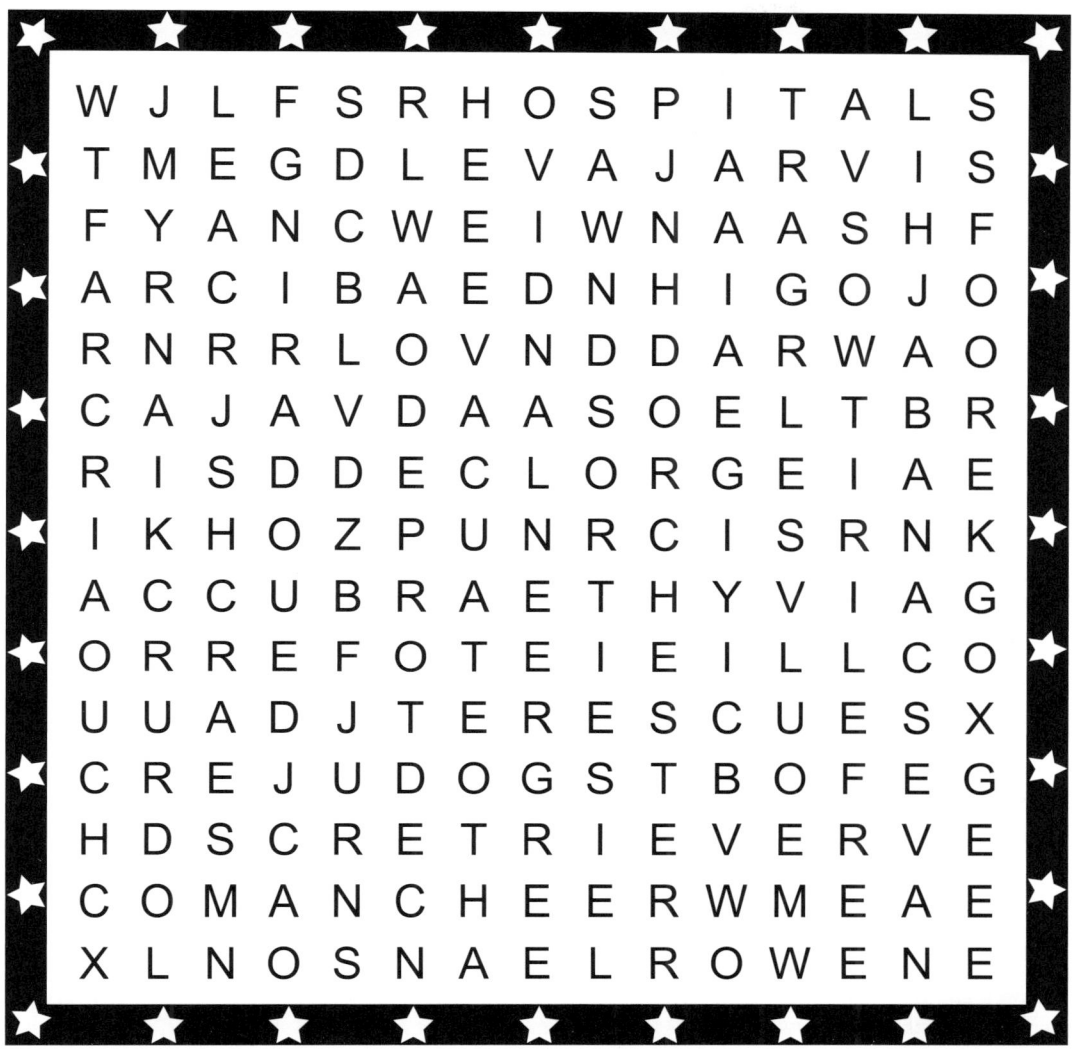

Aircraft
Alaska
Bear
Comanche
Cutter
Daring
Dorchester
Escanaba
Evacuate
Greenland
Hospitals
Jarvis
Katrina
Line
New Orleans
Reindeer
Rescue
Retriever
Roofs
Search
Sled dogs
Sorties
Torpedo
Whaling

VIETNAM WAR MEDAL OF HONOR: ED FREEMAN

★ ★ ★ ★ ★ ★ ★ ★ ★ ★ ★ ★ ★

During the Vietnam War, 248 military personnel were awarded the Medal of Honor for valorous action (156 were awarded posthumously). Each recipient has an extraordinary story—this is just one.

Ed "Too Tall" Freeman was born in Neely, Mississippi, in 1927. He joined the Army at 17 and served through the Korean War as an infantryman. During the war, he found a new goal: becoming an airman. But he was turned down for flight school in 1953 because, at 6'6", he was two inches taller than regulations allowed—a dilemma that gave him his nickname, "Too Tall." The height restriction was eased in 1955, allowing Freeman to become an Army aircraft pilot.

On November 14, 1965, helicopters dropped off about 450 American troops in a clearing in the Ia Drang Valley, a remote area of Vietnam. The troops were of the 1st Battalion, 7th Cavalry, led by Lieutenant Colonel Harold Moore, and the clearing was code-named Landing Zone (LZ) X-Ray. LZ X-Ray turned out to be a sanctuary for the North Vietnamese Army (NVA), and Moore's battalion was surrounded by more than 2,000 NVA troops. They were attacked with machine-gun fire and rocket-propelled grenades. Joseph Galloway, a reporter at Ia Drang, later compared the dire predicament of Moore's troops to a modern version of Custer's Last Stand.

At that time, Captain Freeman was flying an unarmed Huey helicopter with Company A, 229th Assault Helicopter Battalion. Company A's Hueys were a lifeline to American soldiers in Ia Drang, but after the NVA shot up two helicopters so badly that they couldn't fly, Lieutenant Moore ordered the LZ closed.

No helicopters were supposed to fly into the combat zone after the closure because it was too dangerous, but Major Bruce Crandall decided to fly in anyway. He asked for any volunteers to assist him, and only one pilot stepped forward: Too Tall Freeman. At the risk of his own life, Freeman flew into combat fire to transport ammunition, water, and medical supplies. The gunfire was so intense that medical evacuation helicopters wouldn't fly into the LZ, so Freeman took over, evacuating more than 30 severely wounded men—in some instances saving their lives. Though enemy fighters were sometimes as close as 30 yards away, Freeman kept returning to help the battalion. He did it not once or twice, but 14 times.

Thanks in large part to Freeman and his commander, Crandall (who flew in needed ammunition), the Americans staved off the initial attack; by the end of the fighting at Ia Drang, American troops overcame the North Vietnamese.

Freeman initially won the Distinguished Flying Cross for his actions, but Major Crandall and other witnesses believed he deserved an even higher honor. Crandall, with the help of another decorated Vietnam veteran—Arizona senator John McCain—persuaded Congress to award the highest medal to Freeman. On July 16, 2001, he received the Medal of Honor. (Major Crandall also received a Medal of Honor, in 2007.)

VIETNAM WAR MEDAL OF HONOR: ED FREEMAN

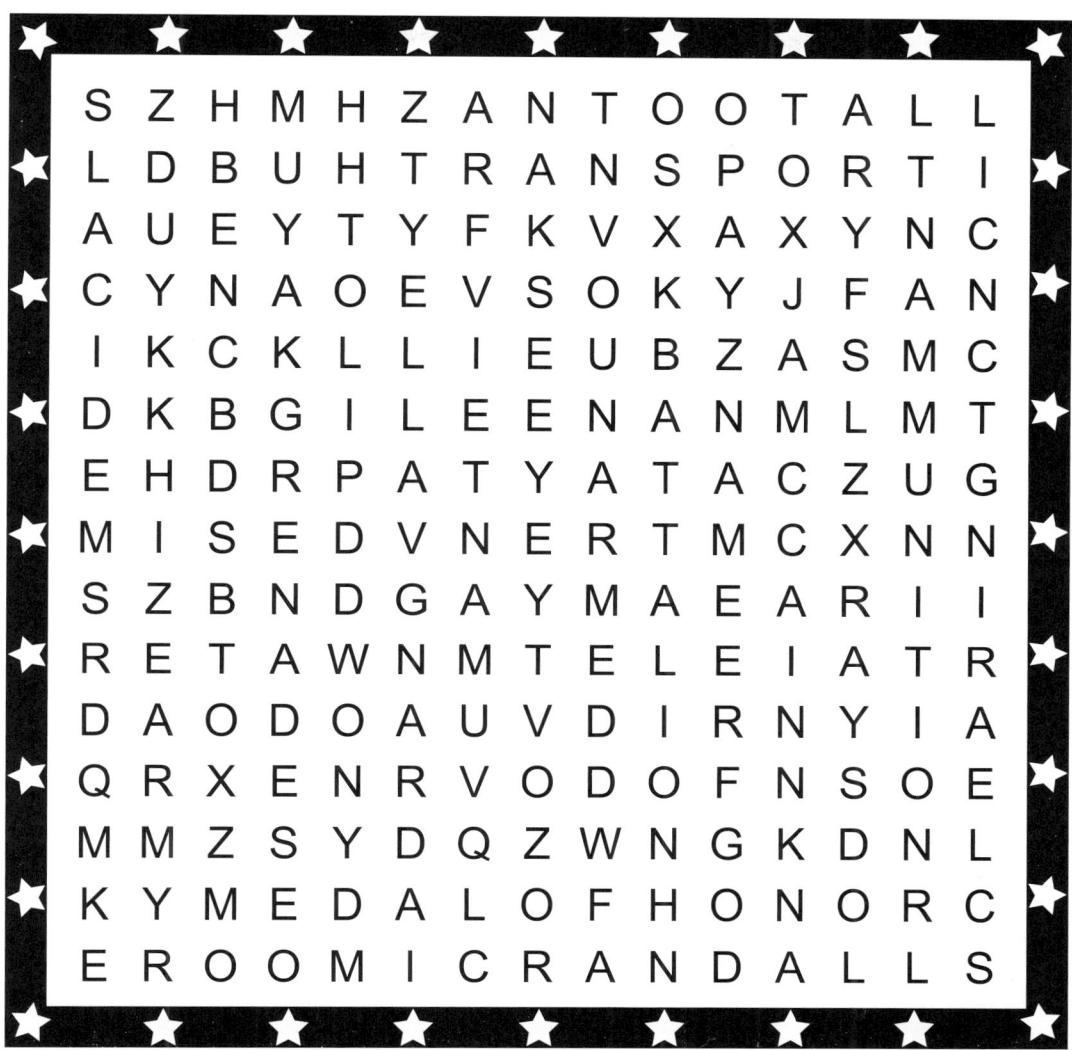

Ammunition	Freeman	McCain	Too Tall
Army	Grenades	Medal of Honor	Transport
Attack	Huey	Medical	Unarmed
Battalion	Ia Drang Valley	Moore	Vietnam
Clearing	Infantryman	Pilot	Water
Crandall	LZ X-Ray	Risk	Wounded

PEARL HARBOR BY THE NUMBERS

★ ★ ★ ★ ★ ★ ★ ★ ★ ★ ★ ★

The Japanese surprise attack on Hawaii's Pearl Harbor Navy base on Sunday, December 7, 1941, launched the United States into World War II's global conflict. It was also one of the most devastating attacks on the U.S. military in the nation's history. Learn more about the "Day of Infamy."

1 hour, 15 minutes: The duration of the attack, which began at 7:55 a.m. Japan had intended to declare war on the United States prior to the attack so as not to violate the Hague Convention of 1907, but the message was delayed until the attack was already in progress.

3: Number of U.S. aircraft carriers that survived the attack. All three were out to sea on maneuvers at the time of the attack. With the Japanese unable to locate them before turning around, the Pacific carrier fleet remained intact.

19: Number of U.S. Navy ships that were damaged or destroyed, including 8 battleships, 3 cruisers, 3 destroyers, and 5 auxiliaries.

34: Number of Japanese craft lost in the attack. There were 29 aircraft and 5 midget submarines lost that day.

61: Total number of Japanese ships involved in the attack, composed of 35 submarines, 11 destroyers, 9 oilers, 2 heavy cruisers, 2 light cruisers, and 2 battleships.

129: Number of Japanese fighters killed. One additional soldier was taken prisoner.

188: Combined number of Army and Navy aircraft completely lost, with an additional 159 damaged.

353: Total number of aircraft in the Japanese strike force, composed of 40 torpedo planes, 103 level bombers, 131 dive bombers, and 79 fighter planes.

2,403: Number of United States personnel killed, including 68 civilians. The Navy suffered the most casualties, with 2,008 dead and 710 wounded; 1,177 were lost on board the USS *Arizona*—which remains sunken at Pearl Harbor to this day—and another 429 were lost on board the USS *Oklahoma*. Other service members killed included 218 Army Air Forces members and 109 Marines.

6 months: Length of time it took for the United States to recover and strike back against Japan, achieving a decisive victory against Japan's Admiral Isoroku Yamamoto at the Battle of Midway in June 1942.

PEARL HARBOR BY THE NUMBERS

```
S E K R T S O D E P R O T A V
R S J E E U P A H H D B F H E
E I T Y E B I R Q D I E A K C
L R A O L M H I T L Z G R M R
I P S R F A S Z W S U S C L O
O R W T R R E O C E M N R R F
E U O S E I L N R I T A I E E
G S U E I N T A D E O I A N K
A T N D R E T W A Y S L G O I
M W D R R S A L C M U I U S R
A U E O A Y B H H A N V U I T
D U D N C K M A M F D I C R S
Z O K L A H O M A N A C Y P C
W S S U R V I V E I Y X D E E
U Q Q B O W Y C K I N T A C T
```

Aircraft
Arizona
Battleship
Carrier fleet
Civilians
Cruiser

Damage
Destroyer
Hague
Infamy
Intact
Marines

Midway
Navy
Oilers
Oklahoma
Prisoner
Strike force

Submarines
Sunday
Surprise
Survive
Torpedo
Wounded

ARMY V. NAVY

★ ★ ★ ★ ★ ★ ★ ★ ★ ★ ★ ★ ★

It's a classic college football rivalry . . . and these quotes about both branches are in competition for the most inspirational.

ARMY

★ "Take time to deliberate; but when the time for action arrives, stop thinking and go in." —Andrew Jackson

★ "The only terms I can accept are immediate and unconditional surrender." —Ulysses S. Grant

★ "It doesn't take a hero to order men into battle. It takes a hero to be one of those men who goes into battle." —General Norman Schwarzkopf

★ "There are no secrets to success. It is the result of preparation, hard work, and learning from failure." —General Colin Powell

★ "No bastard ever won a war by dying for his country. He won it by making the other poor dumb bastard die for his country." —General George S. Patton

★ "Americans never quit."—General Douglas MacArthur

NAVY

★ "The Navy has both a tradition and a future—and we look with pride and confidence in both directions." —Theodore Roosevelt

★ "I wish to have no connection with any ship that does not sail fast, for I intend to go in harm's way." —Captain John Paul Jones

★ "You're only as good as the people who work for you." —Fleet Admiral William D. Leahy

★ "There are no extraordinary men . . . just extraordinary circumstances that ordinary men are forced to deal with." —Fleet Admiral William F. "Bull" Halsey

★ "I can imagine no more rewarding a career. And any man who may be asked in this century what he did to make his life worthwhile, I think can respond with a good deal of pride and satisfaction: 'I served in the United States Navy.'" —John F. Kennedy

★ "No matter what happens, the U.S. Navy won't be caught napping." —Colonel William Franklin Knox

ARMY V. NAVY

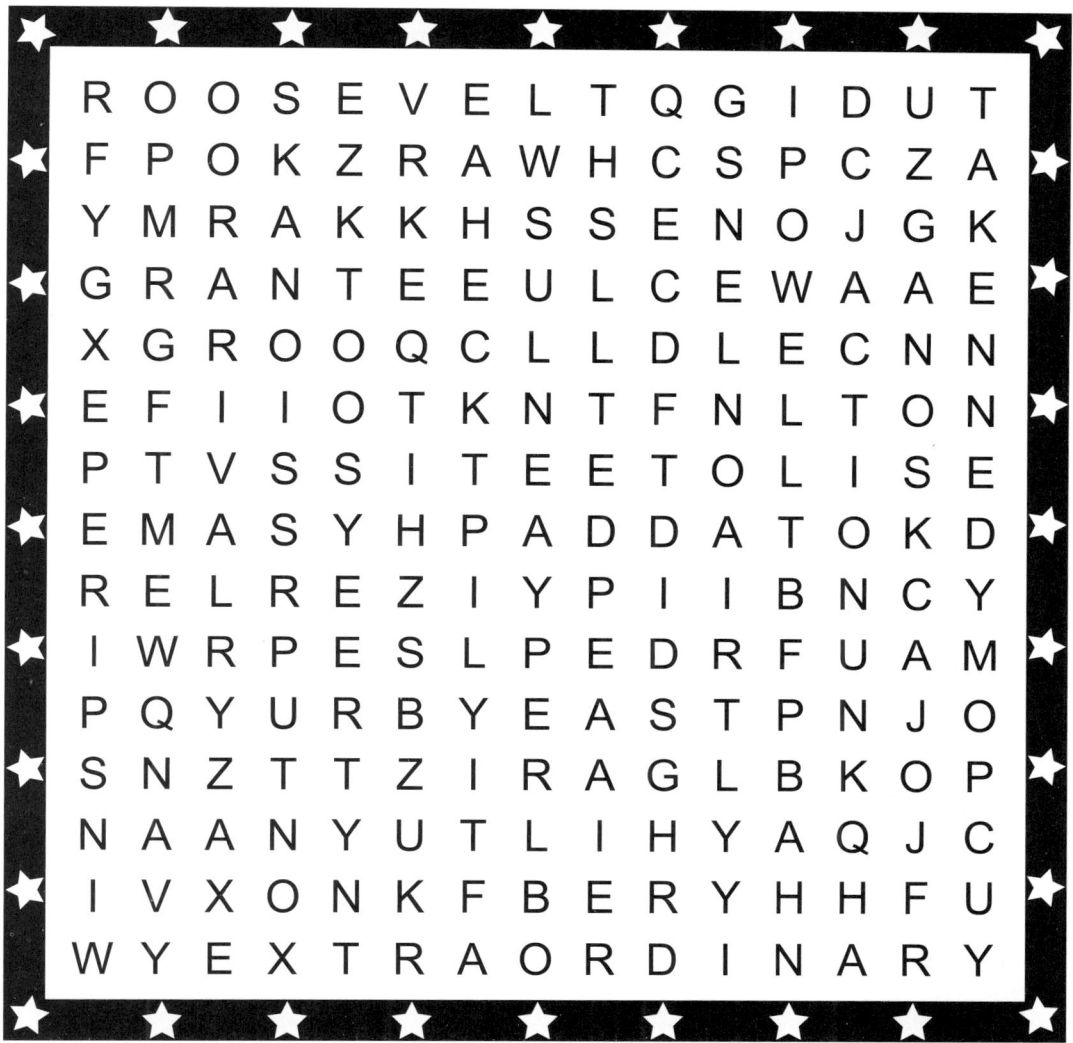

Action	Future	Kennedy	Pride
Army	Grant	Knox	Rivalry
Battle	Halsey	Leahy	Roosevelt
Confidence	Inspire	Navy	Schwarzkopf
Deliberate	Jackson	Patton	Ship
Extraordinary	Jones	Powell	Tradition

UNITED STATES AIR FORCE (USAF) RANKS

★ ★ ★ ★ ★ ★ ★ ★ ★ ★ ★ ★ ★

Airmen in the United States Air Force may be enlisted or commissioned officers. Air Force ranks designate job responsibilities and utilize the below names. At some levels, different positions exist at the same pay grade; the title depends on the Airman's job.

GRADE	RANK	ABBREVIATION
E1	Airman Basic	
E2	Airman	Amn
E3	Airman First Class	A1C
E4	Senior Airman	SrA
E5	Staff Sergeant	SSgt
E6	Technical Sergeant	TSgt
E7	Master Sergeant	MSgt
	First Sergeant	
E8	Senior Master Sergeant	SMSgt
	First Sergeant	
E9	Chief Master Sergeant	CMSgt
	First Sergeant	
	Command Chief Master Sergeant	
	Chief Master Sergeant of the Air Force	CMSAF
O1	Second Lieutenant	2d Lt
O2	First Lieutenant	1st Lt
O3	Captain	Capt
O4	Major	Maj
O5	Lieutenant Colonel	Lt Col
O6	Colonel	Col
O7	Brigadier General	Brig Gen
O8	Major General	Maj Gen
O9	Lieutenant General	Lt Gen
O10	General	Gen
	General of the Air Force (reserved for wartime only)	

UNITED STATES AIR FORCE (USAF) RANKS

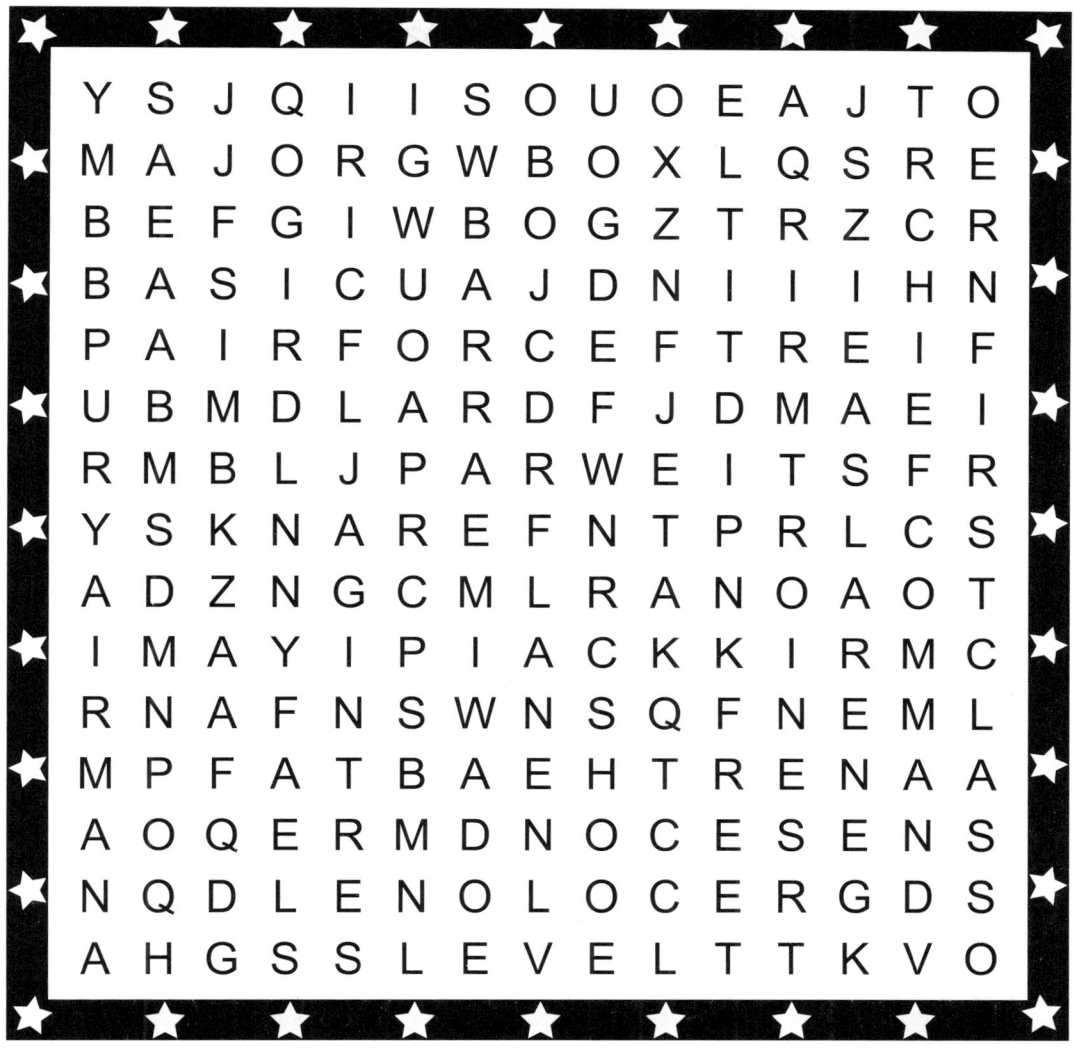

Air Force	Command	Levels	Ranks
Airman	Enlisted	Major	Second
Basic	First	Master	Senior
Captain	First Class	Names	Technical
Chief	General	Officer	Title
Colonel	Job	Pay grade	Wartime

GOT WHAT IT TAKES? U.S. ARMY RANGERS

To be eligible for an elite unit in the Armed Forces, candidates must meet or exceed fitness standards, then go through rigorous training. Learn what it takes to be a member of the U.S. Army Rangers.

The U.S. Army's 75th Ranger Regiment is made up of light infantry forces that can deploy anywhere in the world within 18 hours. Rangers utilize their skills in many ways: airborne assault; direct action; infiltration by land, sea, or air; and support of regular Army forces.

To qualify for the Ranger School, a Soldier must be able to complete:

- 49 push-ups in 2 minutes (80 to be competitive);
- 59 sit-ups in 2 minutes (80 to be competitive);
- 6 pull-ups, no time limit (12 to be competitive);
- 2-mile run in 15:12 (under 13:00 to be competitive);
- 5-mile run in 40:00 (under 35:00 to be competitive);
- 16-mile hike carrying a 65-pound pack in 5 hours 20 minutes (under 5 hours to be competitive);
- 15-meter swim with full gear.

For every Soldier accepted, training at the Ranger School consists of the following:

Camp Benning Phase: 20 days of intense physical training, including marches in full gear, obstacle courses, night and day patrols, reconnaissance, demolitions courses, airborne operations, and close-quarters combat tactics.

Mountain Phase: 20 days in rugged terrain with a small unit, dealing with severe weather, hunger, sleep deprivation, stress, and fatigue while leading a platoon through an exercise designed to simulate what a Ranger would expect to find on a real battlefield.

Florida Phase: 16 days in a marine/swamp environment, learning how to best utilize available skills and equipment in a combat situation and survive in a harsh climate.

Upon successful completion of the course, a Soldier has earned the right to wear the Ranger tab. It is not unusual for a candidate to lose up to 30 pounds in body weight during Ranger School.

GOT WHAT IT TAKES? U.S. ARMY RANGERS

```
R Q D E M O L I T I O N R P S
D E K E L C A T S B O Y W D O
S I H M Z S G L N D M S W I M
H R R T M W Z U M R F N A F S
U E E T A Z Q A A C O K I L C
N S G G E E B S H I C U R O M
G T I H N N W S T A D P B R O
E R M V O A Y A P U P M O I U
R E E O Q O R N N Z E A R D N
Z S N R L T U I O T F W N A T
T S T P L P G I I O Z S E T A
U V E I V O G L P A T R O L I
Q D F A H X E U R V F A K P N
Z N D G F K D R A E G N L C J
I S M D I F A T I G U E L P S
```

Airborne	Fatigue	Mountain	Regiment
Army	Florida	Obstacle	Rugged
Assault	Gear	Pack	Stress
Demolition	Hike	Patrol	Swamp
Deploy	Hunger	Platoon	Swim
Elite	Infiltration	Rangers	Weather

BATTLE OF MIDWAY

★ ★ ★ ★ ★ ★ ★ ★ ★ ★ ★ ★ ★

One of Japan's main objectives during World War II was to install themselves as the main world power in the Pacific. A victory against the United States at Midway would have given them a foothold to do just that. Instead, the battle turned out to be one of the U.S. Navy's greatest victories.

After the attack on Pearl Harbor in December 1941, the Japanese military spent the first half of 1942 planning a major attack on the Allies in the Pacific—and U.S. Navy crypto analysts had already begun Japanese communication codes. After sending out a false message from the American base on the Midway Atoll, just 1,100 miles from Hawaii, the U.S. was able to confirm the location and the approximate date of the Japanese attack. This allowed American forces to prepare in advance, unbeknownst to the Japanese.

On the morning of June 4, four Japanese aircraft carriers attacked and damaged the base; Marine Corps, Navy, and Army Air Forces bombers attempted to damage the Japanese carrier force without success. But U.S. carriers were waiting just east of the island. When the Japanese planes returned to their carriers for rearmament and refueling, the American carriers USS *Yorktown*, USS *Enterprise*, and USS *Hornet* launched their attack, wrecking the Japanese carrier *Soryu* and damaging two others. (A fourth Japanese carrier was fatally struck later in the evening.) Admiral Chūichi Nagumo, commander of Japan's navy, was forced into a critical dilemma: either rearm the returning planes or launch his carrier strike team; his carrier had the capability to do only one of those things at a time. Nagumo's decision to allow the returning planes to land first for refueling and rearming ultimately left them unable to counter the American attacks.

After two more days of combat, with U.S. forces beating the Japanese into a retreat, the attack on Midway was a clear victory for the Americans and considered "the turning point of the Pacific." The U.S. Navy lost the USS *Yorktown*, a cruiser, and 144 aircraft, and suffered just over 300 casualties. But the Japanese lost four carriers, a cruiser, hundreds of aircraft, and more than 3,000 men, losses that were catastrophic to their efforts to establish dominance in the Pacific theater.

BATTLE OF MIDWAY

```
I S E N A L P Z V H M F G J A
B O M B E R S M N H A F Q M T
H Q S O R Y U A O L O W K F O
Z T X S A B E J S D N R A M L
E I S T R I K E T E A M N I L
P C C R Y P T O L V U O K E I
R A N F V J G R H J Y F C H T
E S C A A R E T R E A T L X R
P A X I N D R V I C T O R Y Y
A Z K N F I I N C O D E S W V
R Y A W D I M L E W N Q F R U
E O E C D P C O E E G A M A D
T A B M O C O X D M X D P O N
D N A L S I F U X O M U G A N
O E S I R P R E T N E A B G J
```

Atoll	Dilemma	Island	Planes
Bombers	Dominance	Japan	Prepare
Codes	Enterprise	Midway	Retreat
Combat	False	Nagumo	Soryu
Crypto	Hawaii	Navy	Strike team
Damage	Hornet	Pacific	Victory

FLYING ACE

★ ★ ★ ★ ★ ★ ★ ★ ★ ★ ★ ★ ★

A flying ace is any military member confirmed to have shot down five or more enemy planes during aerial combat. As modern aerial warfare shifts further away from dogfights and closer to unmanned aircraft, the flying ace may be a thing of the past. But their legends live on.

CAPTAIN EDWARD RICKENBACKER, U.S. ARMY AIR SERVICE

World War I saw aircraft used in combat for the first time. "Eddie" Rickenbacker was a well-known race car driver before the United States entered the conflict, and his initial assignment in the U.S. Army was as General John J. Pershing's chauffer. He soon transferred to the U.S. Army Air Service and was among the first American pilots to leave for the front. As a member of the famed 94th Aero Squadron, he had his first victory on April 29, 1918; his fifth victory occurred on May 28. He went on to become commander of the 94th Aero Squadron and to achieve a remarkable 26 combat victories, making him the leading American ace of the war. Captain Rickenbacker received the Medal of Honor for his service, along with the Legion of Honor and Croix de Guerre, among other decorations.

MAJOR RICHARD BONG, U.S. ARMY AIR FORCES

"Dick" Bong was not only one of the most decorated fighter pilots of World War II, but he was also the nation's top flying ace of that war. He earned his pilot wings in January 1942; by November, he was serving in the Pacific based in New Guinea. His initial victory came on December 27, when he shot down a Japanese "Zero" and an "Oscar" in the Battle of Buna-Gona, an action that earned him a Silver Star. By December 17, 1944, he had increased his aerial victories to 40, making him the "Ace of Aces" of World War II. Bong received the Medal of Honor in 1944 before being sent home for good in January 1945. He became a test pilot for Lockheed and was tragically killed during a flight on August 6, 1945, the same day the United States dropped an atomic bomb on Hiroshima.

BRIGADIER GENERAL RICHARD RITCHIE, U.S. AIR FORCE

"Steve" Ritchie was one of only five service members—and one of only two pilots—confirmed as an ace during the Vietnam War. A graduate of the U.S. Air Force Academy, Ritchie first deployed to South Vietnam in 1968. After spending some time stateside as an instructor at Air Force Fighter Weapons School, he volunteered for a second combat tour in 1972 and was assigned to the 432nd Tactical Reconnaissance Wing in Thailand. His first victory came on May 10, 1972; his second followed on May 31. By August 28, he had his fifth victory, making him the Air Force's first and only pilot ace of the War, and one of the most decorated. (Ritchie may also be America's last flying ace—no service member has achieved "ace" status since.)

FLYING ACE

```
G N I Y L F A N P Q T N O R F
R C D J A C O R I S G N I W O
D G Y F E R P C M F X E F G V
I E V L D C C K A Y B W W R I
K A T A U R R N A N G G K A E
I S U A U F O O E F N U M T T
A Q L O R G I D F R O I L S N
S T T O A O T G I R B N A R A
V V A N O H C T H S I E D E M
I T U B G Z C E X T R A V V M
C B N I M H L H D C E I T L Z
T I L H I O Q N R Y F R O I E
O F N E R A C S O V T D L S R
R F M C F J Q M T X M H I A O
Y N F D O G F I G H T D P D A
```

Ace	Decorated	Front	Squadron
Air Force	Dogfight	New Guinea	Tour
Army	Fighter	Oscar	Victory
Bong	Five	Pilot	Vietnam
Buna-Gona	Flight	Ritchie	Wings
Combat	Flying	Silver Star	Zero

KILROY WAS HERE

★ ★ ★ ★ ★ ★ ★ ★ ★ ★ ★ ★

His most daring appearance was in the bathroom reserved for President Harry Truman, Josef Stalin, and Prime Minister Clement Atlee during the "Big Three" conference in Potsdam, Germany, in July 1945. An agitated Stalin returned from the bathroom and asked his translator, "Who is Kilroy?" Wouldn't we all like to know?

WHO IS KILROY?

World War II's best-known GI didn't earn any medals or carry a weapon, but he did get around. The simple graffiti cartoon of a bald man with a long nose peeking over a wall (sometimes gripping the wall with his fingertips) and accompanied by the words "Kilroy was here" has been spotted everywhere from the Statue of Liberty to Hitler's Eagles' Nest retreat. For whatever reason—maybe because they liked the idea that one of them was always ahead of the enemy—something about Kilroy appealed to American GIs. So they left his imprint everywhere.

BUT WHERE DID HE BEGIN?

There are plenty of stories to explain Kilroy's existence. At least 62 men with the surname Kilroy served in the military during World War II, and at least one—Sergeant Francis J. Kilroy Jr.—claims to be the cartoon's inspiration, but his story couldn't be corroborated. There's a rumor that the real Kilroy went AWOL and his friends drew the cartoons in various places to throw off military police. There's the popular but implausible theory that the Kilroy cartoons were a secret agent's means of communicating with other spies. It's also unlikely that Kilroy was a copycat of a similar British graffito from the 1930s called Mr. Chad. (How would American GIs be familiar with the old British cartoon, and why change his name?)

The most widely accepted origin is a real live Kilroy from Halifax, Massachusetts. James J. Kilroy inspected riveting work at the Fore River Shipyard in Quincy, marking each riveted section with a checkmark. Because welders were paid by the number of approved—and marked—sections, some began erasing the checkmark after approval, hoping to get a second payment. Kilroy began marking his sections "Kilroy was here," which couldn't be erased without being noticed. Months later, Sailors doing repairs halfway around the world would find "Kilroy was here" in an inaccessible or sealed compartment. In 1946, during a radio contest investigating Kilroy's origins, Fore River workers corroborated Mr. Kilroy's claims about his unique inspection mark.

IS KILROY STILL LEAVING HIS MARK?

Kilroy continued to show up after World War II and during the Korean War. As time passed, Kilroy became a rarity but didn't go extinct, even being seen recently in Iraq and Afghanistan.

KILROY WAS HERE

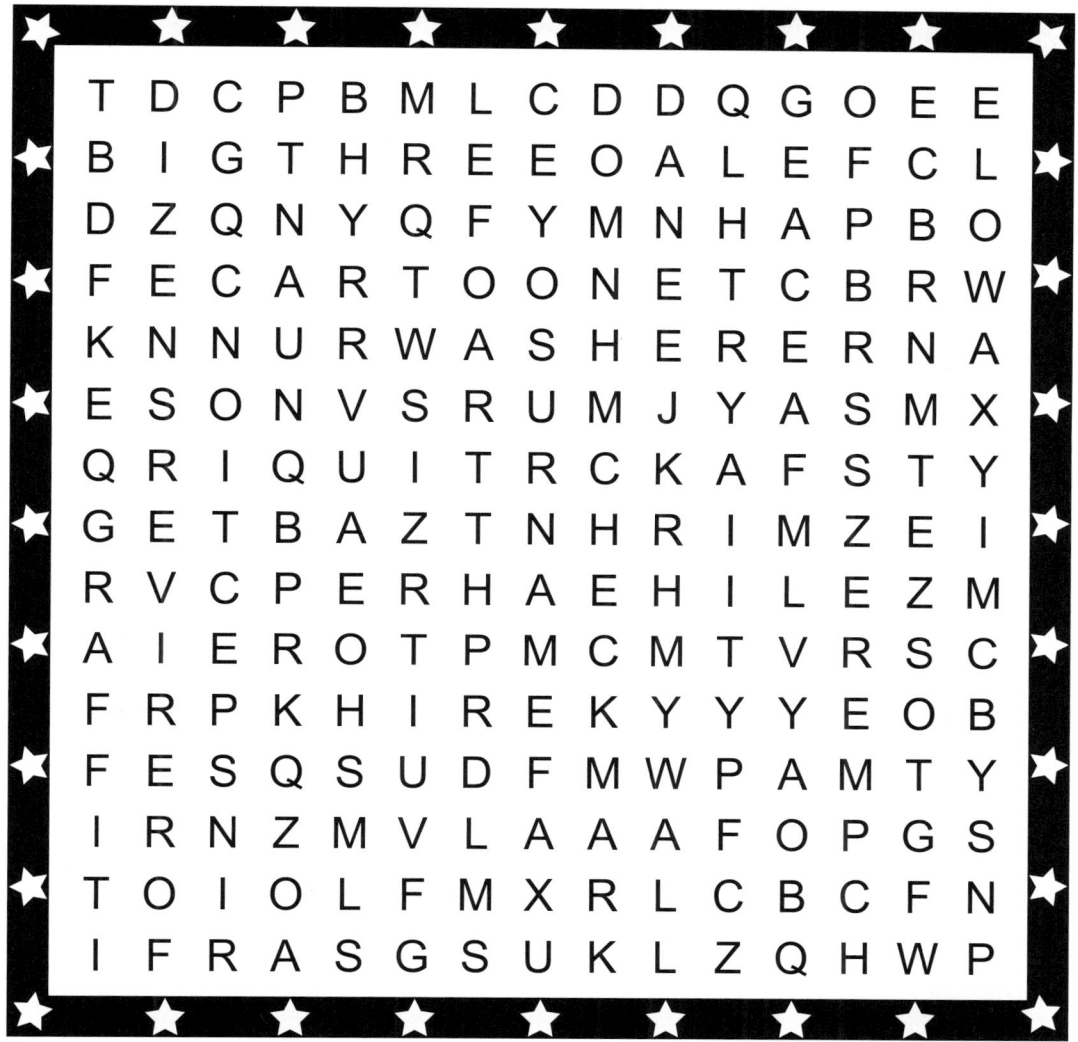

AWOL	Copycat	Kilroy	Repairs
Bald	Erase	Mr. Chad	Rivet
Big Three	Fore River	Myth	Rumor
Cartoon	Graffiti	Nose	Surname
Checkmark	Inspection	Payment	Wall
Contest	James	Radio	Was here

CARE PACKAGES

★ ★ ★ ★ ★ ★ ★ ★ ★ ★ ★ ★

As long as U.S. troops have been away from home, loved ones have been sending care packages. What goes into a care package, and how do you send one to a service member?

BOOT CAMP

Military recruits at basic training are allowed very few personal items; the military provides all basic necessities, and anything sent from home is stored until after graduation. (Drill instructors may even punish an entire unit if one recruit receives anything unauthorized!) At this stage of a service member's career, letters are better (and photos are also OK).

DUTY STATIONS AND DEPLOYMENT

After graduation from basic training, service members can receive care packages at their duty station or on deployment, and many friends and family members love showing their faraway service member how much they're missed. What do service members like to receive? Necessities, such as sunscreen and lip balm, are always welcomed. So are snacks, like chips, nuts, and candy, or homemade goodies such as cookies or "cake in a jar" (baked in a canning jar)—as long as they're packaged in sturdy containers to prevent leaking or being crushed, and as long as they don't contain chocolate or other elements that will melt during transit. Games or other entertainment items—such as crossword books, magazines, or playing cards—will provide a welcome respite from work.

What may be most valuable to service members are personalized notes, letters, or cards that show how much they're missed and that they're top of mind for loved ones. Kids' drawings, photographs, and other sentimental items may be cherished reminders of home. In all instances, shippers should take care to not send anything valuable—packages sometimes get lost—or that they wouldn't want someone else to see, since they may be opened by someone else before the intended recipient.

IN THE MAIL

The United State Postal Service offers free Military Care Kits to anyone who requests them. These kits include priority mail boxes, tape, customs forms, and address labels, all intended to make packaging and shipping care packages as easy as possible. Mail being sent to military addresses (APO or FPO) costs the same as standard domestic postage, even if it's being sent overseas. Overseas shipments do require customs forms, though, and the post office does prohibit the shipment of some items.

Unfortunately, plenty of service members don't have loved ones who can send them packages. Luckily, there are organizations that help boost the morale of these troops, so no one feels left out at mail call. The USO's Care Package program delivered almost 270,000 packages to troops in 72 countries in 2023 alone. Organizations such as Soldiers' Angels and Operation Gratitude also provide care packages to service members (and, in some cases, veterans) through donations and volunteers.

CARE PACKAGES

```
D T N E I P I C E R A M R P N
E V E V M D E L I V E R F G O
S K L Z E V O L O R M F P O T
S W A Q F N I L E Q C W J P E
I E R N A A U S S D R A C S S
M Q O R M N Y C F E J E G T D
E H M Y T H D I G N T N D I L
R Z O E S S R S Q E I S R S S
A A E M A S U P P H K A E M
C R A Q E C T B P O P C W M O
F P H O T O S I U G X A I A T
O G T K W S H J Z I M N N G S
B N E C E S S I T I E S G W U
E D A M E M O H J Y H T S R C
Z A V Z V X T M G S D C G Z I
```

APO	Drawings	Mail	Photos
Basics	FPO	Missed	Recipient
Cards	Games	Morale	Shipping
Care	Home	Necessities	Snacks
Customs	Homemade	Notes	Sturdy
Deliver	Love	Opened	Volunteer

CREED OF THE UNITED STATES COAST GUARDSMAN

★ ★ ★ ★ ★ ★ ★ ★ ★ ★ ★ ★

I am proud to be a United States Coast Guardsman.

I revere that long line of expert seamen who, by their devotion to duty and sacrifice of self, have made it possible for me to be a member of a service honored and respected, in peace and in war, throughout the world.

I never, by word or deed, will bring reproach upon the fair name of my service, nor permit others to do so unchallenged.

I will cheerfully and willingly obey all lawful orders.

I will always be on time to relieve, and shall endeavor to do more, rather than less, than my share.

I will always be at my station, alert and attending to my duties.

I shall, so far as I am able, bring to my seniors solutions, not problems.

I shall live joyously, but always with due regard for the rights and privileges of others.

I shall endeavor to be a model citizen in the community in which I live.

I shall sell life dearly to an enemy of my country, but give it freely to rescue those in peril.

With God's help, I shall endeavor to be one of His noblest Works . . .

A UNITED STATES COAST GUARDSMAN.

The Coast Guardsman's Creed was penned in 1938 by Vice Admiral Harry G. Hamlet, just months before he retired following more than 40 years in Coast Guard service; it was adopted by the Coast Guard in 1950. As a decorated Word War I veteran and former occupant of two of the most prestigious positions in the Service—Superintendent of the Coast Guard Academy and Commandant of the United States Coast Guard—Hamlet himself embodied the values of "honor, respect, and devotion to duty."

The Creed is straightforward and powerful; it describes, in concise terms, the values and the ideal behavior of every member of the Coast Guard. It provides inspiration for Guardsmen to uphold the highest standards in every area of their service.

CREED OF THE UNITED STATES COAST GUARDSMAN

```
S O L U T I O N S R E S C U E
T C X J X S I S L H S Y U M O
A B N Y Y X G U O L S M R O V
N Q D D E B F O A E V C I D T
D R E T B W O E U T S T U E P
A E A E A A D L V E S K T L E
R G R L S I A D R E X P Z R R
D A L M V V E V L D W R T T I
S R Y A S V I B V C S E K U L
G D T H O C O A S T G U A R D
X S A T E N D E A V O R I N M
K R I V D G Q T L L M G J C D
E O Q X Y O I R E S P E C T F
N V O N C O S A R E L I E V E
C R H O N O R W T C R E E D K
```

Alert	Endeavor	Noblest	Service
Coast Guard	Hamlet	Peril	Share
Creed	Honor	Regards	Solutions
Dearly	Ideals	Relieve	Standards
Devotion	Lawful	Rescue	Station
Duty	Model	Respect	Values

CARBINE WILLIAMS

★ ★ ★ ★ ★ ★ ★ ★ ★ ★ ★ ★

The ubiquitous gun was designed by an ex-con—and helped win World War II.

David Marshall "Marsh" Williams had a whiskey still in Cumberland County, North Carolina; when the sheriff and his deputies destroyed it on July 21, 1921, one deputy was killed. Williams was charged with murder and sentenced to 30 years in the Caledonia Correctional Institute.

Williams had always had a talent for machinery, especially firearms. While serving out his sentence, he was eventually put to work fixing farm machinery. After gaining the warden's trust, Williams was given a job in the machine shop repairing guards' weapons, then allowed to design guns. Williams made a semiautomatic rifle that worked on the short-stroke gas piston system. A gas piston was located under the middle of the rifle's barrel. When the gun was fired, the gases from the ejected bullet exploded and propelled the piston violently to the rear. The slam of the piston initiated a slide-bolt action in the gun and automatically loaded another bullet into the ejection chamber.

After eight years in prison, Williams went home and started working on more designs and getting patents, leading to a job at the Winchester Repeating Arms Company as a weapons designer.

In 1941, with war looming, the Army needed to address a problem: the traditional M1 rifle, or Garand rifle, weighed about 10 pounds. It was too cumbersome for medics, radio operators, vehicle drivers, and officers—any troops who weren't frontline riflemen. These "second-line" troops usually carried the M1911A1 .45-caliber pistol. At 3 pounds when loaded, this handgun was lightweight, but didn't have the range or firepower needed for defense.

So the Army held a competition to design a lightweight, semiautomatic shoulder weapon, which Winchester intended to win by providing a lightweight carbine. (Carbines, developed for cavalry troops, were shorter than standard rifles.) It was Marsh Williams who suggested using the short-stroke piston system he'd developed in prison. The result was the M1 Carbine. It weighed in at 5 pounds, 7 ounces. But its accurate range and firepower was much greater than any pistol. The Army accepted Winchester's design less than three months before December 7, 1941, when the United States went to war.

The first M1 Carbines were delivered to the Army in 1942. Six million would be produced by 1945. Standard issue during World War II, and used in Korea and even Vietnam, the carbine became "the war baby," the most-produced small-arms weapon in American military history. (The Soviet Kalashnikov AK-47 is the most-produced small-arms weapon in the world.) The M1 took on mud, rain, rust, and rough treatment—and kept shooting. General Douglas MacArthur called the M1 Carbine "one of the strongest contributing factors in our victory in the Pacific."

CARBINE WILLIAMS

```
D R E Q K Z A L T M X B V L B
W E U L R E W O P E R I F S S
H Q V K F V N D R K Y N S L T
I S C A L I B E R B F W M I N
S M F F P J R Y A K B C O D E
K R Z J R B N W V B U L L E T
E A O I X E Y R O T C I V B A
Y L A P E C N E T N E S A O P
H L C R G C H G A R A N D L V
A A C O N O T S I P S A G T P
N M U P E G N A R S F O W X T
D S R E L Q S M R A E R I F R
G B A L E R R A B S M D M D P
U S T A N D A R D P I S T O L
N W E A P O N S C H A M B E R
```

Accurate   Firearms   Patents   Slide-bolt
Barrel   Firepower   Pistol   Small arms
Bullet   Garand   Propel   Standard
Caliber   Gas piston   Range   Victory
Chamber   Handgun   Rifle   Weapons
Designer   Marsh   Sentence   Whiskey

BIRTH OF THE AIR FORCE, PART I

★ ★ ★ ★ ★ ★ ★ ★ ★ ★ ★ ★ ★

For the first 40 years of its existence, the U.S. Air Force was part of the U.S. Army. Find out how it became its own branch of service.

Attempts to separate the United States' airpower from the Army were initiated before World War I, but not everyone supported the split: creating a new administration would be time-consuming and costly. Only when aviation technology developed to the point that it played a more significant role in war did people realize the importance of giving aviators unique support.

The first step came in August 1907 with the formation of an aerial unit within the Army: the Aeronautical Division, established by Brigadier General James Allen and staffed by one officer and two enlisted men responsible for "all matters pertaining to military ballooning, air machines, and all kindred subjects." The only things it didn't have were airplanes.

In 1914, Congress created the Aviation Section to replace the Aeronautical Division, which had been operating within the Army's Signal Corps. The Army had only a few airplanes, training for combat was inadequate, and manpower was lacking. In April 1917, the evolving air unit was manned by 131 officers and 1,087 enlisted in seven squadrons that flew 55 aircraft, most of which were obsolete. Essentially, American airpower didn't exist.

By May 1918, the War Department recognized the importance of aviation in warfare; the unit was renamed the Division of Military Aeronautics, then the U.S. Army Air Service. Brigadier General William Mitchell's armada of nearly 1,500 airplanes was flying over the trench-bound stalemate of World War I. During that war, Americans shot down more than 750 enemy aircraft and dropped more than 130 tons of bombs while flying approximately 35,000 hours. In operations near the end of the war, Americans commanded and participated in the first mass aerial attacks in history.

By 1920, two years after World War I, the Air Service was elevated to a combatant arm of the Army. A mass demobilization had gutted the Army after war's end, but over the next few years, pilots trained with what little equipment was left over.

The Air Corps Act of 1926 changed the unit's name yet again to the U.S. Army Air Corps (AAC). Over the next 10 years, the AAC established a training center and primary flying school in San Antonio, Texas. What is today Randolph Air Force Base remains the "West Point of the Air" as envisioned by AAC leadership in the 1930s. But it wasn't until 1935 when the General Headquarters (GHQ) Air Force was formed that there was the first hint of an independent air arm. The GHQ Air Force was responsible for the first truly independent mission within the Army: strategic targeting. The tactical (ground support) versus strategic (long-range bombardment) argument between surface forces and air forces was resolved with the establishment of the GHQ Air Force as part of the U.S. Army's combat structure.

Turn the page to learn more about the establishment of the U.S. Air Force.

BIRTH OF THE AIR FORCE, PART I

```
R N E L L A A R M A D A R G K
Y V S E R N S U R F A C E R E
A M T R G V N N Q A D E W O C
E A R S A N A N T O N I O U R
R C U A O C A T G E J S P N O
I H C B H V A R V T N P R D F
A I T U M C I L G E S R I L R
L N U I K N B T T N N O A L I
U E R S S S E R G N O C X E A
N S E H R T R A N D O L P H A
I N Y G E T A R T S L A S C V
T E H S U P P O R T L N B T U
T X A V I A T I O N A G M I X
T R A I N I N G O Q B I O M G
I N D E P E N D E N T S B T Y
```

Aerial unit	Attacks	Independent	Signal Corps
Air Force	Aviation	Long-range	Strategy
Airpower	Balloons	Machines	Structure
Allen	Bombs	Mitchell	Support
Armada	Congress	Randolph	Surface
Army	Ground	San Antonio	Training

BIRTH OF THE AIR FORCE, PART II

★ ★ ★ ★ ★ ★ ★ ★ ★ ★ ★

For the first 40 years of its existence, the U.S. Air Force was part of the U.S. Army. Continued from the previous page, find out more about how the Air Force became its own branch of service.

When Major General Henry Arnold officially took command of the AAC in September 1938, he immediately accelerated research and development already under consideration, including radar, rocket boosters to assist takeoffs, and a host of aircraft and engine design modifications.

By the 1940s, the AAC had made leaps in technology, developed policies in the use of its new weapons, and established contacts with scientists and industrialists who would make the expansion of aeronautical research and aircraft production run smoothly when the need arose.

As the Air Corps expanded, reorganization and restructuring of the War Department became an obvious necessity. When the U.S. Army Air Forces was established in June 1941, General Arnold was named overall commander and acting deputy chief of staff for Air. Under the War Department General Staff reorganization in March 1942, the Army Air Forces were recognized as being equal in status to the Army Ground Forces and the equally new Army Services of Supply branch. Arnold became a member of the Joint Chiefs of Staff, directly responsible to the secretary of war and to the Army's chief of staff for all Army air operations.

During World War II, 2.4 million airmen flew some 300,000 aircraft, but America's air forces would never need to be that large again: the large numbers were a result of a combination of weapons technology, aircraft capability, and the need for large crews on each aircraft. Immediately after the Japanese surrendered in 1945, the Army Air Forces began to demobilize, and in less than one year had released 1.7 million airmen.

The establishment of the U.S. Air Force seemed inevitable after World War II, but the Navy wasn't happy about it. Arguments reached a flashpoint when monies were cut from the Navy's carrier budget and transferred to the AAF's heavy B-36 Peacemaker program. The postwar interservice fighting over budgets and missions was typified by the "Revolt of the Admirals," a well-publicized rebellion by some of the Navy's top brass who felt the Navy was being stripped of its powers by Congress, the secretary of Defense, the Joint Chiefs of Staff, and the president.

The 1947 National Security Act and Executive Order 9877 created the independent U.S. Air Force, but it left holes—which were eventually filled—in the definition of unique roles and missions expected of each service. Since then, the U.S. Air Force has cemented its place as a vital component of the nation's armed forces through combat, reconnaissance, cargo transport, and humanitarian missions.

BIRTH OF THE AIR FORCE, PART II

```
U O P E R A T I O N S N R J R
W S W A R E C O M B A T E S E
Q S D R G B Z I W H D S O C K
K A N D B N T Z I L F R R I A
R R U E A A F Q O E Q E G T M
V B M M I I A N I T J T A U E
N P P O T R R H O A R S N A C
E O L B R A C H F O E O I N A
M T H I A T R C S E D O Z O E
R Z K L N I I R Y R N B A R P
I M M I S N A A L C E G T E D
A N O Z F A X E P A R W I A V
P J A E E M Z S P R R F O N O
S V X V R U P E U G U M N P E
A N S L Y H Z R S O S Z Y J Y
```

Aeronautics
Aircraft
Airmen
Army
Arnold
Boosters

Budget
Cargo
Combat
Demobilize
Engine
Humanitarian

Joint chiefs
Navy
Operations
Peacemaker
Powers
Radar

Reorganization
Research
Supply
Surrender
Top brass
Transfer

CELEBRITIES WHO SERVED

★ ★ ★ ★ ★ ★ ★ ★ ★ ★ ★ ★

Audie Murphy (pages 52 and 54) wasn't the only famous Soldier. Here are some other celebrities who are military veterans.

Two Golden Girls: Betty White, the "First Lady of Television," served in the American Women's Voluntary Services (AWVS) during World War II. White served as a driver in motor transport services until the end of the war in 1945. Her costar Bea Arthur was a typist and truck driver in the Marine Corps from 1943 to 1945 and was one of the first members of the Women's Reserve.

Bob Barker: Before becoming the longtime host of *The Price Is Right*, Bob Barker was a Navy fighter pilot during World War II. (His successor on the game show, Drew Carey, served in the Marine Corps from 1980 to 1986.)

Morgan Freeman: The future Oscar winner spent four years in the Air Force during the 1950s, serving as a radar technician.

Adam Driver: Driver joined the Marine Corps at age 17 shortly after the September 11, 2001, terrorist attacks. He "loved" being a Marine, but he was medically discharged after two years of service.

Tony Bennett: The legendary crooner spent two years in the Army, in Germany and France, during World War II.

Rob Riggle: The actor and comedian joined the Marine Corps in 1990 and retired after 23 years of service in the Reserves.

Ice-T: Tracy Lauren Marrow—better known as rapper and actor Ice-T—spent four years in the Army's 25th Infantry Division after high school.

Humphrey Bogart: As a Sailor in the U.S. Navy during World War I, the future Hollywood leading man spent time on ships ferrying troops between the United States and Europe.

James Earl Jones: Perhaps best known as the voice of Darth Vader, the future actor attended the University of Michigan in the school's Reserve Officers' Training Corps. After graduating in 1955, he spent his time in the Army conducting cold-weather training at Camp Hale in Colorado.

Zach Bryan: The country singer enlisted in the Navy at age 17 in 2013. Bryan was still on active duty in 2021 when he signed his record deal; the Navy honorably discharged him so he could pursue his music career.

CELEBRITIES WHO SERVED

```
S H I I S O X A Q N X F E L F
V R F I L J D C B A I C E T B
W H C R R T X T S Y Y Q L C E
A O E A I R F I T R E T G O A
Q L L W G A N V V B R T G M A
D L E D N G H E P H A E I E R
Z Y B L E O G D I C C N R D T
R W R R D B T U L A W N J I H
C O I O L E P T O Z E E Q A U
O O T W O K U Y T S R B W N R
V D Y C G R E V I R D M A D A
Y R T N A F N I R E S E R V E
D A R T H V A D E R S E N O J
B O B B A R K E R Q I Q R H Z
K B P I D F R E E M A N T X F
```

Active duty	Bob Barker	Freeman	Pilot
Actor	Bogart	Golden Girls	Reserve
Adam Driver	Celebrity	Hollywood	Riggle
AWVS	Comedian	Ice-T	Singer
Bea Arthur	Darth Vader	Infantry	World War II
Bennett	Drew Carey	Jones	Zach Bryan

MREs: THE GOOD, THE BAD, AND THE VOMELET

★ ★ ★ ★ ★ ★ ★ ★ ★ ★ ★ ★

Every veteran has a favorite—and least favorite—meal ration. Have you ever tried one?

The Meal, Ready-to-Eat (MRE) is an individual military ration issued to U.S. service members for use in combat or in other field conditions where fresh food isn't available. Each brown plastic pouch contains a full meal and everything necessary to eat it: a main course ("the main"), a side dish, a snack or dessert (sometimes candy, sometimes an energy bar), crackers or bread with something to spread on it, a powdered beverage mix with mixing bag, utensils, a flameless ration heater (FRH), and an accessory bag with a napkin, seasonings, matchbook, and chewing gum.

Each meal contains about 1,200 calories and is fortified with essential nutrients. MREs are designed to be eaten for up to 21 days and have a minimum shelf life of three years. Vegetarian meals are available, as are religious meals for service members who eat kosher or halal (including a special "Passover Ration" with Matzoh crackers), though the religious meals have a shorter shelf life.

So how do they taste? Some of the nicknames that troops have given MREs over the years are an indicator: "Meals Rejected by Everyone" and "Meals Rarely Edible." (Soldiers in Iraq dubbed 2005's infamous vegetable cheese omelet MRE "the Vomelet"—a play on the words *omelet* and *vomit*—because of its taste and appearance.) But the military consistently seeks feedback on MREs, both to make them more pleasant for troops and to reflect popular food trends. There are 24 menu items, which currently include:

Shredded BBQ Beef

Italian Sausage with Vegetables

Chili and Macaroni

Maple Sausage

Lemon Pepper Tuna

Pepperoni Pizza Slice

Meatballs with Marinara Sauce

Beef Goulash

Chicken Burrito Bowl

Vegetarian Taco Pasta (vegetarian)

Cheese Tortellini (vegetarian)

Spinach Mushrooms & Cream Sauce Fettuccine (vegetarian)

MREs: THE GOOD, THE BAD, AND THE VOMELET

```
T S E A S O N I N G S A E Q B
E S N X I M E G A R E V E B E
L H S H R E D D E D B E E F S
E E I I S E I R O L A C I N N
M L D N D L L K G D V E L O A
O F A U M E I I Q H L T Z I C
V L E T E A D S G D A B X T K
O I R R E R I I N I R L T A X
T F P I M E J N S E O R A R C
A E S E R H D G C H T U L L O
S F I N S S B J F O P U S A M
T Q O T J O K V M R U L S E B
E O G S U K P O U C H R O M A
M A P L E S A U S A G E S Q T
V E G E T A R I A N R E M E E
```

- Beverage mix
- Calories
- Combat
- Field
- FRH
- Halal
- Kosher
- Main course
- Maple sausage
- Meal ration
- MRE
- Nutrients
- Pouch
- Religious
- Seasonings
- Shelf life
- Shredded beef
- Side dish
- Snack
- Spread
- Taste
- Utensils
- Vegetarian
- Vomelet

U.S. MARINE CORPS BASES

★ ★ ★ ★ ★ ★ ★ ★ ★ ★ ★ ★

*The U.S. Marine Corps has numerous stateside bases and installations.
Is there one located near you?*

ARIZONA

Marine Corps Air Station Yuma

CALIFORNIA

Marine Corps Air Ground Combat Center Twentynine Palms
Marine Corps Air Station Miramar
Marine Corps Base Camp Pendleton
Marine Corps Logistics Base Barstow
Marine Corps Recruit Depot San Diego
Mountain Warfare Training Center

GEORGIA

Marine Corps Logistics Base Albany

HAWAII

Marine Corps Base Hawaii
Marine Corps Air Station Kaneohe Bay

NORTH CAROLINA

Marine Corps Air Station Cherry Point
Marine Corps Air Station New River
Marine Corps Base Camp Lejeune

SOUTH CAROLINA

Marine Corps Air Station Beaufort
Marine Corps Recruit Depot Parris Island

VIRGINIA

Henderson Hall
Marine Barracks, Washington, D.C.
Marine Corps Base Quantico

U.S. MARINE CORPS BASES

```
U D S S H B Z A M U Y J T N G
A E T A B M O C D N U O R G Q
L P H J I E E B A R S T O W T
B O C I T N A U Q A I O F R N
A T R A I N I N G M Q H U E I
N S A N D I E G O A F A A V O
Y A N O Z I R A R R B W E I P
M N O I T A T S R I A A B R Y
L O G I S T I C S M V I J W R
O Y F C A L I F O R N I A E R
D S V G C A M P L E J E U N E
B K L L A H N O S R E D N E H
A I Q S K C A R R A B F G G C
S N B Y A B E H O E N A K S J
E P E N D L E T O N I W Y H B
```

Air Station	Beaufort	Hawaii	Pendleton
Albany	California	Henderson Hall	Quantico
Arizona	Camp Lejeune	Kaneohe Bay	San Diego
Barracks	Cherry Point	Logistics	Training
Barstow	Depot	Miramar	Virginia
Base	Ground Combat	New River	Yuma

WHAT'S IN A NICKNAME? PART I

★ ★ ★ ★ ★ ★ ★ ★ ★ ★ ★ ★ ★

Since their inception a century ago, U.S. Navy aircraft carriers have had a variety of names—both official and unofficial, conventional and unconventional. Learn about how these iconic ships get their names.

EARLY CARRIER NAMING CONVENTIONS

The earliest aircraft carriers in the Navy's fleet were converted from other ships. The USS *Lexington* (CV-2), for instance, was formerly a battlecruiser, and battlecruisers were named for famous battles in American military history. Carriers also were named for famous battles, or for famous previous Navy ships, including *Enterprise* and *Hornet*.

There have been exceptions to fleet carrier naming conventions since the beginning. Three early carriers—the USS *Langley* (CV-1), USS *Wright* (CVL-49), and USS *Kitty Hawk* (CVA-63—all paid homage to early advances in aviation. The USS *Hancock* (CV-19), USS *Franklin D. Roosevelt* (CVB-42), and USS *Forrestal* (CVA-59) were named for politicians. And two ships were named USS *Independence* (CVL-22 and CV-62). The most radical exception was probably the USS *Shangri-La* (CV/CVA/CVS-38), named for the fictional paradise described in and made famous by James Hilton's 1933 novel, *Lost Horizon*. How did this name happen? President Roosevelt told a reporter that the famous Doolittle Raid of 1942 had been launched from "Shangri-La." This obviously wasn't true—it was launched from the deck of the USS *Hornet* (CV-8)—but it did, in a sense, continue the tradition of naming a carrier after a battle.

PRESIDENTIAL MONIKERS

Commissioned in 1968, the USS *John F. Kennedy* (CV-67) was named in honor of the recently deceased president and Navy hero. Since then, the majority of carriers have been named for former presidents—again, with exceptions. Some have been named for other politicians; the USS *Doris Miller* (CVN-81) was named for the first Black American to receive the prestigious Navy Cross; and the USS *Nimitz* (CVN-68) honored the commander of the Allied naval forces in the Pacific during World War II. And three ships named the *Enterprise* (CV-6, CVN-65, and the in-construction CVN-80) have continued the tradition—in place since the Revolutionary War—of using this name for U.S. Navy ships.

ESCORT CARRIERS

Escort carriers have their own naming conventions. These ships were smaller than fleet carriers and were used to defend merchant ships, transportation of aircraft, and backups for fleet carriers. The earliest of these carriers were named for bodies of water—bays and sounds—such as the USS *Long Island* (CVE-1). But, like early fleet carriers, were later named for famous battles, including the USS *Guadalcanal* (CVE-60). (The last escort carrier remaining in service was sold for scrap in 1979.)

Turn the page to learn about these ships' numerous nicknames.

WHAT'S IN A NICKNAME? PART I

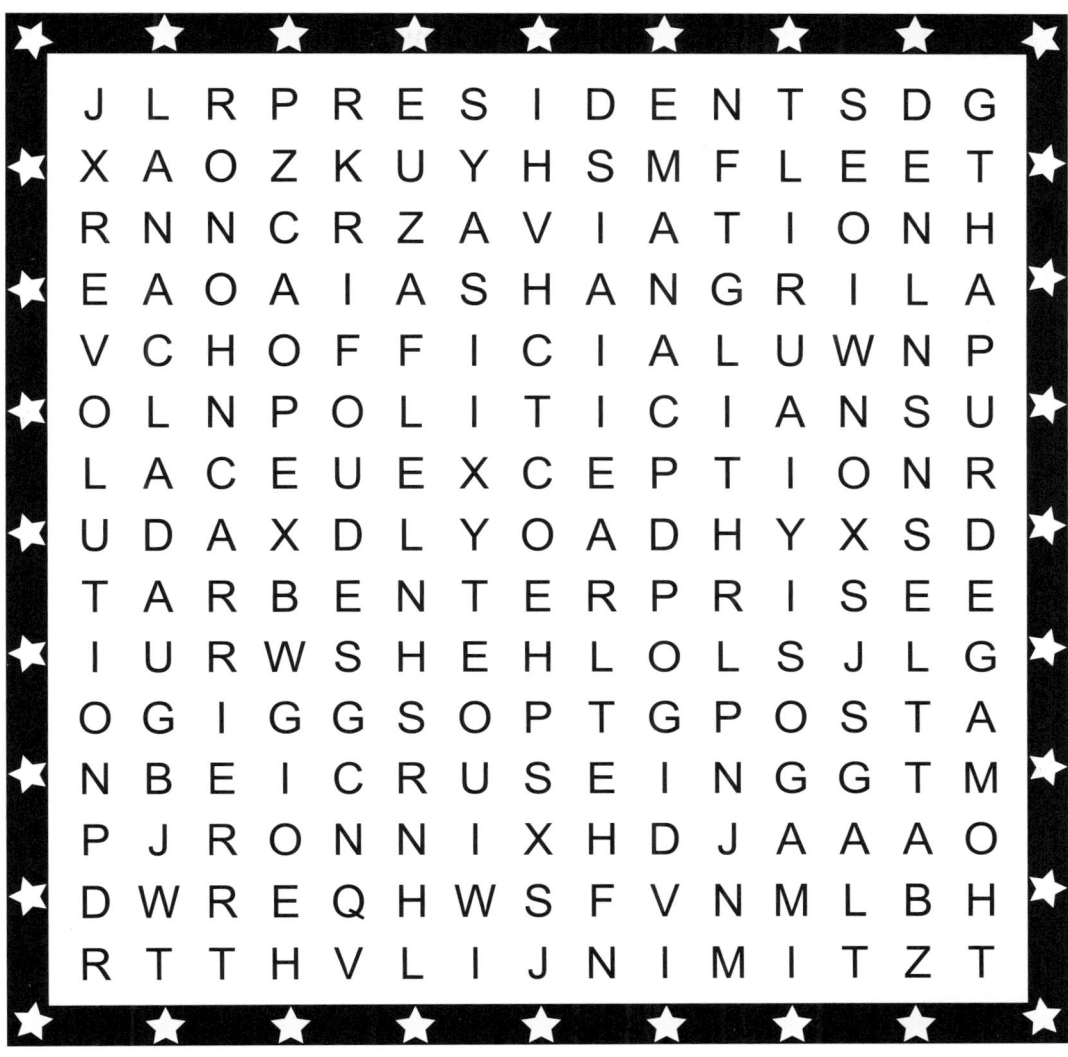

Aviation	Fleet	Independence	Politicians
Battles	Guadalcanal	Langley	Presidents
Carrier	History	Name	Revolution
Enterprise	Homage	Nimitz	Shangri-La
Escort	Honor	Official	Ships
Exception	Hornet	Pacific	Wright

WHAT'S IN A NICKNAME? PART II

★ ★ ★ ★ ★ ★ ★ ★ ★ ★ ★ ★ ★

Since their inception a century ago, U.S. Navy aircraft carriers have had a variety of names—both official and unofficial, conventional and unconventional. Learn about how these iconic ships get their names . . . and their nicknames.

CREATIVE MINDS

The first aircraft carrier in the Navy's fleet was also the first to earn a nickname: the USS *Langley* (CV-1) was a pioneer in naval technology, so, fittingly, its earliest Sailors called it the "Covered Wagon." Two World War II ships earned their nicknames thanks to the Japanese repeatedly reporting in error that they'd sunk, only to have them reappear: the USS *Lexington* (CV-16), nicknamed the "Blue Ghost," and the USS *Enterprise* (CV-6), called the "Galloping Ghost of the Oahu Coast." The former was also called the "Big E," a nickname retained by Sailors on the second USS *Enterprise* (CVN-65).

Other nicknames were less flattering, but equally creative. The USS *Intrepid* (CV-11) saw more than 30 years of service, but the shape it was in by the time it was decommissioned inspired its crew to call it the "Decrepit."

Some other carrier nicknames include the following.

   USS *Yorktown* (CV-10): The Fighting Lady

   USS *Cabot* (CVL-28): The Iron Woman

   USS *Franklin D. Roosevelt* (CVB-42): Rosie, Foo-De-Roo

   USS *Bon Homme Richard* (CV-31): Bonnie Dick

   USS *Cowpens* (CVL-25): Mighty Moo

   USS *Dwight D. Eisenhower* (CVN-69): Iron Ike

   USS *Ronald Reagan* (CVN-76): Gipper

   USS *Abraham Lincoln* (CVN-72): Abe, Stink'n Lincoln

   USS *Coral Sea* (CV/CVB/CVA-43): Ageless Warrior

   USS *Kitty Hawk* (CV-63): Battle Cat

   USS *Carl Vinson* (CVN-70): America's Favorite Carrier, Battle Barge, Battle Star, Chuck Bucket, Chuckie V, Cellblock 70, Dirty V, the Gold Eagle, Starship Vinson

WHAT'S IN A NICKNAME? PART II

```
Y O R K T O W N C O W P E N S
C E L L B L O C K K A N T J Q
F V E I K C U H C R C A B O T
N O G A W D E R E V O C H T Q
T E O A S Z X B V F F N O H B
A B R D L X S Y A I R A T S P
C T Z O E L T T I D H M J J T
E G W E M R O R A U Q I X S T
L I Y A I B O P C R R Z O N I
T P S D R N A O I O S H U B P
T P J O W R A R N N G H L R E
A E Z O R S I I G E G M I L R
B R M U T C K O U E K S M P C
M A H C E E V L R U H S P F E
N C H U C K B U C K E T A E D
```

Abe
Barge
Battle Cat
Big E
Blue Ghost
Cabot

Cellblock
Chuck Bucket
Chuckie V
Covered Wagon
Cowpens
Decrepit

Dirty V
Foo-de-roo
Galloping
Gipper
Iron Ike
Iron Woman

Oahu Coast
Rosie
Star
Starship
Warrior
Yorktown

THIS SPUD'S FOR YOU

★ ★ ★ ★ ★ ★ ★ ★ ★ ★ ★ ★ ★ ★

***Who would think that lowly potatoes could save a warship?
But that's exactly what happened at the height of World War II.***

On April 5, 1943, the destroyer USS *O'Bannon*, on patrol near the Solomon Islands, was sent to investigate a blip on the radar. The blip turned out to be a Japanese submarine casually floating on the surface. The Japanese sailors, unaware that they had been discovered, were sleeping on the deck—even the lookouts were asleep on their watch.

The Americans were poised to ram the sub, but at the last minute the captain, worried that the sub might be filled with explosives, gave the order to swing the rudder hard to avoid a collision. With the *O'Bannon* so close to the sub, an explosion would have dispatched both vessels at the same time.

When the sleeping sailors opened their eyes, they were startled to find an American warship alongside them. The two ships were so close that the *O'Bannon*'s guns could not be lowered enough to fire upon the sub. For a time no one seemed to know what to do; sailors on both sides just stood and stared at one another.

Suddenly, the spell was broken and the Japanese made for their guns. Unwilling to be sitting ducks, the American sailors looked for something, anything, that could be used as projectiles. What they found were measly potatoes in a nearby storage locker. In a stroke of genius, some sailors reached into the storage bins and started pelting the enemy with the tubers. The Japanese, probably thinking that the potatoes were grenades, busied themselves catching them and throwing them back at the *O'Bannon* or overboard into the water. They were kept so busy battling the potatoes that they had no time to man their guns.

With the enemy occupied, the *O'Bannon* was able to maneuver into a position from which her guns could be used. Several shots were fired and the sub's conning tower—the compartment that houses the periscope—was hit. Nevertheless, the sub was able to get below the surface, but it was too late for the Japanese. The destroyer moved into a position just above the sub and set off a depth charge. The sub was sunk, and the potatoes were credited with the victory.

When the Association of Potato Growers of Maine heard the story of the *O'Bannon*'s exploit, they had a commemorative plaque made, which read:

A TRIBUTE TO
THE OFFICERS AND MEN
OF THE
U.S.S. *O'BANNON*
FOR THEIR INGENUITY IN
USING OUR NOW PROUD POTATO
TO "SINK" A JAP SUBMARINE
IN THE SPRING OF 1943
PRESENTED BY
POTATO GROWERS
OF THE STATE OF MAINE
JUNE 14, 1945

The plaque was awarded to the *O'Bannon*, where it was proudly displayed near the mess hall and was perhaps the only time in history that a potato was credited with winning a naval encounter.

THIS SPUD'S FOR YOU

```
W R E Y O R T S E D N U B F E
O S O L O M O N I S L A N D S
R E X P L O S I O N U F A H M
H Q R T G Q E S W C T S I X H
T A N O L N R R W T L E P R R
M O U B G E E F N E J S L E E
W X K V W V K L E I P E A H P
G W V O U Q L P N E T P Q S R
Z U R E P A O G R U M J U O O
X G N S H S E I B G O A E B U
A A U S I N S I S V W I I A D
M N S T U C R K G Z G O R N I
K E I I O T S T O R A G E N E
M O T P G U S P U D S M L O J
N Y E S U B M A R I N E Z N J
```

Asleep	Ingenuity	Periscope	Spuds
Destroyer	Maine	Plaque	Storage
Explosion	Maneuver	Position	Submarine
Fire	Mess hall	Proud	Sunk
Growers	O'Bannon	Ram	Throw
Guns	Pelt	Solomon Islands	Tribute

SEAL TEAMS

★ ★ ★ ★ ★ ★ ★ ★ ★ ★ ★ ★ ★

The Navy's piece of Special Operations Command (USSOCOM) has numerous teams divided into four groups. Learn more about them here.

NSW PERSONNEL

Naval Special Warfare Command is headquartered in Coronado, California, with responsibility for the Naval Special Warfare (NSW) forces: SEAL (Sea, Air, and Land), SWCC (Special Boat operators), and SDV (SEAL Delivery Vehicle) personnel. It also oversees the development of NSW's specialized equipment, weapons, and vehicles.

There are more than 10,000 people assigned to the NSW; about 2,900 are active-duty SEALs, another 200 are SEALs in reserve, and the remainder are support personnel, including civilian employees. The SEALs are divided into eight different teams, each composed of a headquarters and eight 16-man platoons.

THE BREAKDOWN

All odd-numbered SEAL teams are headquartered in Coronado; all even-numbered SEAL teams are headquartered in Little Creek, Virginia. Each one has a geographic region for which they are responsible, but the small size of this elite force means all SEALs must be ready for missions in any circumstances at any time.

Naval Special Warfare Group One (Coronado)
SEAL Team 1: Western Pacific; jungle, desert, and urban environments
SEAL Team 3: Middle East; desert and urban environments
SEAL Team 5: Korea; arctic, desert, and urban environments
SEAL Team 7: Western Pacific; jungle, desert, and urban environments

Naval Special Warfare Group Two (Little Creek)
SEAL Team 2: Northern Europe; desert and urban environments
SEAL Team 4: South and Central America; desert and urban environments
SEAL Team 8: Mediterranean and Southern Europe; desert and urban environments
SEAL Team 10: Mediterranean and Southern Europe; desert and urban environments

Naval Special Warfare Group Three (Coronado)
SEAL Delivery Vehicle Team 1 (SDVT-1): Pacific
SEAL Delivery Vehicle Team 2 (SDVT-2): Atlantic and Mediterranean

Naval Special Warfare Group Four (Little Creek)
Special Boat Team 12 (SBU-12): Pacific and Middle East; maritime and coastal environments
Special Boat Team 20 (SBU-20): Europe, Mediterranean, and Middle East; maritime and coastal environments
Special Boat Team 22 (SBU-22): Worldwide; riverine environments

SEAL Team 6, or DEVGRU (Naval Special Warfare Development Group)—which entered America's collective consciousness after its role in killing former al-Qaeda leader Osama bin Laden in 2011—is a specialized counterterrorism unit composed of personnel selected from existing SEAL teams.

SEAL TEAMS

```
D M I S S I O N S N O P A E W
N X J O N G O Y A Z P U L X M
A Y T U D E V I T C A G M N U
M G X M J D V E J R N K E O Y
M K U E M Y A E C U C O M B W
O I I B V M G T J C W D I K A
C F D A B R I D W N S A T Y R
V I N D E C X S R O U N I R F
Q L N G L I P E J O K O R E A
U W I E D E S E R T N R A V R
N O S D F E E Y P A G O M I E
N E C G R S V A B L R C L L E
Y Z R V K E R R S P O X D E R
L Q E X G A U K K T U U J D Q
Y W R S M L W H A F P G R H A
```

Active duty	Even	Mission	Seal
Arctic	Group	Navy	SWCC
Command	Jungle	Odd	Team
Coronado	Korea	Platoon	Urban
Delivery	Maritime	Region	Warfare
Desert	Middle East	Reserve	Weapons

BRAVO ZULU

★ ★ ★ ★ ★ ★ ★ ★ ★ ★ ★

In the modern U.S. Navy, "Bravo Zulu" is an accolade much appreciated by those who serve well. But where did the expression come from?

An active Navy myth is that Fleet Admiral William "Bull" Halsey Jr. originated the expression "Bravo Zulu" in complimenting the performance of Task Force 38 during combat against Japan, when Halsey commanded the U.S. 3rd Fleet during World War II. Halsey was known for his quips and slogans such as "Hit hard, hit fast, hit often" and "Strike, repeat, strike."

The British navy has its own origin stories: One is that the expression was improvised as a "well done" signal to HMS *Zulu* for an accomplishment during World War II. Another is that "Bravo Zulu" was a signal flag used in the Royal Navy meaning "Issue an extra tot of rum to the crew."

All three stories are false. "Bravo Zulu" didn't become a naval term until many years later. It began as a system of communication between foreign allied navies that developed after World War II.

The original expression for "well done" in the U.S. Navy was hoisting signal flags indicating "TVG," or "Tare Victor George" in the phonetic alphabet of the Navy used over voice radio at that time. After World War II, "Tare Victor George" evolved into "Baker Zebra." The change came from the Allied Naval Signal Book, known as the ACP 175 series, adopted after the North Atlantic Treaty Organization was founded in 1949. Wartime experiences convinced commanders that a uniform system of communication involving signal flags was necessary to ease communications when so many foreign languages were involved among allied navies working together.

ACP 175 codified visual flag signals between ships. Signals with the letter *B* coming first indicated administrative signals. Flags with "BZ," the last of a series of administrative codes, represented "well done"—or, expressed orally, "Baker Zebra."

In the 1950s, the International Civil Aviation Organization (ICAO) adopted English as the international language for air traffic control. Some expressions taken from the ACP 175 series were difficult for some foreign pilots and controllers to say. One of those was "Baker Zebra." Thus, the ICAO devised a more "pronounceable" signal code using a new radio alphabet: "Alpha," "Bravo," "Charlie," "Delta," and so on. In 1956, the Navy realized the benefit of the new command code and adopted it. As a result, "Baker Zebra" became "Bravo Zulu." Well done!

Over the years, "Bravo Zulu" has become a colloquialism for anything done right. And, naturally, not everything is praiseworthy, so today there is an expression for "not so well done"—"NEGAT Bravo Zulu."

BRAVO ZULU

```
U D V F I V I S U A L P O R T
C L L J T L H H T D H W Y A N
O O U R W I Z U X A R P C S E
D G Q Z P O K E J X U H P K M
E C L S O L U L D W M O A C I
S O B A K E R Z E B R A E Q L
N O I T A C I N U M M O C U P
V I M D B L Y E S L A H W I M
D T H R A S N A G O L S C P O
X O A N M R O F I N U X H S C
S V G R J F M N G D C Q A P G
O I E N O D L L E W F U R A A
S C O D I F Y L C G L R L U V
S R S R E T T E L E A F I N B
L A N G U A G E S Z X T E R Y
```

Baker zebra	Compliment	Letters	Signal
Bravo	Delta	Negat	Slogans
Charlie	Flag	Quips	Uniform
Codes	Halsey	Radio	Visual
Codify	ICAO	Rum	Well done
Communication	Languages	Ships	Zulu

UNITED STATES SPACE FORCE (USSF) RANKS

Airmen in the United States Space Force may be enlisted or commissioned officers. Space Force ranks designate job responsibilities and utilize the below names.

GRADE	RANK	ABBREVIATION
E1	Specialist 1	Spc1
E2	Specialist 2	Spc2
E3	Specialist 3	Spc3
E4	Specialist 4	Spc4
E5	Sergeant	Sgt
E6	Technical Sergeant	TSgt
E7	Master Sergeant	MSgt
E8	Senior Master Sergeant	SMSgt
E9	Chief Master Sergeant	CMSgt
	Chief Master Sergeant of the Space Force	CMSSF
O1	Second Lieutenant	2d Lt
O2	First Lieutenant	1st Lt
O3	Captain	Capt
O4	Major	Maj
O5	Lieutenant Colonel	Lt Col
O6	Colonel	Col
O7	Brigadier General	Brig Gen
O8	Major General	Maj Gen
O9	Lieutenant General	Lt Gen
O10	General	Gen

UNITED STATES SPACE FORCE (USSF) RANKS

```
B M D X O M R E N L I S T E D
T B B Q K A I O M L N A Z O N
S M M I P S B K I A X A Y C O
I W N V O T L N I N N T N O C
L A R E N E G D S P E K O L E
A A P N V R R T B C R S I O S
I S A E R A N K H D E F T N B
C L L G U A N N G F C E A E R
E C P G E L I K R B I I I L I
P T A G J C M F A H F H V R G
S G R P A Q Y S D I F C E C A
M E X L T V P S E W O K R Z D
S L R O J A M X F Y J O B X I
F P R U C Q I T S R I F B R E
L L I E U T E N A N T T A Y R
```

Abbreviation
Brigadier
Captain
Chief
Colonel
Enlisted
First
General
Grade
Guardian
Job
Level
Lieutenant
Major
Master
Name
Officer
Rank
Second
Senior
Sergeant
Space
Specialist
Technical

CODE TALKERS: WORLD WAR I

★ ★ ★ ★ ★ ★ ★ ★ ★ ★ ★ ★ ★

In World Wars I and II, Native Americans helped the U.S. say "Nin hokeh bi-kheh a-na-ih-la" ("we have conquered our enemies").

A BRILLIANT PLAN

In October 1918, the American Expeditionary Force in France was in trouble. They'd been sent to help the British and French in World War I but got bogged down in hilly terrain, were surrounded by Germans, and took heavy casualties. American officers couldn't coordinate attacks or retreats without the Germans knowing their plans. If they tried to communicate by telephone, the Germans listened and broke their code. Sending communications by runners was no better: about 25 percent were caught and their communiqués easily deciphered.

But then, according to Private Solomon Louis, he and a friend were conversing in Choctaw when an officer overheard them and realized he couldn't understand anything they were saying. The officer's confusion was the beginning of one of America's greatest military intelligence coups.

THANK THE CHOCTAW

In 1918, Native Americans weren't allowed to vote. They weren't even considered U.S. citizens, and most had been forced as children to attend boarding schools that punished them for speaking their native languages. But now they were asked to use their language to save lives.

Colonel A. W. Bloor, commanding the 142nd Infantry, 36th Division, assigned Louis, his friend, and six other Choctaw to manage communications. They were so successful that 18 Choctaw code talkers got jobs with the military telephoning messages, writing field orders for runners, and translating communications for English-speaking officers. The men adapted their language into a code. Army companies were called different grains of corn—"one grain," "two grains," and so on. A machine gun became "little gun shoots fast." As for casualties, they were translated as "scalps."

The first successful test of the new code was a secret movement of American troops during the night; the second was a surprise attack on the Germans. Neither message was successfully intercepted. Thanks to the Choctaw, the United States finally had a code that stumped the Germans, and the tide of war immediately turned in favor of the Allies. In fact, the war ended only weeks after the Choctaw code breakers started managing Allied communications.

The men came home to no recognition for their accomplishments, however, and very few people knew how much the Army had depended on them. The Germans knew, though. Adolf Hitler sent "students" to the United States to study Native Americans and their dialects. He didn't want German generals outfoxed by code talkers again . . .

Turn the page to find out how code talkers aided Allied troops in World War II.

CODE TALKERS: WORLD WAR I

M	N	F	J	S	M	E	V	I	T	A	N	A	K	D
E	D	X	I	R	A	X	E	M	K	P	P	H	E	I
C	S	S	R	E	K	L	A	T	Q	I	A	C	P	A
N	Z	N	G	D	B	C	O	R	N	B	I	D	Q	L
A	C	C	A	R	H	Z	O	T	F	P	L	N	A	E
R	O	H	E	O	A	S	E	N	H	R	G	O	X	C
F	V	A	C	L	C	R	O	E	Q	T	R	O	O	T
P	K	T	L	F	C	U	R	L	O	U	I	S	F	R
T	A	I	T	E	V	E	G	A	S	S	E	M	T	G
W	E	K	P	E	K	F	L	W	H	W	N	R	U	Z
S	P	T	N	U	G	E	L	T	T	I	L	O	O	E
N	S	Q	H	I	T	L	E	R	P	Z	C	O	D	E
A	R	X	Q	J	C	O	O	R	D	I	N	A	T	E
M	D	D	X	S	C	A	L	P	S	M	H	L	M	Q
J	A	A	E	G	A	U	G	N	A	L	D	V	P	Z

Adapt
Allies
Bloor
Break
Choctaw
Code
Conquer
Coordinate
Corn
Decipher
Dialect
France
Hitler
Intercept
Language
Little gun
Louis
Message
Native
Orders
Outfox
Scalps
Speak
Talkers

CODE TALKERS: WORLD WAR II

★ ★ ★ ★ ★ ★ ★ ★ ★ ★ ★ ★ ★

Navajo troops were integral to the success of Allied forces during World War II.

HERE WE GO AGAIN

Despite the lack of public recognition for the Choctaw role in World War I, the U.S. Army hadn't forgotten the code talkers. By the 1940s, the military used cipher machines to encrypt messages and make them unreadable to the enemy, but it was a slow process: one message could take nearly an hour to complete, too much time to waste on the front lines.

Looking for a better way to transmit codes, the Army again turned to Native American tribes. In 1941, 17 Comanche recruits at Fort Benning, Georgia, developed a coded language for use in Europe. They created a 100-word dictionary and adapted their language to translate military terms. The word for "machine gun" in Comanche code was "sewing machine," and "pregnant airplane" was code for a bomber. As for Hitler, his code name was *posah-tai-vo*, meaning "crazy white man."

On D-Day, the Comanche code talkers landed at Normandy, and despite Hitler's best efforts, the Nazis couldn't understand the messages they were sending. The Germans never broke the Comanche code.

TELL IT TO THE MARINES

U.S. troops in the Pacific relied heavily on their code talkers, too. These men were Navajo. The idea for using the Navajo language—called *Diné bizaad* by native speakers—came from Philip Johnston, a city engineer from Los Angeles. Johnston wasn't Navajo, but he'd grown up on a Navajo reservation where his father was a missionary, and he'd learned to speak the language.

With no connection to any European or Asian language, *Diné bizaad* had tonal variations and a complicated syntax that mystified people who were unfamiliar with it. It was also a language the Germans hadn't yet learned.

To show how well *Diné bizaad* worked as a military code, Johnston and four volunteer Navajos gave a demonstration for Major General Clayton Vogel and his staff. The men could deliver a three-line Navajo message in under a minute; cipher machines needed at least half an hour. On Vogel's recommendation, Navajos were recruited into the Marines and sent to Camp Pendleton for training as radio signalmen.

Find out more about Navajo code talkers on the next page.

CODE TALKERS: WORLD WAR II

```
T R A N S M I T R T Z Y C N R
S S W O Z N Q Y Q U Y O T T T
T O E C H O C T A W D W M S S
E V K N B N E G H I N O A E Y
X N O K I D E I L L A I N B X
A H I G T H Y M R A M I C I I
T P W D E P C S L C R D H R I
N H E R R L Y A R A O S E T L
Y Z H I T L E R M E N X C P C
S M H O Y A D D C H K G E M I
P E N D L E T O N N V L I Z P
N A V A J O Z H A X E A A S H
L D I C T I O N A R Y Y I T E
U N R E A D A B L E A X I Q R
R F Z G T Y M Y I P R A D I O
```

Allied
Army
Choctaw
Cipher
Comanche
D-Day
Dictionary
Diné
Encrypt
Hitler
Machines
Marines
Navajo
Normandy
Pendleton
Radio
Signalmen
Syntax
Talkers
Tonal
Transmit
Tribes
Unreadable
Vogel

Fun fact

CODE TALKERS: THE PACIFIC THEATER

★ ★ ★ ★ ★ ★ ★ ★ ★ ★ ★ ★ ★

Navajo code talkers foiled the Japanese.

WATCH OUT FOR FALLING BUZZARD EGGS

Navajo code talkers had eight weeks to learn the complex code. Because there were no equivalents for standard military terms, they coined new terms: planes were "birds," a bomber was a "buzzard," and bombs were "eggs."

Eventually, the Navajo code talkers developed more than 400 military terms. They also used a coded alphabet for spelling out words that were difficult to translate. For example, they could spell out Iwo Jima as "Ice-Weasel-Owl-Jackass-Itch-Mouse-Ant." But they did it by substituting the Navajo word for each English word. To make the code even more complicated, a talker had more than one choice for words that represented common letters and vowels. For example, to avoid repeating *ice* for the letter *I* in "Iwo Jima," the codebook gave the option of using the word *itch* or *intestine*. The men memorized this so no books could fall into enemy hands.

When Navy intelligence was asked to break the Navajo code, they called it a "weird succession of guttural, nasal, tongue-twisting sounds" they couldn't even write down. Later, the Marines discovered that not even native Navajos could break the code. Sergeant Joe Kieyoomia, a Navajo POW held by the Japanese on Bataan, was tortured to reveal the secrets of the messages coming over the radio. But though Kieyoomia could pick up certain words, he had no clue what they stood for.

TOUGH TALK

After training was over, the first Navajo code talkers began their job at Guadalcanal. Their training had been top secret, and when radio signalmen first heard Navajo code, they panicked, thinking the Japanese had hijacked their frequencies. But the speed and accuracy of the Navajo soon led to requests for additional code talkers.

Before the war was over, about 420 Navajo Marines were transmitting communications in the Pacific. They served in every assault between 1942 and 1945. During the first two days of the Battle of Iwo Jima, six code talkers sent more than 800 messages without any errors.

One Navajo on Iwo Jima had a friend killed right beside him while they were working, but he still sent out an error-free message for help. And when the Marines (who were being fired at from Japanese atop Mount Suribachi) finally took the mountain summit and famously raised the U.S. flag, it was a code-talker message that reported their triumph. According to Major Howard Connor, the 5th Marine Division's signal officer, "Were it not for the Navajos, the Marines would never have taken Iwo Jima." After the war, the Japanese chief of intelligence admitted that his soldiers had been able to decipher some codes used by the Army and Army Air Corps—but they never cracked the code of the Navajo Marines.

CODE TALKERS: THE PACIFIC THEATER

```
S U R I B A C H I L P A L A H
T D A T W M Z W W H Q A A A M
E J H N X W N Y O S C L N K V
R V S O Y V A N J I K I A I S
C C E I D Y Z C I L J K C E C
E O G T S D O Q M G H S L Y Z
S D A P Q D F T A N P E A O V
Y E S O E E R O R E G R D O O
X B S D N I J I L O Y E A M W
N O E Z U A E L B K N Q U I E
N O M M V C I F L A G N G A L
A K P A I N N H V W L D O C S
P H N O G R Z G K Y C R A C K
A U H E C N E G I L L E T N I
J C I I C O M P L I C A T E D
```

Birds	Crack	Japan	Panic
Choice	English	Kieyoomia	Secrets
Codebook	Flag	Messages	Spelling
Coded	Guadalcanal	Navajo	Suribachi
Complicated	Intelligence	Navy	Triumph
Connor	Iwo Jima	Option	Vowels

BLACK HAWK DOWN

★ ★ ★ ★ ★ ★ ★ ★ ★ ★ ★ ★ ★

The phrase became famous thanks to the 2001 movie of the same name. What really happened during the Battle of Mogadishu?

In 1993, United Nations relief efforts in Somalia were being hampered by local warlords. UN troops were sent to protect humanitarian workers; among the armed forces were a group of Pakistani troops who were ambushed and killed. Army Rangers and Delta Force launched a mission to capture the most powerful warlord—General Mohamed Farrah Adid—and several of his lieutenants. Unfortunately, two Black Hawk helicopters were shot down during the mission. That mission then changed to rescuing the crews from the downed choppers.

Two Delta snipers circling above in another helicopter volunteered to defend one of the crash sites that was about to be overrun by Somali gunmen. They knew it was probably a suicide mission, but they agreed to be dropped off at the site because they could see that at least one of the American soldiers there was still alive. They held off hundreds of Somali gunmen until they were overrun and killed; in the process, they saved the life of the chopper pilot, Michael Durant, who was captured by the gunmen but later released. The snipers, Master Sergeant Gary Ivan Gordon and Sergeant First Class Randall D. Shughart, were each posthumously awarded the Medal of Honor for their extraordinary heroism.

By the time the Rangers and Delta Force operators arrived at the crash areas and set up defensive perimeters, they were surrounded by hostile locals and under near-constant attack. They were trapped in the city overnight and suffered heavy casualties. But the next morning, a relief force arrived, led by the 10th Infantry Division, and they managed to fight their way out along what became known as the "Mogadishu Mile."

BLACK HAWK DOWN

```
K W A H K C A L B A I V C Q H
S N I P E R S S X A M B U S H
T N A R U D D U N F U S A S V
M R E T E M I R E P K R D P G
S X E T W V R T I C C E O O
I N I S P Q O O E G A H L N R
O P M P C V S U L T T O T N D
R R B G I U E N I H T P A E O
E J E V U R E D T G A P F S N
H Z R L U N C L S I R E O O O
J U S T I N M Z O F N R R M I
S Z P A K E X E H D Q C C A S
O A E M F A F U N A G N E L S
C B R E T P O C I L E H L I I
X E D W V O L U N T E E R A M
```

Ambush
Attack
Black Hawk
Capture
Chopper
Crash

Defend
Delta Force
Durant
Fight
Gordon
Gunmen

Helicopter
Heroism
Hostile
Mission
Perimeter
Relief

Rescue
Snipers
Somalia
Surround
Survivor
Volunteer

NOTABLE QUOTABLES: GOING TO WAR

★ ★ ★ ★ ★ ★ ★ ★ ★ ★ ★ ★ ★ ★

- ★ "The object of war is not to die for your country but to make the other bastard die for his."
 —General George S. Patton, Jr.

- ★ "Hit the enemy twice: First to find out what he's got; then, to take it away from him."
 —General Omar N. Bradley

- ★ "The true soldier fights not because he hates what is in front of him, but because he loves what is behind him." —G. K. Chesterton

- ★ "The more you sweat in peace, the less you bleed in battle."
 —General Norman Schwarzkopf

- ★ "In war, you win or lose, live or die, and the difference is just an eyelash."
 —General Douglas MacArthur

- ★ "If you find yourself in a fair fight, you didn't plan your mission properly."
 —Colonel David Hackworth

- ★ "It is fatal to enter a war without the will to win it." —General Douglas MacArthur

- ★ "Perpetual optimism is a force multiplier." —General Colin Powell

- ★ "No army can be efficient unless it be a unit for action; and the power must come from above, not from below." —General William Tecumseh Sherman

- ★ "It is not enough to fight. It is the spirit which we bring to the fight that decides the issue. It is morale that wins the victory." —General George C. Marshall

- ★ "Nothing is easy in war. Mistakes are always paid for in casualties and troops are quick to sense any blunder made by their commanders." —General Dwight D. Eisenhower

- ★ "In war there is no second prize for the runner-up." —General Omar N. Bradley

- ★ "However fine the weapon, however adequate the equipment, neither represent any more strength than the hearts of the men who use them." —General Matthew B. Ridgway

- ★ "Many, who should know better, think that wars can be decided by soulless machines, rather than by the blood and anguish of brave men." —General George S. Patton, Jr.

- ★ "Courage on the battlefield is the greatest single factor in the winning of battles and the waging of war." —General Raymond S. McClain

NOTABLE QUOTABLES: GOING TO WAR

```
C F E V O R H Q P R E W O P K
M E V S X K X M A V E O H S M
Q Y O O X L I S T E L A R O M
V E L L M H N I T W T D Z Z B
I L D D A A M M O N T P J R M
C A E I R C X I N O A D A E E
T S G E S K S T L T B D M W B
O H A R H W S P F R L S G O S
R Y R A A O W O T E D M M H P
Y K U D L R E Y Y T O L E N I
L D O G L T A G M S R A W E R
B B C I J H T G N E R T S S I
V A B L E E D R K H N X N I T
M C C L A I N D L C Y E M E S
D S A N G U I S H P O W E L L
```

Anguish	Eisenhower	McClain	Soldier
Battle	Enemy	Morale	Spirit
Bleed	Eyelash	Optimism	Strength
Bradley	Hackworth	Patton	Sweat
Chesterton	Love	Powell	Victory
Courage	Marshall	Power	War

BASE FACTS

★ ★ ★ ★ ★ ★ ★ ★ ★ ★ ★ ★

Here are some fun facts about U.S. military bases of all branches.

Fort Liberty in North Carolina is the largest of all the bases in the continental United States. The Army base just west of Fayetteville is home to more than 52,000 military personnel and covers more than 251 square miles—that's larger than the city of Chicago!

The largest overseas military base is Camp Humphreys, located about 40 miles south of Seoul in South Korea. This Army garrison covers an area of 3,454 acres containing more than 500 buildings.

The most remote military base is Pituffik Space Base. The former Air Force air base—now a Space Force base—is the U.S. military's northernmost installation, situated just 947 miles from the North Pole in remote Greenland. The surrounding environment includes Wolstenholme Fjord, the only place on the planet where four active glaciers join.

California is the state with the most military bases. There are 32 bases across all branches of the Armed Forces, along with National Guard/Reserve bases.

The Navy's largest complex is Naval Air Weapons Station China Lake. This base in California's Mojave Desert covers more than 1.1 million acres of land across three different counties. The restricted airspace above the base is 19,600 square miles, which totals 12 percent of California's airspace.

Also in California's desert is Marine Corps Air Ground Combat Center Twentynine Palms, the Marine Corps' largest base. Encompassing 1,102 square miles, the installation near Joshua Tree National Park was a census-designated place until 2010 and has its own zip code (92278).

U.S. Army Garrison West Point, home to the United States Military Academy, is the oldest continuously occupied military base in the United States. The Continental Army first occupied the New York installation in 1778. It was initially called Fort Arnold, after its commanding officer, Benedict Arnold; after Arnold's infamous treasonous acts of attempting to turn the fort over to the British, it was renamed Fort Clinton in honor of General James Clinton.

BASE FACTS

```
O C C U P I E D R E S E R V E
S P A C E B A S E M O J A V E
Y S Z I P C O D E D A P Y I J
E E R E S T R I C T E D T G W
R O V E R S E A S L O F R R O
H U H L B W W R E M O T E E L
P L G F J O R D C I C I B E S
M J O S H U A T R E E G I N T
U W E S T P O I N T L S L L E
H P I T U F F I K A G Y T A N
P I A I R S P A C E X L R N H
M A I N R O F I L A C H O D O
A J M E V N E W Y O R K F J L
C T S E G R A L C E N S U S M
C D Z V S V G A R R I S O N E
```

Airspace
California
Camp Humphreys
Census
Fjord
Fort Liberty
Garrison
Glaciers
Greenland
Joshua Tree
Largest
Mojave
New York
Occupied
Overseas
Pituffik
Remote
Reserve
Restricted
Seoul
Space Base
West Point
Wolstenholme
Zip code

GOT WHAT IT TAKES?
U.S. AIR FORCE SPECIAL TACTICS

★ ★ ★ ★ ★ ★ ★ ★ ★ ★ ★ ★ ★

To be eligible for an elite unit in the Armed Forces, candidates must meet or exceed fitness standards, then go through rigorous training. Learn what it takes to be a U.S. Air Force Special Tactics Officer.

There are two specialties in U.S. Air Force Special Tactics. Combat controllers are sent on advance deployments to establish battlefield parameters. Pararescuemen are trained to recover personnel in hostile territory and provide medical treatment.

To qualify for Special Tactics training, an Airman must be able to complete:

- 20-meter underwater swim, done twice (pass/fail);
- 500-meter swim using freestyle, breaststroke, or sidestroke in 14:00 (under 9:00 to be competitive);
- 1½-mile run in 10:45 (under 9:00 to be competitive);
- 6 pull-ups in 1 minute (13 to be competitive);
- 45 sit-ups in 2 minutes (100 to be competitive);
- 45 push-ups in 2 minutes (100 to be competitive);
- 45 flutter-kicks in 2 minutes (100 to be competitive).

Combat controllers undergo a 35-week training program that covers a wide range of skills, including air-traffic control, parachuting, survival, and combat tactics. Once this has been completed successfully, a combat controller will spend the next 12 months in an advanced program that includes free-fall parachuting, combat diving, and further mental and physical training.

Pararescuemen spend 14 months in a training program to learn emergency medical techniques, mountaineering, recovery, and how to escape from an aircraft that has been ditched into the water. Pararescuemen also go through some of the same training as combat controllers, such as free-fall parachuting, combat diving, and survival. Both specialties attend the U.S. Army Airborne School at Fort Benning, Georgia, to learn basic parachuting skills.

GOT WHAT IT TAKES?
U.S. AIR FORCE SPECIAL TACTICS

```
Z M B Q K P H Y S I C A L J D
E M E R G E N C Y P S U M D O
K G T F L C E E F N U E E B A
E N U I K F N L F D D L M S N
U I H M S R X U I I C L P A
C V C M O P A T C T F M L U S
S I A B R Y A A S I E E R T P
E D R X S B L O N R U N E I U
R I A Q M W H B L W Q T T S H
A E P O S C I T C A T A A J S
R E C O V E R M C F N L W M U
A B U N D E R W A T E R E F P
P Y U R G L S U R V I V A L B
A I R F O R C E T Z P J I W P
S P E C I A L T Y E P A C S E
```

Air Force	Escape	Physical	Specialty
Airborne	Hostile	Pull-ups	Survival
Combat	Medical	Push-ups	Swim
Diving	Mental	Recover	Tactics
Elite	Parachute	Run	Underwater
Emergency	Pararescue	Sit-ups	Water

THE COAST GUARD'S MEDAL OF HONOR: DOUGLAS A. MUNRO

★ ★ ★ ★ ★ ★ ★ ★ ★ ★ ★ ★ ★

The Medal of Honor is the highest accolade awarded by the United States Military. Of the 3,517 recipients, only one has gone to a member of the Coast Guard. Here is his story.

Douglas Munro was born in 1919 in Vancouver, Canada, to an American father and a British mother; the family moved to the small town of Cle Elum in Washington state when Munro was two years old. Growing up, Douglas excelled in sports and had a passion for helping others in need. By mid-1939, Munro was aware of the difficult situation in Europe and the increasing possibility of military conscription. He enlisted in the Coast Guard in September 1939 and immediately made friends with Raymond J. Evans, a fellow recruit; the two became inseparable and were stationed together throughout their service.

By August 1942, Munro had been promoted to Signalman First Class and was assigned to Naval Operating Base Cactus at Lunga Point, participating in the Guadalcanal Campaign. At the Second Battle of Matanikau on September 27, he was responsible for two Higgins boats transporting Marines to their landing point; he also transported injured Sailors and Marines away from the fighting. Boat crews were refueling at the staging area when they received word that the Marines—overwhelmed and being driven back to the beach—needed to be pulled out immediately. Munro led the way back to the beach.

The Coast Guard ships were quickly overcome by enemy fire, and Munro was told to fall back: the rescue wouldn't be possible. Munro refused to turn around, instead positioning his boat so that Evans could provide cover for the retreating Marines while they swam out to the landing craft. When all the Marines were on board, Munro began his return to Lunga Point, but noticed another landing craft full of Marines stuck on the nearby reef. Munro pulled alongside it and the Marines on board with him tied a tow rope to it, managing to extract it—but coming under increasingly heavy machine-gun fire from the Japanese while doing so. Just as they freed the other boat and began heading back, Munro was struck with a single bullet and fell unconscious. After Evans sped the boat back to Lunga Point, Munro regained consciousness just long enough to ask his friend "Did they get off?" Those were the 22-year-old's last words before he perished.

Thanks to Douglas Munro's efforts, no Marines—including the wounded—were left behind. He was posthumously awarded the Medal of Honor in May 1943.

THE COAST GUARD'S MEDAL OF HONOR: DOUGLAS A. MUNRO

```
H I G G I N S N C K A R E E F
S F T M V W H V Q R X R Z B Y
K Q L A E Q H L G L I L C G D
Q Y T R V T N K T F A R O I L
T K C I C H E O L N E E V D G
R T A N K S W L D N T T E O N
A U R E Q R Y I L I Y R R R I
N O T S O C N I U U U E E N L
S L X P B G S R Y J B A T U E
P L E R P T C V N B F T W M U
O U K O E E N I S P O R T S F
R P I V R M A T A N I K A U E
T N A M E D A L O F H O N O R
T N I N S E P A R A B L E A F
S O M S N W K C A B L L A F O
```

Bullet
Cover
Crews
Enlist
Evans
Extract

Fall back
Fire
Higgins
Injured
Inseparable
Landing point

Marines
Matanikau
Medal of Honor
Munro
Pull out
Recruit

Reef
Refueling
Retreat
Sports
Tow rope
Transport

ONE DAY THAT CHANGED THE COURSE OF THE WAR: D-DAY BY THE NUMBERS

★ ★ ★ ★ ★ ★ ★ ★ ★ ★ ★ ★ ★

The Invasion of Normandy (code name: Operation Overlord) on June 6, 1944, brought together Allied land, air, and sea forces in the largest amphibious assault in military history and changed the course of World War II. Here are some of the key numbers from that historic day.

5: Number of beaches in Normandy where Allied troops landed. These were given the code names Utah, Omaha, Gold, Juno, and Sword.

50: Number of miles in the stretch of beach along Normandy targeted by Operation Overlord.

2,400: American casualties suffered on Omaha Beach, the six-mile-long stretch of beach between Sainte-Honorine-des-Pertes and Vierville-sur-Mer. The 1st Army, 5th Corps was responsible for taking this beach, aided by the U.S. Navy and Royal Navy. The 34,000 Americans involved in this assault suffered the worst ordeal of all D-Day operations.

6,000: Ships and landing craft that participated, including 1,213 naval combat ships, 736 ancillary craft, and 864 merchant vessels.

8,230: American casualties (killed, wounded, missing, or captured). An additional 3,774 casualties were suffered by U.K. and Canadian troops. Germany's casualties are estimated between 4,000 and 9,000.

11,000: Aircraft that participated.

23,400: Number of Allied airborne troops.

50,000: Approximate number of German forces involved in the fighting.

50,000: Vehicles that participated.

100,000: Tons of military equipment that had crossed the beachheads by June 11.

156,000: Number of troops from the United States, United Kingdom, Canada, Norway, Australia, and other Allied countries who landed in Normandy.

ONE DAY THAT CHANGED THE COURSE OF THE WAR: D-DAY BY THE NUMBERS

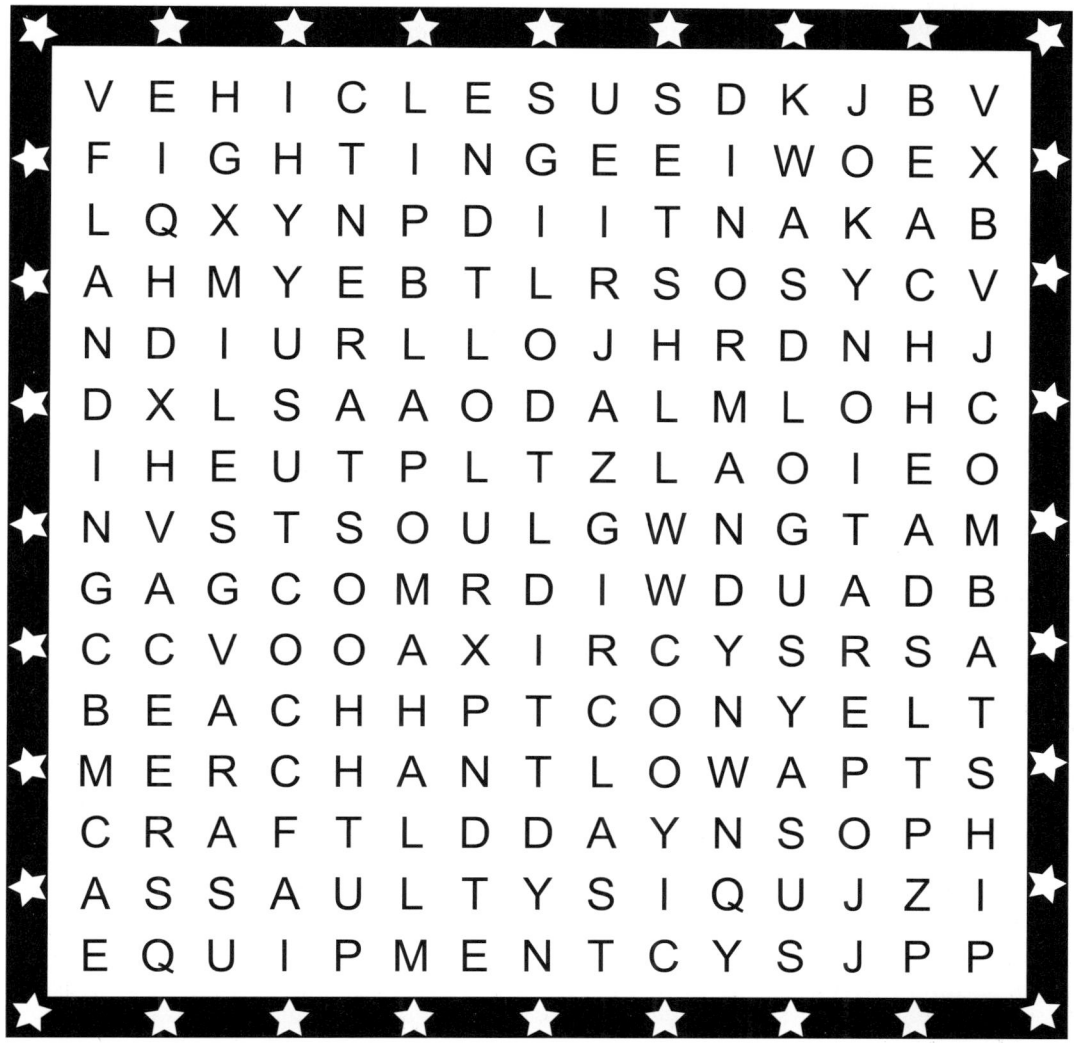

Allied	Combat ship	Historic	Omaha
Ancillary	Craft	Juno	Operation
Assault	D-Day	Landing	Sword
Beach	Equipment	Merchant	Troops
Beachheads	Fighting	Miles	Utah
Casualties	Gold	Normandy	Vehicles

JAMES N. ROWE: AN EXTRAORDINARY ESCAPE

★ ★ ★ ★ ★ ★ ★ ★ ★ ★ ★ ★ ★

Hundreds of American service members were taken prisoner during the Vietnam War, many of them subject to severe treatment—including torture—in violation of the Geneva Convention guidelines. Here is the story of one of only 34 who managed to escape captivity.

Lieutenant James "Nick" Rowe was a graduate of West Point and member of the elite U.S. Army Special Forces (Green Berets) who had been in Vietnam for only three months when he was captured by Viet Cong forces on October 29, 1963. Rowe was separated from his fellow POWs and held in the U Minh Forest; for 62 months he was held captive, primarily in a small bamboo cage, with only brief encounters with other American prisoners. As an intelligence officer, he possessed critical information about American defenses, friendly Vietnamese, and the location of American mine fields, but he managed to convince his captors that he was merely an engineer who had been drafted to build schools. In addition to starving him, withholding medical treatment, and holding him in solitary confinement, the Viet Cong tortured him continually, attempting to get him to break his story, but without success—they even gave Rowe engineering problems to solve, which he was able to work out thanks to the basic engineering studies he'd undertaken at West Point.

Unfortunately, Rowe's biography was included in a list of "high-value" American POWs that was released, and his captors discovered his true identity as an intelligence officer. Enraged, the Viet Cong ordered his execution. On December 31, 1968, Rowe was led deep into the nearby jungle to be shot. In a twist of fate, his guards were surprised by fire from nearby American gunships. Rowe was able to knock one of his guards unconscious, escape the area, and flag down one of the helicopter pilots, leading to his rescue after 1,903 days. According to the citation for the Silver Star he earned for these actions, "his first action after rescue was to request permission to re-enter the area with combat troops and to continue the fight based on his intimate knowledge of the area."

After returning to the United States, Major Rowe (he had been promoted during his time in captivity) served on the Army Staff for Intelligence as principal planner for Operation Homecoming, the plan to bring home the remaining 591 American prisoners in North Vietnam. He then transitioned to the Army Reserve, but in 1981, he was recalled to active duty as a Lieutenant Colonel, charged with designing and building the rigorous Survival, Evasion, Resistance, and Escape (SERE) course at Fort Bragg. The course is a requirement for all U.S. Army Special Forces personnel, and the Navy, Air Force, and Marines have similar courses based on it for their special operations team members. The course is critical for those personnel serving in positions at high risk of capture by enemy forces.

Nick Rowe was assassinated on April 21, 1989, while serving as Ground Forces Director for the Joint U.S. Military Advisory Group in the Philippines. He is buried in Arlington National Cemetery.

JAMES N. ROWE: AN EXTRAORDINARY ESCAPE

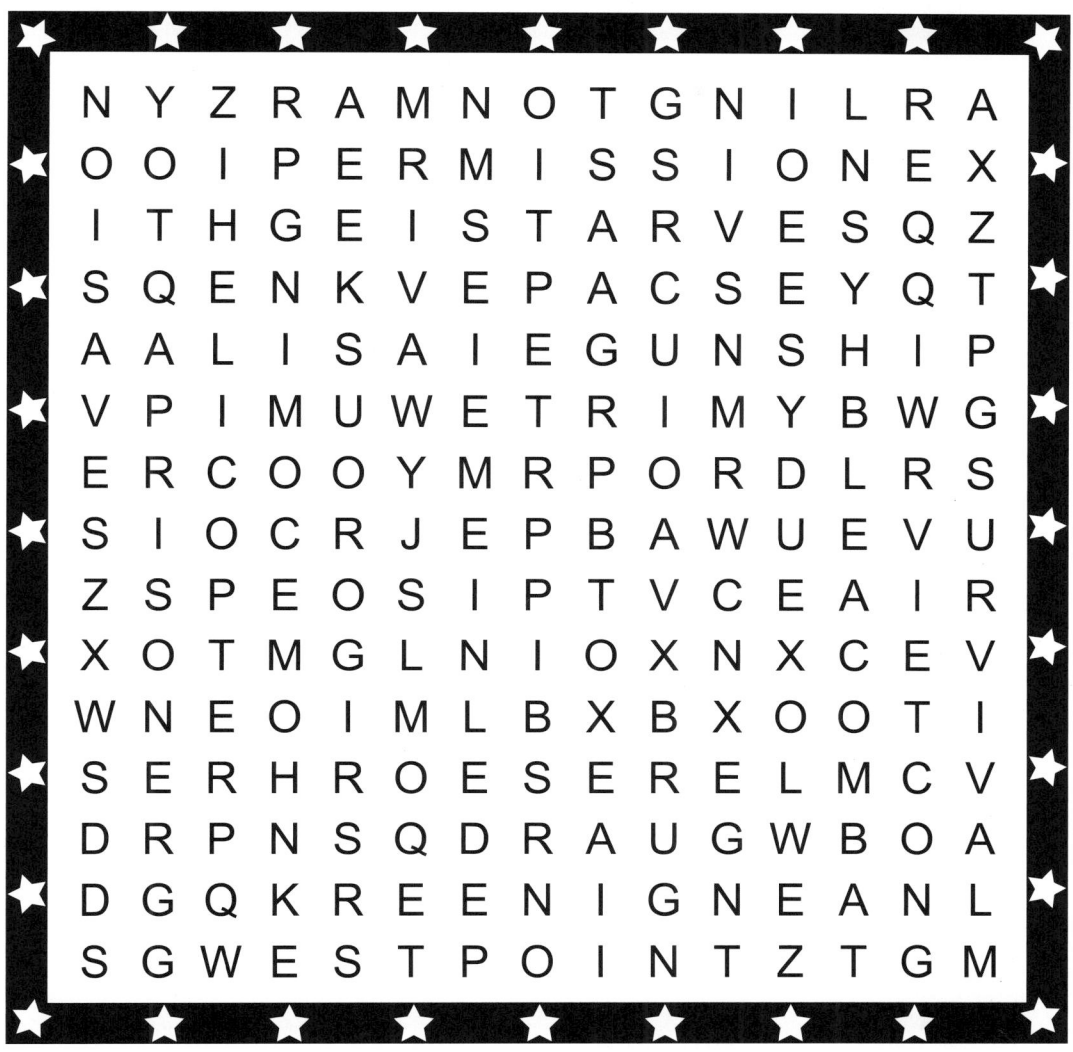

Arlington
Break
Captive
Combat
Engineer
Escape

Evasion
Green Beret
Guard
Gunship
Helicopter
Homecoming

Permission
Philippines
POW
Prisoner
Rigorous
Rowe

SERE
Solitary
Starve
Survival
Viet Cong
West Point

BY THE (HULL) NUMBERS

★ ★ ★ ★ ★ ★ ★ ★ ★ ★ ★ ★ ★

Most civilians recognize the name of at least a few famous Navy ships, but may not recognize—or understand—the codes associated with them. Read on to learn about hull numbers, the military's method for identifying ocean-going craft.

After a century of referring to ships only by type and name, the U.S. Navy realized the need for a new system that was less confusing (by 1874, there had already been five ships named *Enterprise*). The first attempt at a system of categorization came in the 1890s, when the Navy instituted "naval registry identification numbers," a system that identified each ship by its name, then its type (spelled out), then the number for the individual ship of that type. One example was the second cruiser in the fleet, identified as *Charleston* (Cruiser No. 2). In 1907, the system employed abbreviations for ship type.

The modern system was adopted in the 1920s, when the Navy began using a two-letter identifier for ship type (the "hull classification symbol") followed by a number for the individual ship; numbers are assigned sequentially by ship type—the first being assigned number 1, the second being assigned number 2, and so on. The letters and numbers combined are referred to popularly as "hull numbers." Some ships had letter classifications based on what they were—"BB" for battleships or "SS" for submarines. Others are seemingly unrelated—aircraft carriers are "CV." With time, the letters have changed or been updated as new ships are developed and others become obsolete. But each individual ship usually retains its hull number for the course of its time in service.

Because some ships were renamed or reclassified, deciphering historical hull numbers can require some research. But current ships are included in the Navy's online Naval Vessel Register. For a brief overview, here are the hull classifications for some common ship types, both retired and current.

BB: battleship
CA: heavy cruiser
CL: light cruiser
CV, CVA, CVN: aircraft carrier
CVE: escort carrier
DD, DDE, DDK, DDR: destroyer
DL: destroyer leader
DEG: guided missile destroyer escort
FF: frigate
FFG: guided missile frigate
LCS: littoral combat ship
PG: gun boat
SS, SSN, SSBN, SSGN: submarine

BY THE (HULL) NUMBERS

```
N E S I R P R E T N E F A E L
J V E S S E L E J W Z W T K Y
X P P Q R C D Y B Y Q A U C P
M F Y E V E D A A M G P E V Q
E I T S Z C S C E I U G R K I
T D V U L I O I R L K N B R D
S E W B L M R F U N H E A V Y
Y N L M B A L O G R A H N T N
S T P A Y R R L G U C V U Z Y
F I T R Y O G O X E N C A L U
I F X I Y C T B T Z T B O L L
S Y G N Q F K M E T J A O D N
O H N E A A Q Y P U I H C A E
R E I R R A C S D M M L M Q T
M E C P T R O C S E N E K A A
```

Carrier	Enterprise	Identify	Ship
Categorize	Escort	Leader	Submarine
Code	Frigate	Littoral	Symbol
Combat	Gun boat	Name	System
Craft	Heavy	Naval	Type
Cruiser	Hull	Number	Vessel

THE MISSING MAN

★ ★ ★ ★ ★ ★ ★ ★ ★ ★ ★ ★ ★

*Also sometimes referred to as the "Fallen Comrade Table,"
the Missing Man Table is a sign that no comrade is ever forgotten.*

You may have seen it in a military dining facility, at a military function, or even at a bar or restaurant on Veterans Day or Memorial Day: a set table with a single, empty chair. This "Missing Man" table is a ceremony and memorial set up as a reminder to all present of the fallen, missing, or imprisoned U.S. military service members who cannot be present to join in festivities.

No item is placed on the table by chance—each has a symbolic meaning. None of them are required, but are elements of tradition.

Empty chair: remains the unclaimed seat at the table. Only one chair represents the isolation of the missing service member.

Round table: the shape, without beginning or end, demonstrates everlasting concern.

White tablecloth: the color symbolizes the purity of the service members' motives when called to serve.

Single red rose: represents the blood shed of these service members, and also the enduring faith of their friends and loved ones while searching for answers.

Red ribbon: symbolizes the continued determination to account for the missing.

Slice of lemon: a symbol of their bitter fate—captured, missing, or killed in a foreign land.

Pinch of salt: represents the tears of the missing and of the families who long for answers.

Lighted candle: reflects hope for their return, alive or dead.

Inverted glass: the glass being empty and upside down represents their inability to share in a toast.

At large functions, the table may have seven place settings—one to represent each branch of service, along with civilians who died during conflict. In these cases, there is often a head covering at each place, one from each branch's dress uniform. Private displays may also include a Bible or other religious text, symbolizing the strength of the service members that they gained through their faith.

THE MISSING MAN

```
E A X C H H F P Z N E X R J S
P T D K A A H X O T M E Q Y E
O E A E I L H B I F D P M D G
H L Y T M B B H P R F B A N P
B B H G L I W V O B O R I R F
W A Z E R T A S Q L M T B E K
E T M I S T E L I O S E P D D
X O G Y L E K S C A R O U N D
N U L X L R M N L N F Q R I I
S R A E T D E R J M U J I M N
G E S L V L E L D N A C T E I
T B S Z L V B L O O D Y R N
Q O L A E M P T Y C H A I R G
A V F N L U P S I D E D O W N
I S O L A T I O N U Y T V O C
```

Bitter
Blood
Candle
Dining
Empty chair
Everlasting

Faith
Fallen comrade
Glass
Hope
Isolation
Lemon

Purity
Red rose
Reminder
Ribbon
Round
Salt

Symbolism
Table
Tears
Unclaimed
Upside down
White

THE SAILOR'S CREED

★ ★ ★ ★ ★ ★ ★ ★ ★ ★ ★ ★ ★

I am a United States Sailor.

*I will support and defend the Constitution of the United States of America
and I will obey the orders of those appointed over me.*

*I represent the fighting spirit of the Navy and those who have gone before me
to defend freedom and democracy around the world.*

I proudly serve my country's Navy combat team with Honor, Courage, and Commitment.

I am committed to excellence and the fair treatment of all.

    The current version of the Sailor's Creed was written in 1993 at the directive of Chief of Naval Operations Admiral Frank B. Kelso II. Every member of the U.S. Navy coming out of basic training is required to memorize the creed, and it is incorporated into officer training, as well.

    The creed embodies the spirit of today's Navy: each member, regardless of rank or role, is a sailor first and foremost. It is a code of ethics, calling all sailors to follow a path of personal excellence, focusing on the branch's core values: honor, courage, and commitment.

THE SAILOR'S CREED

```
C O M M I T M E N T L S T B S
A V K Y O O S E R V E T U Z E
O D C O N S T I T U T I O N U
R I A F Z K F Y C O D E O Z L
A G G E S R E R J V C L I M A
R Z E C N E L L E C X E P S V
F C G C R E E D S E H F K P X
N I O N B D S F H O D V T I I
G G G U I X C K V D R O G R Y
D M F H R N X C L U O M M I E
E O N Y T A I R O O N L G T B
F R V T B I G A W R O E H Z O
E A S E C M N E R P H I O R P
N L R A N K P G T T C D Z G G
D E W M D U P Q A S R E D R O
```

Code	Ethics	Kelso	Rank
Commitment	Excellence	Morale	Serve
Constitution	Fair	Navy	Spirit
Courage	Fighting	Obey	Team
Creed	Freedom	Orders	Training
Defend	Honor	Proud	Values

THE CUTTING EDGE, PART I

★ ★ ★ ★ ★ ★ ★ ★ ★ ★ ★ ★

A Marine's most trusted weapon might be the rifle—but the KA-BAR knife is a close second.

On December 9, 1942, a year after the United States entered World War II, the Union Cutlery Company of Olean, New York, approached the U.S. Marine Corps with a design for a "fighting knife" that it hoped the Corps would adopt. The knife was designed as part of the company's KA-BAR line, so named because one devoted client claimed he'd used such a knife to kill a bear—or as he had written in a letter to the company, "k a bar."

Union Cutlery was earnest in its desire to assist in the U.S. war effort, and their timing was perfect. Many Marines had joined the fray carrying weapons of their own selection. After the August 1942 Battle of Guadalcanal, the Corps was closer to formulating a list of the characteristics that they required in a fighting and utility knife. Jungle combat in the Pacific was unlike any they had faced before, and ground forces needed a knife that was up to the challenge.

Colonel John M. Davis and Major Howard E. America worked with Union Cutlery to refine its proposed design, devising a tough, reliable knife that could serve countless purposes in the field. It was a weapon viable for attack or defense, but it could also be a tool for everything from digging trenches to pounding tent stakes to opening ration cans and chopping food for cooking. World War II Marines found dozens of uses for it—and today's Marines still do.

Besides the Marines, the Army, the Navy, and the Coast Guard, the KA-BAR was also standard issue for the Navy's Underwater Demolition Teams (UDTs) in World War II. Those brave frogmen—known with admiration as "naked warriors"—were generally issued not much more than swim trunks, canvas sneakers, face masks, and KA-BAR knives, then sent into the waters of the Pacific to do reconnaissance, clear enemy mines and obstacles, and set charges. Their KA-BAR knives proved to be useful tools and valuable companions.

In a 2008 newspaper interview, one World War II veteran recounted his experience working with a UDT setting charges at Peleliu Island on September 15, 1944, when, suddenly, he found himself engaged in hand-to-hand combat with a Japanese soldier. With nothing but his KA-BAR to protect him, the Sailor drew the knife and did what he had to do. "I still have the KA-BAR that saved my life," the vet told the newspaper reporter. He added, "I treasure that knife."

Even when the UDTs evolved into the elite group known as the Navy SEALs, with all the high-tech equipment available to them, the KA-BAR was still their knife of choice.

Turn the page to learn more about this iconic weapon.

THE CUTTING EDGE, PART I

Attack	Engaged	Knife	Tool
Bear	Fighting	Olean	Tough
Combat	Frogmen	Peleliu	Treasure
Companion	Hand-to-hand	Reliable	Uses
Defense	Jungle	SEAL	Utility
Digging	KA-BAR	Tent stakes	Weapons

THE CUTTING EDGE, PART II

★ ★ ★ ★ ★ ★ ★ ★ ★ ★ ★ ★ ★

Learn more about the iconic World War II–era knife still treasured today.

The Marine-issue KA-BAR knife—designated 1219C2—is 11.875 inches long with a 7-inch blade made of high-carbon steel that is hardened and tempered to resist breakage and to retain sharpness. Its leather handle is formed from 22 slotted cowhide disks compressed to form a shockproof, moisture-resistant surface. The elliptical hand guard that separates the handle from the blade is sometimes curved slightly downward to protect the hand. The pommel, or butt cap, at the end of the handle is made from solid steel attached to the handle with a steel pin. Although the design has been altered slightly over the years, the KA-BAR remains true to its original conception.

More than a million KA-BAR knives were produced during World War II, by Union Cutlery and by other firms who came on as subcontractors to meet the immediate demand. (True KA-BAR knives—stamped with the KA-BAR mark on their tangs, or ricassos, just above the hand guard—remain the most prized.) KA-BAR knives were still being issued to SEAL trainees during the Vietnam War. Even though the frogmen knew the knives were "leftovers" from World War II, they soon discovered that the good old knives were still the best knives and they kept the KA-BAR legacy alive.

In the same way, the sons and grandsons of the first Marines to carry KA-BAR knives are entering battle today bearing the same knives their forefathers did. Said one Marine who deployed to Kuwait in 2003 carrying the KA-BAR his father had used in Vietnam from 1968 to 1972: "I'd go ballistic if this knife got lost."

Today KA-BAR knives have taken on a symbolic significance in the Marine Corps—they're often given as presentation pieces to outstanding personnel, celebrities, or dignitaries, and numerous special-edition commemorative versions have been made especially for collectors. Yet the reliable, all-purpose KA-BAR has not outlived its usefulness.

THE CUTTING EDGE, PART II

```
S P E C I A L E D I T I O N M
U G D C E Q L U F E S U Y Y G
Y W W D F A L L P U R P O S E
C Q O E I B E E S B D W I J N
Y S R N N U G A R I C A S S O
S T L E K X A T X B O H Y B X
U T D D G R C H D P O M M E L
M I W R I D Y E C C S T B T Y
A A A A F S R R K B E W O S F
R W R H Z E N P R A H S L N A
K U I I P U R X R F F K I O I
I K I M N O H A N D L E C B S
K Z E A O E B D E S I G N R S
I T H F Y A S T E E L U D A U
V R K K K V I E T N A M Z C E
```

All purpose	KA-BAR	Mark	Steel
Carbon	Knife	Pommel	Symbolic
Design	Kuwait	Ricasso	Tempered
Handle	Leather	Sharp	Useful
Hardened	Legacy	Shockproof	Vietnam
Issue	Marines	Special edition	World War II

A SUPERIOR GENERAL: JOHN J. PERSHING

★ ★ ★ ★ ★ ★ ★ ★ ★ ★ ★ ★ ★

There have been innumerable excellent leaders in the U.S. Army through the years. This is the story of one.

John J. Pershing grew up on a farm in Laclede, Missouri, and displayed a high level of intelligence as a child. He received an appointment to West Point in 1882 and later served in four military campaigns.

The Indian Wars: As a Second Lieutenant in the 6th Cavalry Regiment in 1886, he served in the West during the Indian wars. In 1895, he commanded the famous African American Buffalo Soldiers, where he got the nickname "Black Jack."

The Spanish- and Philippine-American Wars: During the Spanish-American War, Pershing served with the 10th Cavalry at San Juan Hill and also commanded troops in the Philippine-American War from 1899 to 1901.

The Mexican War: When the Mexican civil war of 1914 spilled across the border, Pershing led a 4,800-man brigade and for 10 months unsuccessfully pursued Pancho Villa's forces into Mexico.

World War I: In 1917, President Woodrow Wilson decided that Pershing would command the American Expeditionary Force (AEF) in Europe. Pershing arrived in France on June 23 to begin a massive buildup of U.S. forces. Pershing refused France's demand that American units fight under French field commanders, instead preserving the AEF as an independent fighting force. He directed three major AEF offensives in 1918: Aisne-Marne from July 25 to August 2, Saint-Mihiel from September 12 to 19, and the final Meuse-Argonne offensive from September 26 to November 11.

Pershing didn't use the same trench-warfare tactics employed by the French, which, after four years, had failed to dislodge the enemy and had resulted in enormous casualties. Instead he operated on the flanks of the enemy. He was also the first to use air power to soften fortified positions through bombing instead of relying entirely on artillery. The French and British thought the war could be won by 1919 or 1920, but Pershing said the AEF would end the war in 1918—which they did.

His appointment as General of the Armies of the United States in July 1919 made him the first and only general to receive the rank in his lifetime.

A SUPERIOR GENERAL: JOHN J. PERSHING

AEF	Buildup	France	Pancho Villa
Air power	Campaigns	General	Pershing
Army	Cavalry	Independent	Philippines
Black Jack	Dislodge	Meuse-Argonne	Rank
Bombing	Flanks	Mexican War	San Juan Hill
Brigade	Forces	Offensive	Spanish

MODERN DOGS OF WAR

★ ★ ★ ★ ★ ★ ★ ★ ★ ★ ★ ★ ★

Today's military has 1,600 working dogs serving on active duty. They are highly trained warriors and engage in land, air, and sea operations with their human handlers. What does it take to be a four-legged member of the Armed Forces?

THE PUPPY PROGRAM

Military dogs begin their training in puppyhood. The Department of Defense sources dogs from breeders and also runs the Military Working Dog Breeding Program (a.k.a. the Puppy Program). Between 50 and 90 puppies are born into the program every year at the 341st Training Squadron at Joint Base San Antonio. The program exclusively breeds and raises Belgian Malinois, which are ideal for military work. While the new pups are still nursing, Puppy Development Specialists start examining them for traits that indicate suitability for military service, including being sociable and not exhibiting fear of noises. The puppies then spend some time in local foster homes getting socialization, after which they're returned to the base for an intense training program: bite work, obedience, recognition of and response to odors, and exposure to environments like those in combat zones. The final phase is the "consignment test," used on both Puppy Program dogs and those from outside breeders: it determines who is qualified to enter the Military Working Dog Training Program.

THE BIG TIME

The Military Working Dog Training Program is also run by the 341st Training Squadron, which has been training dogs since the 1950s. This comprehensive 120-day program qualifies its graduates—including Belgian Malinois, German shepherds, and Labrador retrievers—to patrol, to detect illegal drugs, and to detect explosives. Handlers train up to 18 dogs at a time, preparing them for active-duty service. Upon graduation, each dog is sent to its assigned service branch, where it will stay for the course of its career in a specialized role.

ON DUTY

Dogs serve in all branches of the military. They serve as sentries for troops in the field and at airports or other important areas or storage facilities. (The Coast Guard uses them to detect enemy submarines!) Particularly quiet dogs are used for scouting and patrolling, detecting snipers or ambushes. Casualty dogs assist in search-and-rescue efforts. Dogs trained to detect explosives specialize in bombs, improvised explosive devices (IEDs), or, in the Army, buried mines and artillery.

OUTRANKED

The bond between a military working dog, or MWD, and its handler is uniquely special and strong. MWDs are considered noncommissioned officers, or NCOs, and a dog's rank is always one rank higher than its handler's: this tradition ensures that the dog, as the higher-ranking officer, does not receive any mistreatment from its handler, which would result in stern discipline for the human servicemember. But dog handlers have the utmost respect for their canine charges, and consider their dogs not just their comrades but their friends—many handlers end up adopting their former MWDs when the dogs enter retirement.

MODERN DOGS OF WAR

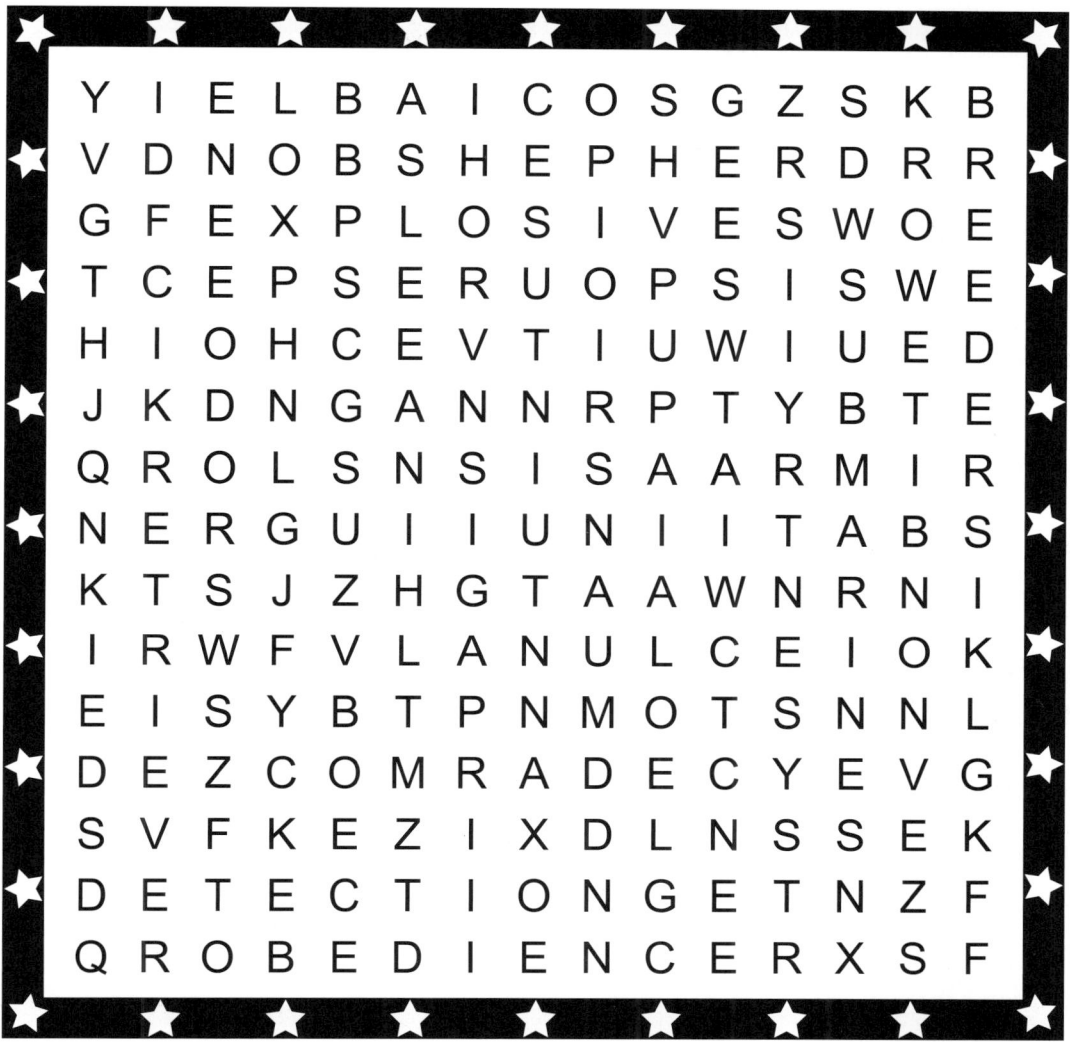

Bite work	Consignment	Odors	Sentry
Bond	Detection	Outrank	Shepherd
Breeders	Explosives	Patrol	Snipers
Canine	Handler	Respect	Sociable
Casualty	IEDs	Retriever	Submarines
Comrade	Obedience	Scouting	Training

IN THE CROSSHAIRS

★ ★ ★ ★ ★ ★ ★ ★ ★ ★ ★ ★ ★

A single sniper in the right place at the right time can change the course of a battle. Here are just a few of the many who have served in the U.S. Armed Forces.

ARMY STAFF SERGEANT ADELBERT WALDRON

Waldron served for 12 years in the U.S. Navy before enlisting in the Army. During the Vietnam War, he was a member of the 3rd Battalion, 9th Infantry Division, and was assigned to PBR boats patrolling the Mekong Delta. He had 109 confirmed kills in just eight months—at the time, the record for a U.S. sniper—with one of his kills coming from a moving boat at 900 yards. He was a rare double recipient of the Distinguished Service Cross, awarded for separate actions in 1969.

NAVY CHIEF PETTY OFFICER CHRIS KYLE

Kyle, a Navy SEAL who served four tours during the Iraq War with SEAL Team 3, broke Adelbert Waldron's record with 160 kills confirmed by the Department of Defense. One of those kills came when he hit a target from 1.2 miles away. After Kyle recorded 91 kills in the city of Ramadi, Iraqi combatants there nicknamed him the "Devil of Ramadi" and put a $20,000 bounty on his head.

MARINE CORPS GUNNERY SERGEANT CARLOS NORMAN HATHCOCK II

A "confirmed" kill for a Vietnam War sniper was one for which an officer was present to witness, in addition to the sniper's spotter. Hathcock had 93 confirmed kills, but it's estimated he killed between 300 and 400 People's Army of Vietnam (PAVN) and Viet Cong personnel during his two deployments to Vietnam. One of his most famous kills came when he shot an enemy sniper through the enemy's own rifle scope. Hathcock later helped establish the Marine Corps Scout Sniper School in Quantico.

IN THE CROSSHAIRS

```
W Y T Y I H S S E N T I W D D
H Y T Q R B G I G N K V E F T
J K I Y G N O C T E I V L R A
N I C K N A M E S R I R U B O
L N H X Z V G B L L D F A H B
I O V N X Y L W O T D Y C M R
I R R A E Y K F A U T R C X B
O M A T P K R Y Y Q N A D R P
C A S Q A A Q R S N I T B E P
I N H G M P D L S E H Y Y P T
T T L A O D L R C U S M B I O
N E D Z H I A W O N S R P N O
A I E K K X X N P C L A E S H
U V I S P O T T E R E F D Z S
Q E L Y K Y C O N F I R M E D
```

Army	Kills	PAVN	Shoot
Battle	Kyle	PBR boat	Sniper
Bounty	Marine	Quantico	Spotter
Confirmed	Navy	Record	Viet Cong
Devil of Ramadi	Nickname	Scope	Vietnam
Iraq	Patrol	SEAL	Witness

WE ARE ALL JEWS HERE

★ ★ ★ ★ ★ ★ ★ ★ ★ ★ ★ ★ ★

Learn the remarkable but little-known story of Staff Sergeant Roddie Edmonds, who saved 200 Jewish American service members from probable death at the hands of their Nazi captives.

Roderick "Roddie" Edmonds joined the Army in 1941 and was sent to combat in Europe in December 1944 as a member of the 106th Infantry Division. He then fought with the 422nd Infantry Regiment, where he fought in the Battle of the Bulge. On December 19, Edmonds was captured and sent to Stalag IX-B, a German prisoner-of-war camp; in January, he and numerous other enlisted personnel were transferred to Stalag IX-A. As a Master Sergeant, 25-year-old Edmonds was the senior noncommissioned officer in the camp and responsible for the 1,292 American POWs being held there. Edmonds, a devout Christian, relied on his faith to help guide him in keeping morale high.

On January 27, 1945, the Germans ordered all Jewish POWs to report separately the following morning. Edmonds knew what fate likely awaited the Jewish men if they followed this command. Throughout the war, the Germans murdered or sent to extermination camps any Jews among the Allied troops captured on the Eastern Front; those captured on the Western Front were sent to Berga, a slave labor camp where survival rates were dismal. (The U.S. military encouraged Jewish service members to destroy any evidence of their faith—including their dog tags—if they were captured.) With this in mind, Edmonds ordered every one of the 1,292 POWs to line up on the morning of January 28. When the camp's commandant, Major Siegmann, angrily ordered Edmonds to identify the Jewish soldiers, Edmonds gave this defiant response:

"We are all Jews here."

When Major Siegmann repeated the command, this time with a pistol to Edmonds's head, Edmonds still refused to comply. According to one of the men he saved that day, Edmonds then calmly warned the commandant that if he harmed any of the POWs, he would be tried for war crimes for violating the Geneva Conventions, which required prisoners to give only their name, rank, and serial number.

Roddie Edmonds's successful act of defiance emboldened the POWs in Stalag IX-A to maintain hope during the remaining time they spent in captivity before being liberated. After liberation, Edmonds returned home to Tennessee; he passed away in 1985, never having spoken of the incident to any member of his family. It was only after his death, when his granddaughter read his diaries as part of a school project, that they learned of his extraordinary act and began to research the details. In 2015, Edmonds became just the fifth American, and the only American Soldier, to be recognized by Yad Vashem as "Righteous Among the Nations," Israel's highest honor for non-Jews who risked their lives to save Jews during the Holocaust.

WE ARE ALL JEWS HERE

```
M J Z H B H R D K V B U L G E
S E N I O R E J O B E R G A W
M T J Z E I C N E F Y Q R Y H
P K A T L E I C L W L T M F T
X T A L M Q F A K I I V V I N
D F A X A T F M Q I S S Q T A
A V E N E G O P U N Y T H N D
C A P T I V I T Y F J N E E N
E D M O N D S X U A C H B D A
R K O S I E G M A N N T K I M
Z E Y G I C D L O T S I P S M
Y Y P R T D J L K R S A Y E O
B Q A O V A W J L Y M F H O C
A I E M R F G E S U F E R B N
D H C A P T U R E R C O U O X
```

Allied	Commandant	Fate	Pistol
Berga	Diaries	Geneva	Refuse
Bulge	Dog tag	Identify	Report
Camp	Edmonds	Infantry	Senior
Captivity	Enlisted	Jewish	Siegmann
Capture	Faith	Officer	Stalag IX-A

STAYING ALIVE

★ ★ ★ ★ ★ ★ ★ ★ ★ ★ ★ ★ ★

"I am a SERE specialist . . . an expert in Survival, Evasion, Resistance, and Escape. I can survive anywhere in the world and prepare others to do the same."
(The SERE Creed)

Established by the Air Force at the end of the Korean War, the SERE program was expanded during the Vietnam War to include the Army, Navy, and Marine Corps. Service personnel at high risk of being captured and exploited by the enemy—such as Special Forces, Rangers, and Airmen—are taught how to evade capture, survive in hostile territory, resist interrogation, and escape from the enemy. The instructor is typically someone who has lived through one or more phases of the SERE experience. The training course is rigorous. *The Unit*, starring Dennis Haysbert, provides a look at Special Forces operations using SERE training.

Every trainee goes through an intensive three-week "stress inoculation" program to learn basic wilderness survival tactics along with techniques for camouflage, signaling and rescue, escape and evasion, and POW resistance. Training is done under all major climatic conditions including arctic, desert, tropical, ocean, and temperate in remote wilderness locations in all possible weather conditions. Much of the training is directed to Airmen and Navy personnel, so water survival and equipment maintenance is also taught. A resistance training lab simulates conditions in a POW compound, including torture methods. Some techniques taught are still top secret.

The Air Force has four training schools, including Arctic survival training at the Eielson base in Alaska and parachute water survival training in Pensacola, Florida. The Army runs two schools in the South. Lieutenant Commander James Rowe of the Special Forces established the first school at Camp Mackall, North Carolina, after surviving 62 months in a North Vietnamese prison camp before escaping. The Navy runs two highly specialized schools for pilots as well as Sailors, both at remote training sites on the East and West coasts. The Marine Corps operates its own training centers, one in California and the other on Okinawa.

STAYING ALIVE

```
Q E D C A L O C A S N E P C V
U N I Y N T N A Z B M N I R W
N O Q E E R A P E R P T M E T
U I U L L E E V L W C F M S R
T T T Y Q S C V A R V T L I O
E A E R K E O T A S E A E S P
R G R X P D E N X A V E G T I
C O X O P R H G N I A P A A C
E R W H E L E Q V L S A L N A
S R A F S R O R Q O I C F C L
P E P N A T U I E R O S U E R
O T L L G S R T T S N E O E H
T N B W K E T E P E L H M M F
P I L O T S R T S A D P A X J
H O S T I L E S T S C R C V F
```

Arctic
Camouflage
Capture
Desert
Eielson
Escape
Evasion
Exploited
Hostile
Interrogation
Ocean
Pensacola
Pilots
POW
Prepare
Rangers
Resistance
Sailors
SERE
Stress
Survival
Top secret
Tropical
Water

UNITED STATES ARMY RANKS

★ ★ ★ ★ ★ ★ ★ ★ ★ ★ ★

Soldiers in the United States Army may be enlisted, warrant officers, or commissioned officers. Army ranks designate job responsibilities and utilize the below names. At some levels, different positions exist at the same pay grade; the title depends on the Soldier's job. Warrant officers receive a commission upon promotion to chief warrant officer 2, but they remain specialists or experts in their area; commissioned officers are generalists.

GRADE	RANK	ABBREVIATION
E1	Private	PV1
E2	Private	PV2
E3	Private First Class	PFC
E4	Corporal	CPL
	Specialist	SPC
E5	Sergeant	SGT
E6	Staff Sergeant	SSG
E7	Sergeant First Class	SFC
E8	Master Sergeant	MSG
	First Sergeant	1SG
E9	Sergeant Major	SGM
	Command Sergeant Major	CSM
	Sergeant Major of the Army	SMA
W1	Warrant Officer 1	WO1
W2	Chief Warrant Officer 2	CW2
W3	Chief Warrant Officer 3	CW3
W4	Chief Warrant Officer 4	CW4
W5	Chief Warrant Officer 5	CW5
O1	Second Lieutenant	2LT
O2	First Lieutenant	1LT
O3	Captain	CPT
O4	Major	MAJ
O5	Lieutenant Colonel	LTC
O6	Colonel	COL
O7	Brigadier General	BG
O8	Major General	MG
O9	Lieutenant General	LTG
O10	General	GEN
	General of the Army (reserved for wartime only)	GA

UNITED STATES ARMY RANKS

```
Z F S V D J F C O R P O R A L
O A C L Q N S E D A R G Y A P
F S R O E K A X I U N T O U X
R T P M L V S M L H U N F L B
G S B E Y O E M M T C A F R M
E I Q W C F N L W O S E I W V
N L E W A I R E U V C G C F E
E A T V R R A O L C A R E T X
R R A I E S R L J D X E R H P
A E V I T T R A I A K S Z Y E
L N I T S C G E N S M F O R R
V E R S A L R N K T T K R A T
Y G P L M A U D E T S I L N E
D N O C E S R R U L C T K K M
Z D E R D S N I A T P A C S J
```

Army	Corporal	Levels	Ranks
Brigadier	Enlisted	Major	Second
Captain	Expert	Master	Sergeant
Chief	First Class	Officer	Specialist
Colonel	General	Pay grade	Title
Command	Generalist	Private	Warrant

THE BRIDGE AT DONG HA

★ ★ ★ ★ ★ ★ ★ ★ ★ ★ ★ ★

John Ripley had always wanted to blow up a bridge—now he had his chance. But would he survive it?

On Easter Sunday 1972, Captain John Ripley thought he'd received an order to die. The lone Marine advisor to the 3rd Vietnam Marine Corps Battalion had received word that the South Vietnamese regiment to his north had collapsed. Several dozen North Vietnamese Army (NVA) tanks, followed by their soldiers, were barreling south to Dong Ha. If they crossed the bridge over the Bo Dieu River, there would be no Vietnamese or American force standing between them and Hue City to the south; the NVA could then make its way unopposed to the huge air base at Da Nang. They had to be stopped at Dong Ha.

As the tanks approached his position that morning, Ripley called in gunfire from four U.S. Navy destroyers patrolling offshore. They responded with an incredibly accurate barrage of 5-inch shells that destroyed the NVA tanks approaching Ripley and his outnumbered South Vietnamese marines. Throughout the day, Ripley continued to call in fire missions from the destroyers, as well as from South Vietnamese air force jets. The North Vietnamese also understood the strategic importance of moving their tanks and troops across the river, and despite these losses, managed to dispatch a new column of some 200 NVA tanks south. On hearing this news, Ripley quickly realized that the bridge had to be destroyed.

Using TNT and C-4 explosives supplied by the Army of the Republic of Vietnam (ARVN) engineers, Ripley decided the best and quickest method of blowing up the bridge was to place each box of explosives under the bridge's main girders. While under constant fire from the North Vietnamese, he ran onto the bridge over and over again carrying each 50-pound box, which he then pushed into position as he hung from the bridge's I-beams. Exhausted from manhandling each box into its proper spot, Ripley finally had enough explosives in position to blow the bridge, but he needed to stay alive long enough to build and light the fuse.

Running back to the South Vietnamese side of the bridge, Ripley discovered that the ARVN engineers and their U.S. Army advisor were nowhere to be found. Exhausted but seeing that he was running out of time as the NVA tanks were approaching, he quickly built two fuses—one electric and the other burnable—and ran out yet again to place the blasting caps, and fired the electrical fuse. Nothing. He then lit his burnable fuse, which finally blew. The center span of the bridge collapsed with a huge roar into the river, halting the NVA's advancing tanks. The bridge's timbers burned for a week.

For this act of incredible bravery, Captain John Ripley earned the Navy Cross. The NVA tank column eventually crossed the river seven days later but was quickly decimated by an American Army tank unit led by another Marine advisor.

THE BRIDGE AT DONG HA

```
E P G F A X O K Z U Q N E A E
Y E L P I R G H Z H R M A X N
K G B L S D A M F U A N P A Y
C U R K M N C Z B R C L V A Z
I N I M A N T E I V O Y T R O
R F D E E X N H S C C G S A
T I G V B S E Y I R Q F R J E
C R E R I C T V O K U E Y S M
E E U J O I E S J N B G P N K
L Q T R C S S G O M T A N K S
E N P E D K A O I U L R J R L
T S U A T X R T J L V R O S A
A H G N O D M U O O E A E V L
S R F U S E Y C Z C R B N F V
G S N N F A K A U L Z T K R D
```

Army	Column	Halt	Ripley
ARVN	Dong Ha	Hue City	Roar
Barrage	Electric	I-beams	Tanks
Bridge	Explosives	Marine Corps	Timbers
Burn	Fuse	Navy Cross	TNT
Collapse	Gunfire	NVA	Vietnam

OPERATION ENDURING FREEDOM MEDAL OF HONOR: MICHAEL MURPHY

★ ★ ★ ★ ★ ★ ★ ★ ★ ★ ★ ★ ★

During the War on Terrorism, 20 military personnel were awarded the Medal of Honor for valorous action in Afghanistan (five were awarded posthumously). Each recipient has an extraordinary story—this is just one.

Born in 1976, Michael Murphy grew up in Patchogue, a town on New York's Long Island. He attended Penn State University after high school, excelling in sports and academics and graduating with dual degrees in political science and psychology in 1998. The son of a Vietnam veteran, Murphy was accepted into several law schools, but instead set his sights on becoming a Navy SEAL.

After attending Army Jump School, SEAL Qualification Training, and SEAL Delivery Vehicle (SDV) school, Lieutenant Murphy earned his SEAL Trident in July 2002. After deployments to Jordan, Qatar, and Djibouti, Murphy was sent to Afghanistan with SEAL Delivery Team 1. On June 28, 2005, he was the officer in charge of a four-man SEAL team supporting Operation Red Wing, tasked with finding a key enemy militia commander near Asadabad, deep behind enemy lines on the Afghan-Pakistani border at an unforgiving 10,000-foot altitude. The SEALs were immediately spotted by locals and, it's believed, reported to local Taliban.

A fierce firefight between the SEALs and the enemy force resulted in all four SEALs being wounded and pushed deeper into a ravine. Gunner's Mate Second Class Danny Dietz tried to place a distress call back to base, but he was shot in the hand, shattering his thumb. Suffering grave gunshot wounds himself, Murphy then risked his own life to save his teammates: he "unhesitatingly and with complete disregard for his own life" moved into the open, where he could call for assistance.

His deliberate and heroic act made him a target for the enemy, but he was able to contact Bagram Air Base. Shot in the back while making the radio call, he dropped the transmitter—yet picked it up, completed the call, and continued firing at the still-attacking enemy. Severely wounded, Murphy then returned to his men and continued to fight.

An MH-47 Chinook helicopter with reinforcements—eight additional SEALs and eight Army Night Stalkers—was sent to pull out the four wounded SEALs. As the Chinook raced to the battle, attempting to land on the rocky terrain, a rocket-propelled grenade struck the helicopter, killing all 16 men aboard. On the ground and nearly out of ammunition, Murphy and the other SEALs continued the fight, but two hours later, he and two other SEALs were dead. Only a single Navy SEAL—Hospital Corpsman Second Class Marcus Luttrell—survived that day's events, which represented the worst death toll for Navy Special Warfare since World War II.

By his courage, fighting spirit, and devotion to his men in the face of certain death, 29-year-old Lieutenant Michael Murphy was able to relay the position of his unit—a selfless act that led to the rescue of Luttrell and the recovery of the remains of the three SEALs killed in the battle. Murphy was awarded the Medal of Honor on October 22, 2007.

OPERATION ENDURING FREEDOM
MEDAL OF HONOR: MICHAEL MURPHY

```
K K N O I T I S O P W U G D J
L X Y K C H E T C D Y N I N K
X M A R G A B P L L I E V U W
Q Y T E A M W A E W T T R O N
A A R E Y D E A D Z G E T W G
S E E F H S D E J F C C N R K
A G C E P E R P N O I A E N O
D A I Y R E L I V O B N W O O
A R F M U D A E R I A X Z I N
B U F E M R R E L D C E L T I
A O O N R Y H A E B N A N A H
D C S E S E T A M M A E T R C
W F T I K K M V V S T L J E V
N A T S I N A H G F A P H P M
U F L U T T R E L L V A L O R
```

Afghanistan	Enemy	Officer	Taliban
Asadabad	Grenade	Operation	Team
Bagram	Heroic	Position	Teammates
Chinook	Leader	Recovery	Terrain
Courage	Luttrell	Red Wing	Valor
Dietz	Murphy	SEAL	Wound

THUNDERBIRDS FACTS AND FIGURES

★ ★ ★ ★ ★ ★ ★ ★ ★ ★ ★ ★

The U.S. Air Force Demonstration Squadron—known as the Thunderbirds—is an Air Combat command unit that showcases the professional abilities of Airmen, strengthens morale among the Force's members, and supports recruiting and retention programs. Learn more about this impressive group.

The Air Force became its own branch in 1947; just six years later, the Thunderbirds were born. Designated the 3600th Air Demonstration Unit, they were activated on May 25, 1953, at Luke Air Force Base, Arizona. Since 1974, they have been a component of the 57th Wing at Nellis Air Force Base, Nevada.

The team is composed of eight pilots, four support officers, three civilian personnel, and more than 130 enlisted personnel in 25 fields. Officers serve for the team for two years, and enlisted Airmen serve for three or four.

An air demonstration show lasts about 90 minutes. During that time, six pilots perform about 30 maneuvers, including both formation flying and solo routines. The squadron performs about 75 demonstrations per year between March and November.

The squadron has a total of eight formations: the Diamond, Delta, Stinger, Arrowhead, Line-Abreast, Trail, Echelon, and the Five Card. During the Arrowhead, the planes maneuver within 18 inches of each other. All maneuvers are performed at speeds of 450 to 500 miles per hour.

Thunderbirds fly in the Lockheed Martin F-16 Fighting Falcon, one of the best precision tactical bombers and air-to-air combat aircraft in the world. These aircraft are specially modified for the Thunderbirds with smoke-generating systems in place of 20mm cannons; they are also specially painted in Thunderbird colors.

The Thunderbirds squadron is an Air Combat Command that, if required, can be integrated into a fighter unit on short notice. The minimal modifications to the F-16s they fly ensure the planes can be made combat-ready in less than 72 hours.

Visiting Nevada? Nellis Air Force Base maintains a Thunderbirds Museum covering the history of the team. On display is a full-size F-16 gate-guard (display plane) painted in Thunderbirds paint scheme.

THUNDERBIRDS FACTS AND FIGURES

```
Y Y H I S T O R Y I X S C F K
F O R M A T I O N O M I E I O
P O L O S S L Q H U J L E V Z
C T S A E R B A E N I L T E H
W O H S E C O S Q M T E A C M
R E M J S Q U A D R O N R A A
E C G B T M Y F I D O M T R N
B R R K A A L A C F C B S D E
M O H T P T C U T T U U N E U
O F L G E E A T J L R H O E V
B R I L F Z R Y I T E U M P E
D I A M O N D F O C N D E S R
X A R M S R O L O C A I D S N
A P T T D Z I X Z R K L A D J
J V F S I P I P Z Y M T H P Q
```

Air Force	Diamond	Modify	Show
Bomber	Five card	Museum	Solo
Colors	Formation	Nellis	Speed
Combat	History	Paint	Squadron
Delta	Line-abreast	Perform	Tactical
Demonstrate	Maneuver	Pilot	Trail

MY RIFLE—THE CREED OF THE UNITED STATES MARINE

★ ★ ★ ★ ★ ★ ★ ★ ★ ★ ★ ★ ★

This is my rifle. There are many like it, but this one is mine.

My rifle is my best friend. It is my life. I must master it as I must master my life.

*My rifle, without me, is useless. Without my rifle, I am useless. I must fire my rifle true.
I must shoot straighter than my enemy who is trying to kill me.
I must shoot him before he shoots me. I will . . .*

*My rifle and myself know that what counts in this war is not the rounds we fire,
the noise of our burst, nor the smoke we make.
We know that it is the hits that count. We will hit . . .*

*My rifle is human, even as I, because it is my life. Thus, I will learn it as a brother.
I will learn its weaknesses, its strength, its parts, its accessories, its sights and its barrel.
I will ever guard it against the ravages of weather and damage as I will ever guard my legs,
my arms, my eyes and my heart against damage. I will keep my rifle clean and ready.
We will become part of each other. We will . . .*

*Before God, I swear this creed. My rifle and myself are the defenders of my country.
We are the masters of our enemy. We are the saviors of my life.*

So be it, until victory is America's and there is no enemy, but peace!

The Marine's Rifle Creed is credited to Major General William H. Rupertus, Commanding General of Marine Corps Base San Diego in 1942. An experienced marine and expert marksman, he staunchly believed that "the only weapon which stands between [marines] and Death is the rifle . . . they must understand that their rifle is their life . . . It must become a creed with them." Captain Robert P. White, the public relations officer at the base, suggested Major General Rupertus draft such a creed.

Rupertus's words, first penned on a "random scrap of paper," were first published in the San Diego *Marine Corps Chevron* on March 14, 1942. The creed is still taught to all marines undergoing basic training, because it captures the ethos of the Marine Corps: in the words of General Alfred M. Gray Jr. 29th Commandant of the Marine Corps, "Every marine is, first and foremost, a rifleman. All other conditions are secondary."

MY RIFLE—THE CREED OF THE UNITED STATES MARINE

```
Y F W P E T H O S M J L S V S
A Q T Z H H M D W E A P O N N
D D X S T R E N G T H S T J T
N B A R R E L A S Z T R T H S
E U U S R Z C R D R A U G E U
I E Q H E Q N E E I F I N M R
R A Q O H Z Z A N O S I L A A
F G G O T W D I G E M R Q R E
T S G T O Y N E M Q M A R K W
S A V A R G I M M S R Y E S S
E V D E B D K Y E M V V S M N
B I E K N H L F L J D O L A A
U O H A J E O I F C A U I N E
T R S W J J E R I M P Z F Z L
R N M K I R W E R E C A E P C
```

Barrel	Fire	Peace	Sight
Best friend	Guard	Ready	Strength
Brother	Life	Rifle	Swear
Clean	Marksman	San Diego	Training
Enemy	Master	Savior	True
Ethos	Mine	Shoot	Weapon

U.S. ARMY BATTLE TANKS

★ ★ ★ ★ ★ ★ ★ ★ ★ ★ ★ ★

America's Army has a long history of dominating tank warfare.
Here are three of the most important tanks used in service.

M4 SHERMAN

Its official name was Medium Tank, M4, and it was a symbol of America's dominance in combat and in industry during World War II. Between 1942 and 1945, around 50,000 of these cheap, reliable tanks were constructed, making it the most produced tank in American history. In use by U.S. forces in every combat theater around the world—along with British and Soviet Union troops—it was beloved by Soldiers because it was the first tank to have its machine gun on a fully traversing central turret. The U.S. Army replaced the Sherman in 1957, but it continued to be used by other nations' militaries into the 1980s.

M60

This second-generation main battle tank (MBT) evolved from the M48 Patton and came into service at the height of the Cold War. This tank had an integrated fire control system that allowed for rapid fire, a powerful 105mm cannon, and a longer cruising range than any tank that preceded it. A total of about 15,000 M60s were manufactured, beginning in 1960; the largest deployment of M60s by the United States occurred during the Gulf War in 1991, where they were used by Marines to defeat Iraqi armored forces. The U.S. retired the M60 after Operation Desert Storm, but it continues to be used by numerous foreign militaries today.

M551 SHERIDAN

This amphibious light tank made its debut in 1969 during the Vietnam War. The most important feature of the M551 Sheridan was that it was light enough to be transported by air, a first for any tank at the time—this was essential in Vietnam because of the thick jungle environment and lack of infrastructure. The M551 had an M81 launcher capable of firing MGM-51 anti-tank guided missiles, and advanced thermal sights helped Soldiers see better in jungle canopies. However, the aluminum construction that made the tank so lightweight also made it more likely to get damaged by enemy fire, leading the M551 Sheridan to be moved to a support role before being retired in 2003.

U.S. ARMY BATTLE TANKS

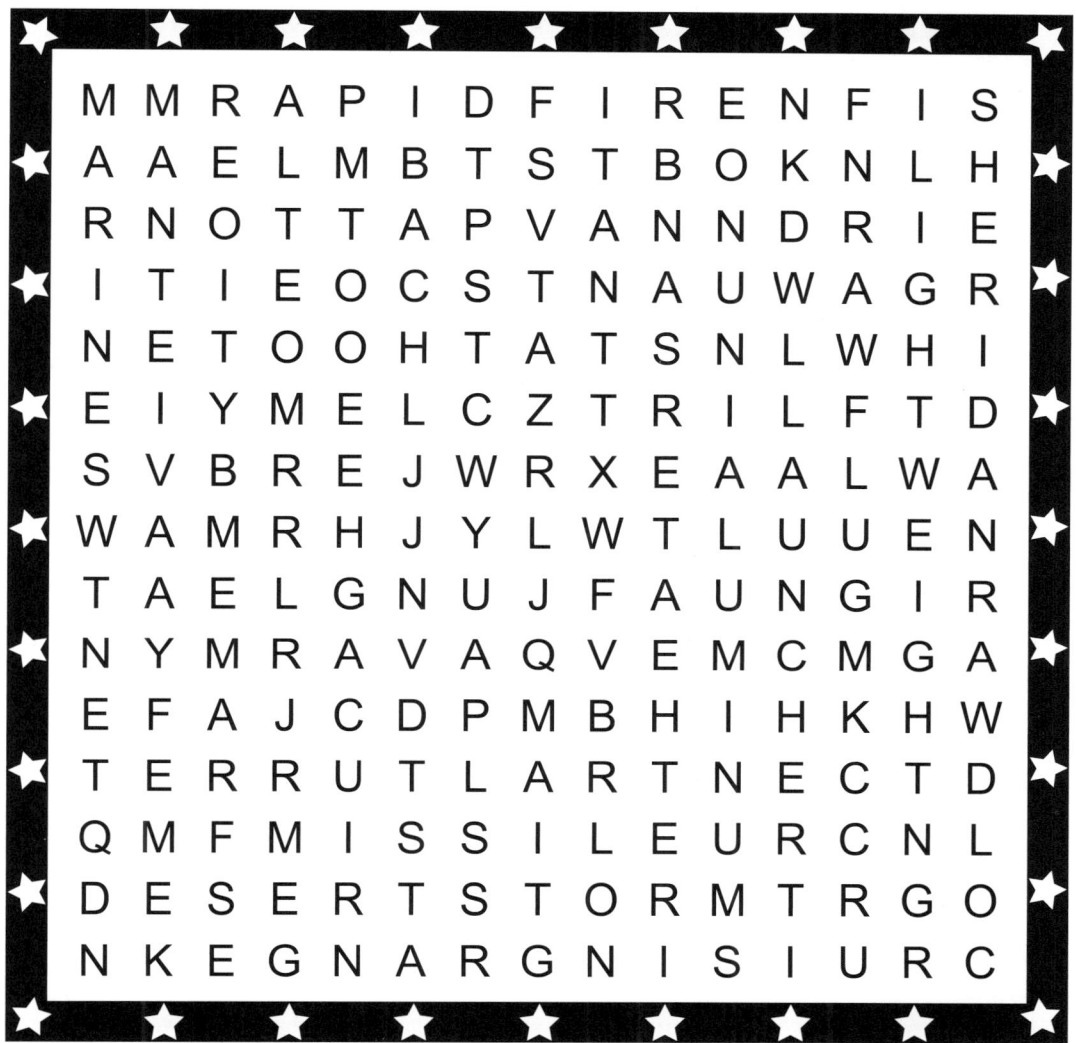

Aluminum	Combat	Launcher	Rapid fire
Army	Cruising range	Lightweight	Sheridan
Battle	Desert Storm	Marines	Sherman
Cannon	Gulf War	MBT	Tank
Central turret	Industry	Missile	Theater
Cold war	Jungle	Patton	Vietnam

TUN TAVERN

★ ★ ★ ★ ★ ★ ★ ★ ★ ★ ★ ★

On Philadelphia's Front Street, a historical marker labels the spot where Tun Tavern once stood, and cites it as the "traditional birthplace of the United States Marine Corps." Was it really?

The United States Marine Corps was born as the Continental Marines on November 10, 1775, during the Second Continental Congress in Philadelphia, where the Founding Fathers were meeting to prepare for their break with England. Where else to find seamen than in Philadelphia, one of the busiest ports in the American colonies?

Samuel Nicholas, the first commandant of the Marine Corps, was tasked with finding appropriate men. According to tradition, he set up shop at Tun Tavern, located at the corner of Water Street and Tun Alley. (*Tun* is an Old English word meaning "cask" or "barrel of beer.")

Nicholas didn't pick Tun Tavern by chance. It had been the original headquarters for organizations such as the first American Masonic lodge as well as the St. Andrew's Society and the St. George's Society, for aid to Scottish and English immigrants, respectively. George Washington, Thomas Jefferson, Benjamin Franklin, and other Founding Fathers met at the tavern and its restaurant (Peggy Mullan's Red Hot Beef Steak Club) to discuss business and draft resolutions for the First and Second Continental Congresses. In 1756, it had been a recruiting center for the Pennsylvania Militia when they were raising forces to fight Native Americans.

The tavern's owner, Robert Mullan, served as chief Marine recruiter and raised two battalions in less than a month. He must have been a natural salesman—or maybe it was the free-flowing beer. No matter what his secret was, for more than 200 years and wherever they're stationed, Marines gather on November 10 to toast the birthday of the Corps and the place where it all began: Tun Tavern. Sadly, Marines can't visit the original Tun Tavern; it burned down in 1781, and its location now lies beneath I-95.

There is conflict about whether the Tun Tavern origin story is accurate. As uncovered by the National Park Service, Robert Mullan sold Tun Tavern in 1773, several years before he supposedly began recruiting Marines there; recruitment posters mentioning Tun Tavern can't be authenticated; and some historians claim that Nicholas operated out of a tavern called the Conestoga Wagon, at Fourth and Market streets. Regardless, the Tun Tavern legend can't be ruled out completely, and Marines are still safe to continue toasting it every November 10. And soon, they'll be able to do so in an authentic reproduction of the establishment in Philadelphia's Old City neighborhood (just 250 yards from the original location). The restaurant, with historical exhibits, is slated to open in November 2025, in time for the Corps' 250th birthday.

TUN TAVERN

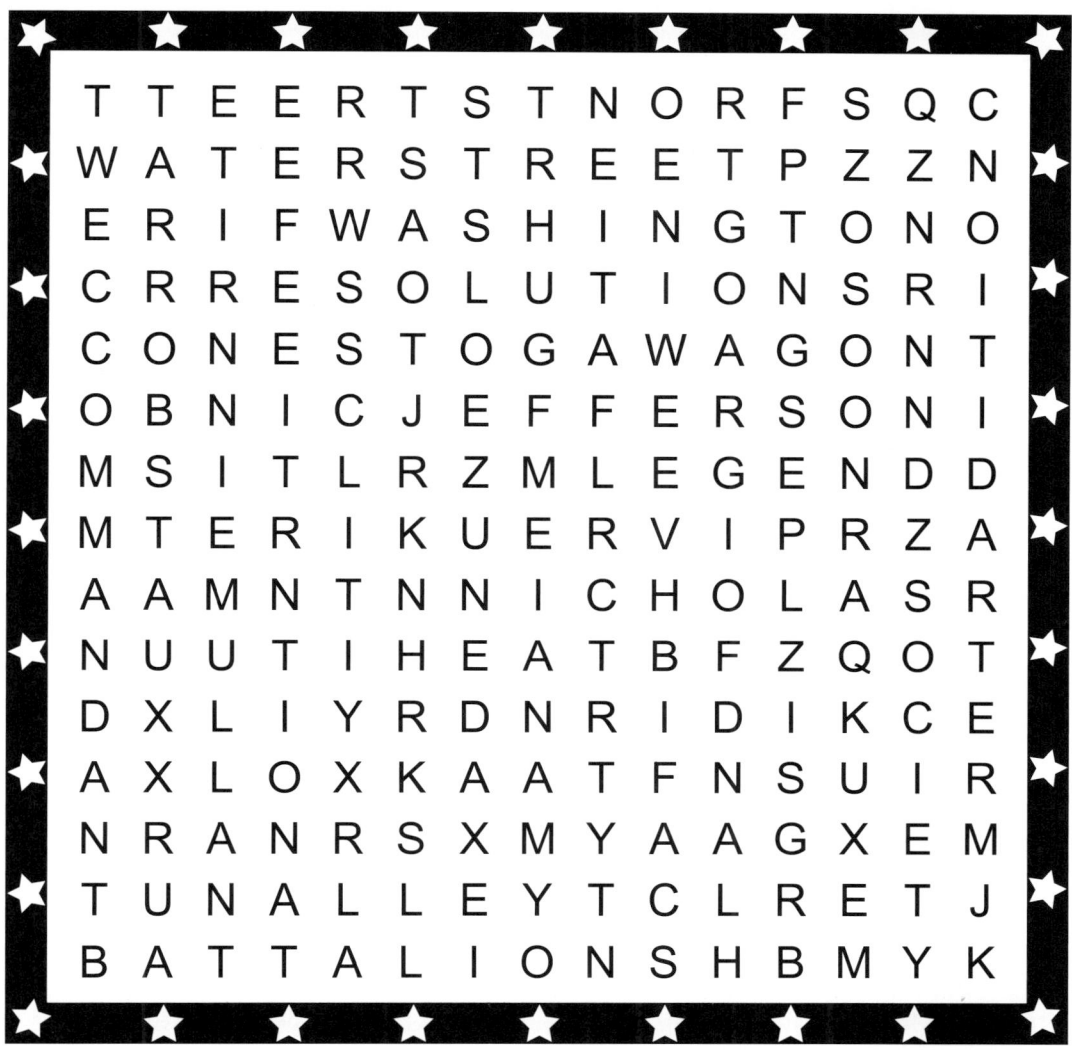

Battalions	Continental	Marines	Society
Beer	Fire	Mullan	Toast
Birthday	Franklin	Nicholas	Tradition
Cask	Front Street	Port	Tun Alley
Commandant	Jefferson	Recruiting	Washington
Conestoga Wagon	Legend	Resolutions	Water Street

GOT WHAT IT TAKES?
U.S. ARMY SPECIAL FORCES

★ ★ ★ ★ ★ ★ ★ ★ ★ ★ ★ ★ ★

To be eligible for an elite unit in the Armed Forces, candidates must meet or exceed fitness standards, then go through rigorous training. Learn what it takes to be a member of the U.S. Army Special Forces (a.k.a. Green Berets).

The U.S. Army Special Forces, better known as the Green Berets, have five key responsibilities: unconventional warfare, foreign internal defense, special reconnaissance, direct action, and counterterrorism. Many activities emphasize cultural skills when working with another country's troops and maintaining a peacekeeping or humanitarian presence on foreign soil.

To qualify for the Special Forces Assessment and Selection Course (SFAS), a Soldier must achieve close to a perfect 300 score on the Army Physical Fitness Test (PFT), which entails:

- 71 push-ups in 2 minutes (100 to be competitive)
- 78 sit-ups in 2 minutes (100 to be competitive)
- 2-mile run in under 13:00 (under 12:00 to be competitive)

If accepted, Soldiers are subjected to two weeks of tough physical training: endless push-ups, sit-ups, and pull-ups; running; swimming; marching with heavy packs; obstacle courses; and orienteering. At the end of two weeks, the instructors decide who moves on to the Special Forces Qualification Course, or "Q Course."

The Q Course lasts from six months to a year, and training for some specialties can last longer. In the Q Course, candidates undergo more physical training, and instruction in direct action (raids and patrols), survival techniques, and foreign languages. The course also includes instruction in an individual's specialty, lasting up to 48 weeks. Once the course is completed, a Soldier is given his green beret and is eligible to be deployed. Of course, the training never ends for a Special Forces Soldier, as there are many advanced courses that can be completed to further hone skills.

GOT WHAT IT TAKES?
U.S. ARMY SPECIAL FORCES

```
M A R C H E S M S Z A O R Q S
U D E F E N S E M J B G P P E
E S W I M M I N G S P L U S C
Y S P E C I A L T Y E H P F N
E L R O J U P A O G S U R O A
R U T U T V C O A U T E Z R S
X N U R O L N U P I E B J E S
Y M H H E C G A S T V Y Q I I
S G T D P N Q M N I O G S G A
W A R F A R E E B L U V K N N
D R F L T P I A P Z I V E Q N
I M E S R R F E F G O V G J O
V Y M B O I D T E R U T L U C
V E T I L E S U R V I V A L E
D I A R G R E E N B E R E T R
```

Army	Green beret	PFT	SFAS
Culture	Language	Push-ups	Sit-ups
Defense	Marches	Q course	Specialty
Deploy	Obstacle	Raid	Survival
Elite	Orienteer	Reconnaissance	Swimming
Foreign	Patrol	Run	Warfare

ON SILENT WINGS, PART I

★ ★ ★ ★ ★ ★ ★ ★ ★ ★ ★ ★

*Learn about military gliders—the silent planes used in World War II—
and the men who piloted them.*

G IS FOR *GLIDER*

An Army Air Forces uniform sporting silver wings with a *G* for *glider* was a one-time phenomenon during World War II. These tough, independent men flew fragile craft—"throwaways" constructed of metal, wood, and fabric—that had no engines. When tow planes "snatched" the glider into the air, one veteran pilot described it as being "violently bounced on the end of a nylon rope 350 feet back." Once released near the landing area, glider pilots hedgehopped in at treetop level to deliver soldiers or equipment on silent wings while bullets often ripped through the fabric. "It was like flying a stick of dynamite through the gates of hell," the pilot said. No wonder these men—all volunteers who dared to fly with no engine, no parachute, and no second chance—claimed the *G* stood for *guts*.

WHY GLIDERS?

Germany turned to gliders after the Versailles treaty in 1919 forbade their building motorized airplanes. By 1922, Germany had constructed the first true sailplane; until the early 1930s, all gliding records were held by Germany and Austria. Although the U.S. Army experimented with gliders in 1923 and the Navy in 1930, both programs were abandoned long before World War II.

To fly without power, gliders use air mass currents for lift. While soaring, the glider can travel a surprisingly long distance. When gliding, it descends on an inclined path toward the ground. Unlike paratroops spread over a large drop zone, glider pilots could make a silent, concentrated landing in the target zone. Pilots were expected to maneuver their craft as close as possible to an open space near the front lines that was often mined or under fire. When Germany's secretly rebuilt air force attacked Belgium, the Netherlands, and Luxembourg in 1940, transport planes towed glider trains, with each glider carrying six soldiers apiece. A year later, General Henry H. "Hap" Arnold and the United States War Department created the American Glider Program.

Turn the page to find out more about how glider pilots participated in World War II.

ON SILENT WINGS, PART I

```
P I E D P N E N B P T E Z N R
K T N E R R U C R I A C J E R
R P A H O Y C I X V R N V A Q
E H L C G L I D E R G U Y M N
N E P T R X R B R O E O N Q P
I C W A A C B E K N T B P G T
L R O N M V A Q A I S Q V F S
T O T S W M F M G R R O A Q T
N F Y D N E C S E D L R S N R
O R I L Y T J I A U C G E A D
R I A L B A D N N R N L Y O P
F A E X X L G T I I I W O H I
U S I M O E E A W S X W E F L
E M E S R E Q U I P M E N T O
O V Q S R S I L V E R K K C T
```

- Air current
- Air Force
- Aircraft
- Bounce
- Danger
- Descend
- Equipment
- Fabric
- Front line
- Glider
- Lift
- Maneuver
- Metal
- Pilot
- Program
- Silent
- Silver
- Snatched
- Soldiers
- Target
- Tow plane
- Volunteer
- Wings
- Wood

ON SILENT WINGS, PART II

★ ★ ★ ★ ★ ★ ★ ★ ★ ★ ★ ★

Learn more about military gliders—the silent planes used in World War II—and the men who piloted them. Part I is on the previous page.

GLIDER PILOT TRAINING

Early gliders used for training were off-the-shelf commercial sailplanes, and training itself was difficult. There were few experienced instructors among the volunteers at California's Twentynine Palms, and many trainees were either enlisted men with no flying experience or washouts from powered airplane pilot programs. The first class graduated only six students. General Arnold upped the number, six other states offered their airfields, and, by early 1942, over 6,000 glider pilots had earned their G wings.

MILITARY GLIDER

Manufacturers—including piano companies and casket factories—that had the necessary material joined the effort and began turning out military gliders. More than 14,000 were built by late 1944. Military gliders came in a variety of models: combat assault and bomb gliders, cargo gliders for carrying troops or equipment, and training gliders, built from 1941 to 1948. The Waco cargo glider was the most widely used by American glider pilots.

In July 1943, gliders participated in the first Allied airborne invasion in Sicily. Two-man crews ferried combat-equipped troops, jeeps, or armament to the front lines from D-day until March 24, 1945, when Operation Varsity at Wesel, Germany, was the last glider mission in the European theater. A total of 1,348 American and British gliders participated in the Rhine River crossing.

Glider pilots, along with airborne forces, were part of all major invasions behind enemy lines. They also served in Luzon, the Philippines, and Burma. By the end of World War II, 221 glider pilots had been killed in action and 151 more in training or other noncombat operations. During the Korean War, military gliders were replaced by helicopters, which could not only extract soldiers but drop light tanks by parachute. The Defense Department ended the glider pilot program in 1952. On October 19, 2002, the Silent Wings Museum opened its doors at Lubbock International Airport (formerly South Plains Army Airfield) in Texas.

ON SILENT WINGS, PART II

```
B V L A I R E T A M B X A R A
N A R U T U A G M F M F R E E
O O U B S W E R C Q O I N V X
R G I P E C R O W F B J O I P
E E W S P R O Y A D D F L R E
B U E I S I K M E G L I D E R
A L E Q N I A V B U C J O N I
I S J X K G M N B A E T M I E
R H T J T O S B O E T Q Z H N
F P I E D R O P P S Y C Y R C
I W U E K C A S S A U L T W E
E B L X K S Z C W L S T A P G
L S Q D Q S A Z T M N C G O O
D Z A O G R A C L P O D F P B
S A I N S T R U C T O R S Q U
```

Airfields
Arnold
Assault
Bomb
Cargo
Caskets

Combat
Crews
D-Day
Experience
Extract
G wings

Glider
Instructors
Jeeps
Korea
Lubbock
Material

Mission
Models
Pianos
Rhine River
Waco
Wesel

QUOTABLE SPECIAL OPS

★ ★ ★ ★ ★ ★ ★ ★ ★ ★ ★ ★ ★

Small, clandestine, and unorthodox military teams involved in high-risk operations have played an important role in the history of warfare. Hear what they have to say about their jobs.

- ★ "Pain is weakness leaving the body." —**Special Ops Instructors**

- ★ "The only easy day was yesterday."—**U.S. Navy SEALs**

- ★ "Death waits in the dark."—U.S. Army Task Force 160 "Night Stalkers"

- ★ "Any time, any place."—**U.S. Air Force 16th SOW**

- ★ "These things we do that others may live."—**U.S. Air Force Pararescue**

- ★ "Elite of the elite." — **U.S. Marine Corps 2nd Force Recon**

- ★ "De oppresso liber." ("To free the oppressed.") —**U.S. Army Special Forces**

- ★ "Sua sponte." ("Of their own accord.") —**U.S. Army Rangers**

- ★ "There is no 'I' in TEAM." —**U.S. Navy SEALs**

- ★ "Anyone can just go in there and kill someone, but you can't get information from a corpse." —**U.S. Navy SEALs**

- ★ "Lo que sea, cuando sea, donde sea." ("Anything, anytime, anywhere.") —**U.S. Army 7th Special Forces Group (Airborne)**

- ★ "We ain't making no goddamn cornflakes here." —**Colonel Charlie Beckwith, U.S. Army 1st Special Forces Operational Detachment–Delta**

- ★ "We want to be in a situation under maximum pressure, maximum intensity, and maximum danger. When it's shared with others, it provides a bond which is stronger than any tie that can exist." —**U.S. Navy SEAL Team Six Officer**

QUOTABLE SPECIAL OPS

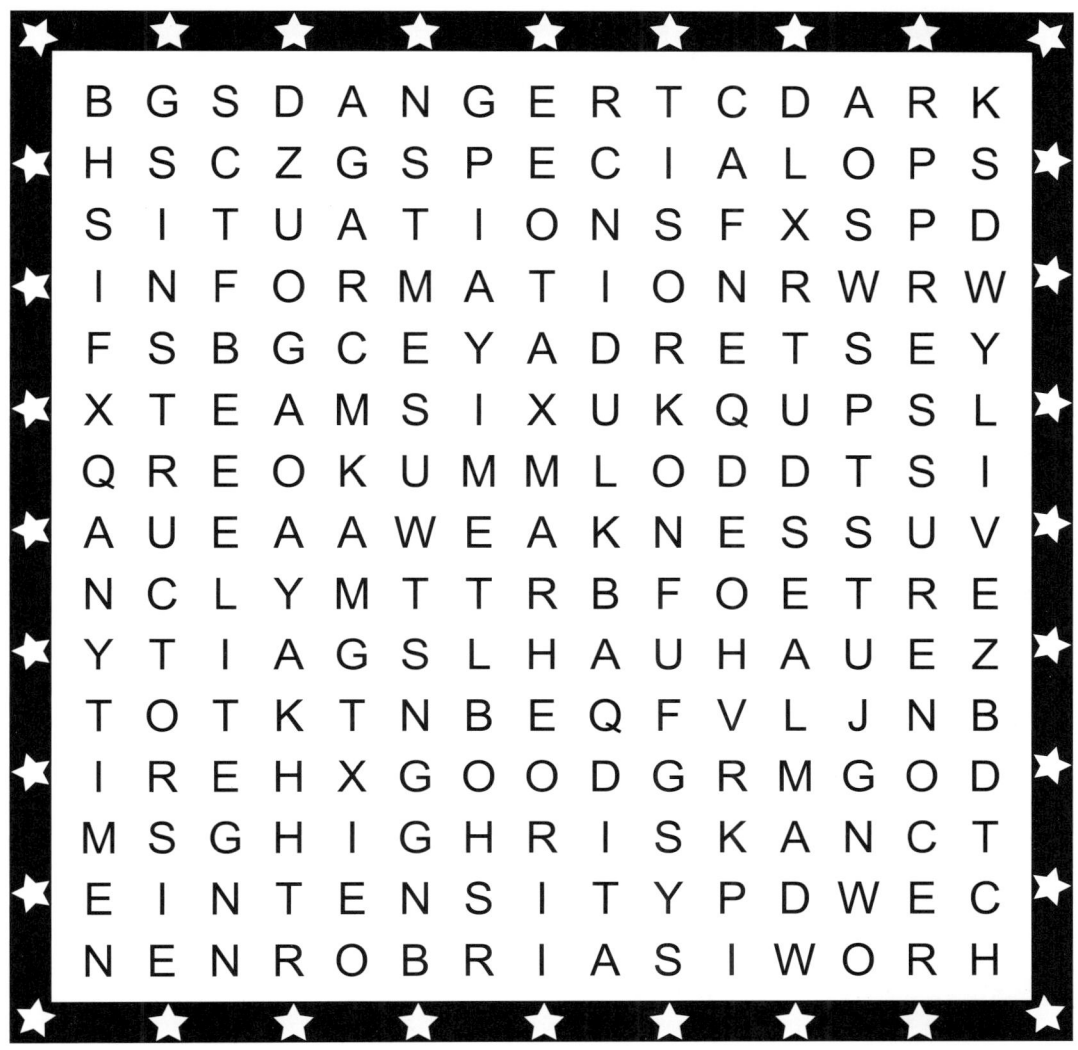

Airborne	Elite	Night Stalkers	Strong
Any time	High risk	Pressure	Team
Bond	Information	Recon	Team Six
Danger	Instructors	SEAL	Warfare
Dark	Intensity	Situation	Weakness
Delta	Live	Special ops	Yesterday

U.S. NAVY BASES

★ ★ ★ ★ ★ ★ ★ ★ ★ ★ ★ ★ ★

The U.S. Navy has numerous stateside bases and installations; these are just some of them. Is there one located near you?

CALIFORNIA
Naval Air Station Lemoore
Naval Air Station North Island
Naval Air Weapons Station China Lake
Naval Base Coronado
Naval Base Point Loma
Naval Base San Diego
Naval Base Ventura County

CONNECTICUT
Naval Submarine Base New London

FLORIDA
Naval Air Station Jacksonville
Naval Air Station Key West
Naval Air Station Pensacola
Naval Air Station Whiting Field
Naval Station Mayport

GEORGIA
Naval Submarine Base Kings Bay

HAWAII
Naval Station Pearl Harbor

ILLINOIS
Naval Station Great Lakes

MARYLAND
Fort George C. Meade
National Naval Medical Center
Naval Air Station Patuxent River
United States Naval Academy

MISSISSIPPI
Naval Air Station Meridian
Naval Construction Battalion Center Gulfport

NEVADA
Naval Air Station Fallon

NEW YORK
Naval Support Activity Saratoga Springs

RHODE ISLAND
Naval Station Newport

SOUTH CAROLINA
Naval Weapons Station, Joint Base Charleston

TEXAS
Naval Air Station Corpus Christi

VIRGINIA
Naval Air Station Oceana
Naval Station Norfolk

WASHINGTON
Naval Air Station Whidbey Island
Naval Base Kitsap
Naval Station Everett

U.S. NAVY BASES

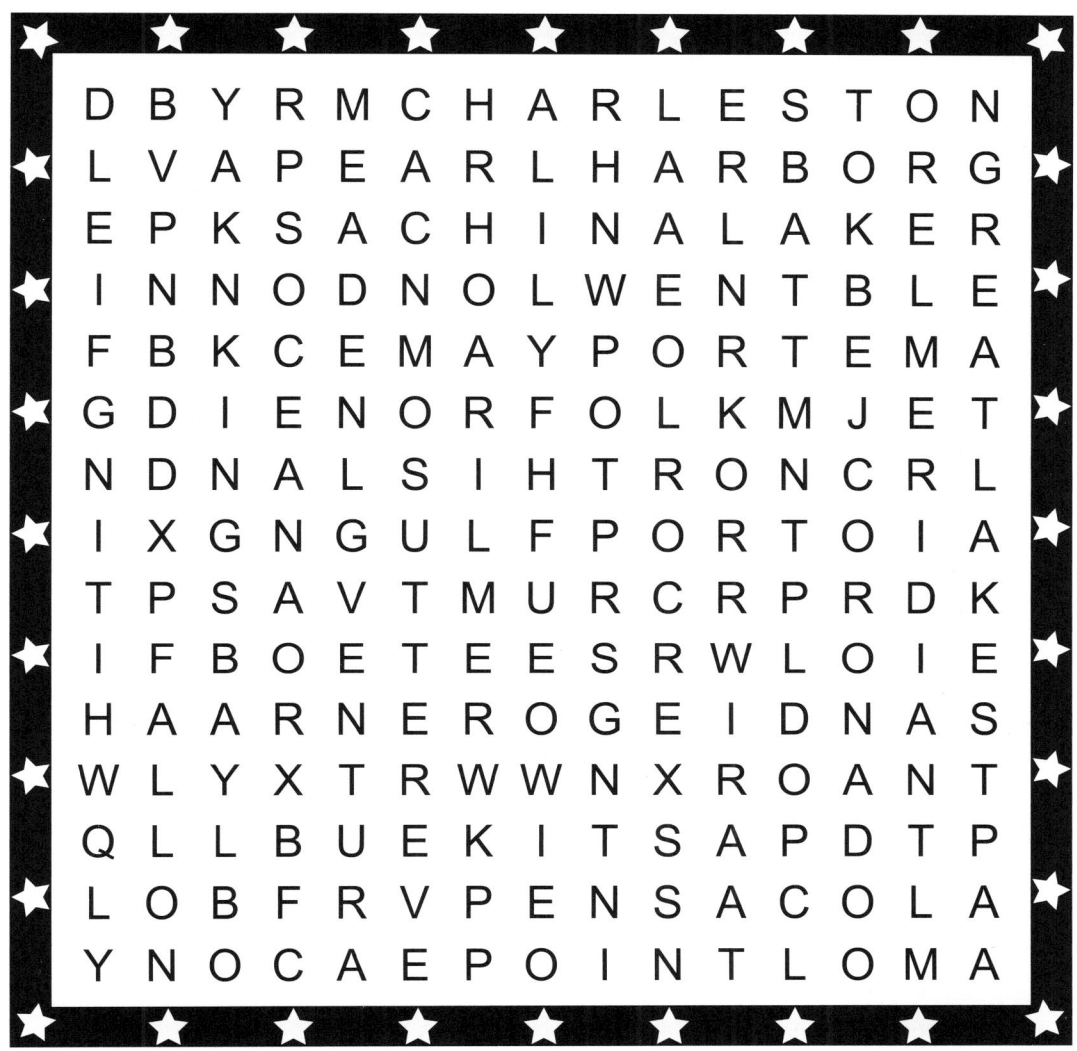

Charleston	Gulfport	Meridian	Pearl Harbor
China Lake	Kings Bay	New London	Pensacola
Coronado	Kitsap	Newport	Point Loma
Everett	Lemoore	Norfolk	San Diego
Fallon	Mayport	North Island	Ventura
Great Lakes	Meade	Oceana	Whiting Field

OPERATION FREQUENT WIND

★ ★ ★ ★ ★ ★ ★ ★ ★ ★ ★ ★ ★

U.S. combat troops left Vietnam in 1973, but the conflict between North and South Vietnam continued for another two years, and American military aid to South Vietnam continued with it. Read on to learn more about the final acts of U.S. service members in Vietnam: the largest evacuation in history.

By April 1975, North Vietnamese forces were advancing in the South. Beginning April 3, U.S. aircraft delivering supplies to Saigon began carrying Vietnamese orphans out of the region on return flights in what became known as Operation Babylift. At the same time, Air Force C-141 aircraft started evacuating U.S. citizens and Vietnamese-born dependents out of the country, with 6,000 taken out of the country by April 16. As the North Vietnamese army closed in on Saigon, U.S. officials simplified the paperwork process for potential evacuees, and, more importantly, President Gerald Ford approved the evacuation of thousands of "at-risk" Vietnamese who were not American citizens. C-130s from Clark Air Base in the Philippines joined the evacuation efforts. Between April 20 and April 28, twenty C-141s filled with evacuees left each day, and twenty C-130s departed each night, each plane with 180 or more passengers. By the end of April, the U.S. Air Force had flown 201 C-141 missions and 174 C-130 missions with more than 45,000 people, including 5,600 U.S. citizens.

On April 27, North Vietnamese rocket launches into Saigon precluded the Air Force from flying additional C-141 missions because of their vulnerability. The next day, April 28, the North Vietnamese bombed Tan Son Nhut Airport and destroyed a C-130. Desperate people flooded the runways, and the remaining citizens and refugees—including the U.S. ambassador and his staff—had to be evacuated by helicopter. The operation required a cooperative effort from the U.S. Air Force, U.S. Marine Corps, and U.S. Navy. The Navy assembled a massive force of ships off the coast. The carriers USS *Hancock* (CVA-19) and USS *Midway* (CV-41) each carried Marine and Air Force CH-53 and HH-53 helicopters. Navy and Air Force fighters, along with Air Force AC-130 gunships and KC-135 tankers, flew as escorts. More than 800 Marines provided security at the airport. On April 29 and 30, 71 U.S. helicopters flew 660 sorties between Saigon and the fleet of Navy ships, evacuating more than 7,800 people from the Embassy and the Defense Attaché Office. The deck of the *Midway* was so crowded with aircraft that some had to be pushed overboard to make room for more, and some pilots had to abandon their aircraft and crash-land in the ocean.

Operation Frequent Wind ended at 9:00 a.m. on April 30; by noon, the North Vietnamese flag flew over Saigon's Presidential Palace. The Vietnam War was officially at an end.

OPERATION FREQUENT WIND

```
G R K I G K Y E C E F F O R T
T R O C S E S G L L D V X C R
B L K B A E V M A R I N E S V
M I S S I O N S R V T K I Z X
O Z L T R Y R B K S A C S W T
B G R Y C S E O A P N O P H A
E O G G R S F R I I S C I S N
S C I C A A U P R H O N H E K
A J R I F B G H B S N A S C E
B B G O T M E A A F N H N U R
E O P M F E E N S K H P U R S
N C N K Y R S S E P U J G I F
O P E R A T I O N K T T U T W
G W K R L E V A C U A T E Y L
Y V A N Z G P S M I D W A Y T
```

- Air Force
- Aircraft
- Bomb
- Clark Air Base
- Effort
- Embassy
- Escort
- Evacuate
- Gunships
- Hancock
- Marines
- Midway
- Missions
- Navy
- Operation
- Orphans
- Refugees
- Saigon
- Security
- Ships
- Sorties
- Tan Son Nhut
- Tankers
- Wind

COAST GUARD TRIVIA

★ ★ ★ ★ ★ ★ ★ ★ ★ ★ ★ ★ ★

Did you know that the U.S. Coast Guard is the only branch of the Armed Forces that operates under the Department of Homeland Security during peacetime? Learn more facts about this organization.

1. From its founding in 1915 until 1963, the Coast Guard operated under the Department of the Treasury; from 1967 until 2003, it operated under the Department of Transportation. The Coast Guard can be transferred in whole or in part to the Department of the Navy by order of the president or an act of Congress during times of war (as happened during World War I and World War II).

2. The Coast Guard has about 43,000 active-duty personnel and 8,000 reservists.

3. The historic Boston Light, in Boston Harbor's Little Brewster Island, is the last lighthouse still operated by the Coast Guard.

4. The Coast Guard patrols and maintains inland waterways, from the Great Lakes to the Mississippi River, in addition to 4,500,000 square miles of ocean water in the U.S. Exclusive Economic Zone. The Ninth Coast Guard District in the Great Lakes area assists with shipping and navigation during ice season, among other duties.

5. The branch is in charge of about 250 cutters (ships of at least 65 feet in length that can house crewmembers) and more than 1,600 other boats, along with 200 aircraft.

6. The Coast Guard seizes an average of one drug-smuggling vessel every five days.

7. Comics legend Popeye wasn't always a sailor man—he was originally a member of the Coast Guard.

COAST GUARD TRIVIA

```
G F G D I C E S E A S O N B G
N W A R T I M E H P H D J R P
I J V A F O U N D I N G A R N
L D Q U T A O B C A P O U E O
G M R G N N F M L U Y P Y F I
G Q L U W B A N P L T H I S T
U P P C G J I V D I U T Z N A
M A O C K S A M Y G D N E A G
S T P S V E I F A H E I T R I
G R E Y J I R X J T V N P T V
U O Y E N Z C V R H I S H B A
R L E T Q E R T N O T S O B N
D M A I N T A I N U C O H D B
Z P S R W E F J V S A B H H A
E S U O H S T T R E A S U R Y
```

Active duty
Aircraft
Boat
Boston
Cutter
Drug smuggling
Drugs
Founding
Guard
House
Ice season
Inland
Lighthouse
Maintain
Navigation
Navy
Ninth
Patrol
Popeye
Seize
Shipping
Transfer
Treasury
Wartime

CHESTY XVI

★ ★ ★ ★ ★ ★ ★ ★ ★ ★ ★ ★ ★

English bulldogs have been beloved by the Marine Corps since 1922. The current mascot, Chesty XVI, is a "mostly good boy" who was promoted to Lance Corporal in January 2024. Learn more about the history of the Marine Corps' mascot.

Legend has it that, after their ferocious performance in World War I's Battle of Belleau Wood, the U.S. Marines were nicknamed *teufel hunden*, or "devil dogs," by their German enemies. That nickname stuck. Bulldogs had also been an unofficial Marine Corps mascot since an early recruiting poster showed a bulldog wearing a U.S. helmet chasing a dachshund in a German helmet.

Thanks in part to this tradition, Marine Barracks in Quantico, Virginia, has long had a bulldog mascot. Two-time Medal of Honor recipient Brigadier General Smedley Butler enlisted the first one, Private Jiggs, into the Marine Corps on October 14, 1922. When Jiggs died in 1927—at the rank of Sergeant Major—he was buried with military honors and succeeded by Jiggs II. After Jiggs II died in 1937, a number of mascots were named Smedley, in honor of the man who started the tradition. Then Private First Class Chauncy was enlisted in 1956, followed by Chesty I, who made his debut in 1957.

Every mascot since 1957 have borne the name Chesty. Named for legendary Lieutenant General Lewis "Chesty" Puller, the most decorated Marine in the history of the Corps, this succession of dogs has played a key role in boosting morale among Marines and interacting with the public at events, and they also represent the connection between the fighting spirit of legendary Marines of the past and Marines today. The current Chesty, Chesty XVI, enlisted in the Corps in February 2022, and was promoted to Sergeant. Scott Rogers, Chesty's handler, says he likes pizza, belly rubs, and playing with other dogs. (His predecessor, Chesty XV, lacked the discipline necessary to be an effective Marine, so he was retired after four years of service.)

Other installations also have bulldog mascots. Named for the first female Marine, Opha May became the first female bulldog mascot in 2017 and served at Parris Island until retirement in 2022; Opha May II has taken over duties.

(Not all dogs serve with distinction. Chesty VI was demoted from private first class to private in 1979 for destroying a punching bag and disobeying an order; he then received nonjudicial punishment in 1981 for biting two corporals on the foot. And Chesty XIII gained notoriety in 2012 for snarling at Defense Secretary Leon Panetta's golden retriever.)

CHESTY XVI

Bite	Helmet	Nickname	Rank
Bulldog	Honors	Parris Island	Recruit
Butler	Interact	Pizza	Retire
Decorated	Jiggs	Promotion	Rogers
Devil dog	Mascot	Puller	Snarl
Event	Morale	Quantico	Spirit

SEMPER SUPRA

The newest branch of the Armed Forces has the newest march.

We're the mighty watchful eye,
Guardians beyond the blue,
The invisible front line,
Warfighters brave and true.

Boldly reaching into space,
There's no limit to our sky.
Standing guard both night and day,
We're the Space Force from on high.

The Space Force's motto is "*Semper Supra*," meaning "always above." After creation of the Space Force in December 2019, former member of the United States Air Force Band James Teachenor began working with Chief of Space Operations, General John W. Raymond, to craft a song that would "encompass all the capabilities that the Space Force offers and its vision." Teachenor then collaborated with Chief Musician Sean Nelson, a trombonist and staff arranger with the United States Coast Guard Band. The two worked together for months to finalize the song.

The song was publicly unveiled in September 2022. The United States Department of the Air Force stated the song "was created to capture the esprit de corps of both current and future Guardians, and intends to bring together service members by giving them a sense of pride."

SEMPER SUPRA

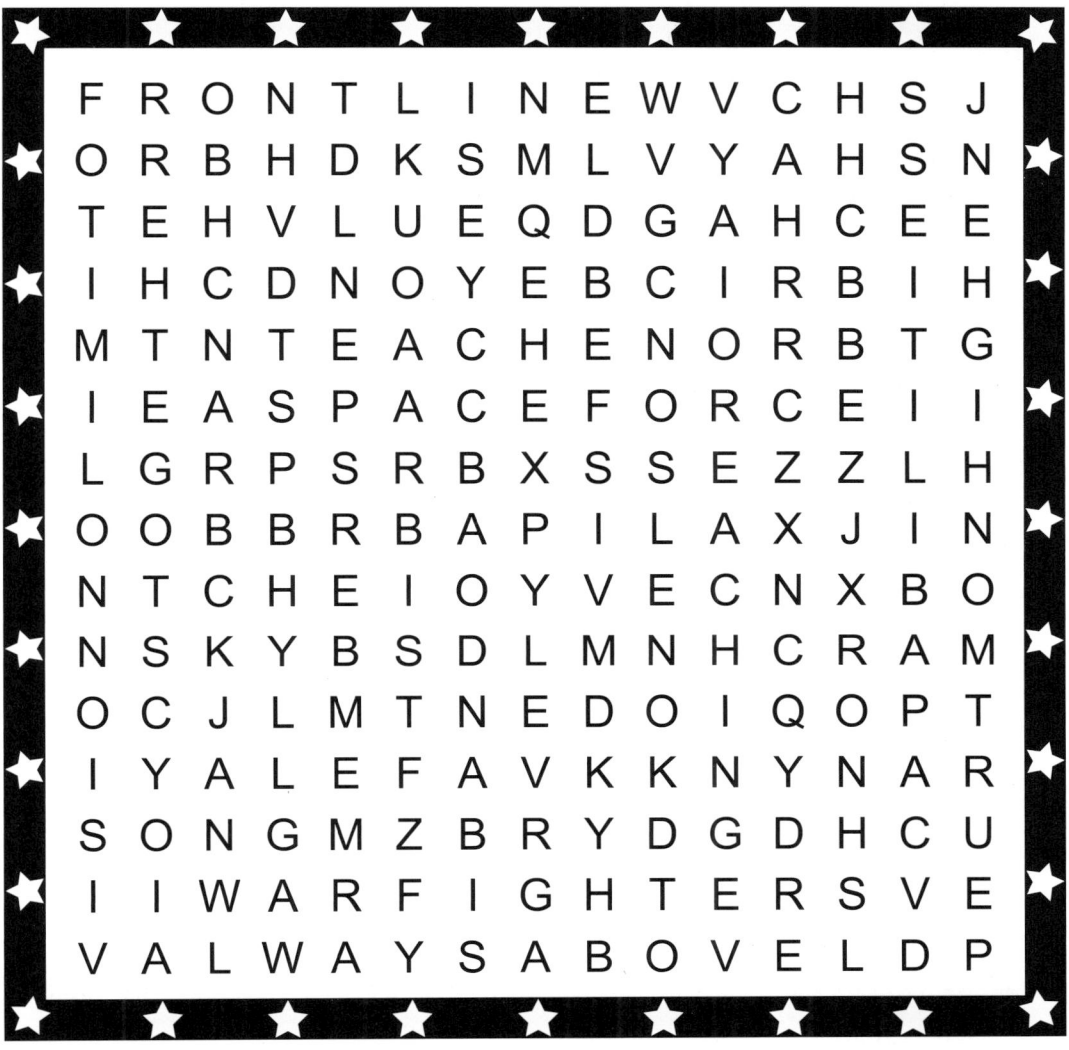

Always above	Capabilities	On high	Space Force
Band	Front line	Pride	Teachenor
Beyond	March	Raymond	Together
Bold	Members	Reaching	True
Branch	Nelson	Sky	Vision
Brave	No limit	Song	Warfighters

GOT WHAT IT TAKES?
U.S. NAVY SEALS

★ ★ ★ ★ ★ ★ ★ ★ ★ ★ ★ ★ ★

To be eligible for an elite unit in the Armed Forces, candidates must meet or exceed fitness standards, then go through rigorous training. Learn what it takes to be a member of the U.S. Navy SEALs.

Navy SEALs (Sea, Air, and Land Forces) work in small units, deploying from the sea to conduct a variety of clandestine missions: unconventional warfare, direct action, counterterrorism, foreign internal defense, and personnel recovery. They comprise less than 1 percent of U.S. Navy personnel. (Highly qualified U.S. Coast Guard personnel are also sometimes accepted into the SEALs.)

To qualify for the training program, a Sailor must be able to complete:

- 500-yard swim using breast- or sidestroke in 12:30 (under 10:00 to be competitive);
- 42 push-ups in 2 minutes (100 to be competitive);
- 52 sit-ups in 2 minutes (100 to be competitive);
- 8 pull ups, no time limit (15 to be competitive);
- 1½-mile run in boots and trousers in 11:30 (under 10:20 to be competitive).

If accepted, training consists of:

- 8 weeks at the Special Warfare Preparatory School.
- 3 weeks at the Indoctrination Course.
- 24 weeks of Basic Underwater Demolition/SEAL training (physical conditioning, diving, and land warfare), including "Hell Week," 132 hours of continuous physical activity. A typical class loses 70–80 percent of its trainees in this phase.
- 15 weeks of SEAL Qualification Training (learning special skills and tactics, as well as developing the ability to lead men), including 4 weeks of cold-weather training in Kodiak, Alaska; those left standing are awarded the SEAL trident and assigned to a team—but the training isn't over yet.

Prior to deployment, a SEAL goes through 18 months of individual and team training to develop specialized skills (such as sniping, surveillance, advanced driving, and foreign languages) and the ability to function within a cohesive unit.

GOT WHAT IT TAKES?
U.S. NAVY SEALS

```
C Y H D K T S E G A U G N A L
O R Z G N R M T B U D S U N P
H E H E P A A Y K O D I A K T
E V S S C I L W R P F I M N A
S O J N O N L A L U X I E U C
I C K E L E U I F V W M H L T
V E G F D E N G S S Y P E A I
E R D E W S I N L O B T L E C
O Y R D E S T I L A I R L S S
D V I W A X V P I O J I W L H
X A V G T L E I K D I D E D B
Q N I A H D T N S M V E E M D
D T N Z E J I S U K K N K J S
B J G V R T L A S E A T S N Z
U C L A N D E S T I N E M I Z
```

Air	Deployment	Languages	Small unit
BUDS	Driving	Navy	Sniping
Clandestine	Elite	Recovery	Swim
Cohesive	Hell Week	Sea	Tactics
Cold weather	Kodiak	SEAL	Trainees
Defense	Land	Skills	Trident

U.S. NAVY BATTLESHIPS

★ ★ ★ ★ ★ ★ ★ ★ ★ ★ ★ ★ ★

Aircraft carriers rose in prominence during World War II, displacing battleships as the preeminent ships used by the U.S. military. But battleships—armored warships with large-caliber guns—once dominated the U.S. Navy.

USS *ALABAMA* (BB-60)

The final member of the *South Dakota*–class battleships, designed for providing shore bombardment and antiaircraft defense for carriers, the USS *Alabama*'s first deployment was to the European Theater in 1943, where it assisted British naval forces in the North Atlantic protecting the Soviet fleet. Later that year, it was sent to the South Pacific, where it engaged in operations in the Gilbert Islands, Marshall Islands, the Marianas, the capture of Saipan, and the liberation of the Philippines, among others. The "Mighty A" earned nine Battle stars before being decommissioned in 1947. The ship was moved to Mobile, Alabama, in 1964 and today serves as a museum and memorial.

USS *NEW JERSEY* (BB-62)

The most decorated battleship in U.S. history made its debut in the Pacific Theater during World War II. Launched on the one-year anniversary of the Pearl Harbor attack in December 1942 as one of four *Iowa*-class ships, the USS *New Jersey* alone played a role in every major amphibious invasion in the Pacific Theater, including the Marshall Islands, New Guinea, Iwo Jima, and Okinawa. It was also responsible for the Allied victory in the Battle of the Philippine Sea—the largest carrier battle in history—before leading the Navy's main fleet in the Battle for Leyte Gulf—the largest sea battle of all time. Through later service in Korea, Vietnam, Lebanon, and the Persian Gulf, the ship traveled more miles, fought in more battles, and fired more shells than any other battleship in history, and earned 19 Battle and Campaign stars. The USS *New Jersey* is now a museum and memorial in Camden, New Jersey.

USS *MISSOURI* (BB-63)

The last U.S. Navy battleship to be commissioned was also the last to be decommissioned. It headed to the Pacific Theater from Hawaii in January 1945, where it supported the invasion of Iwo Jima, participated in strikes against Tokyo and Okinawa, and thwarted repeated Japanese kamikaze attacks before becoming a flagship for the Third Fleet; the USS *Missouri* famously became the site of the Japanese surrender, officially bringing World War II to a close, on September 2, 1945. But that wasn't the end of the *Missouri*'s service: it also served in Korea, then was recommissioned in 1986 to assist in military defense in the Middle East, including during Operation Desert Shield and Desert Storm. The ship was decommissioned in 1992 and is now a museum in Pearl Harbor.

U.S. NAVY BATTLESHIPS

```
S U R R E N D E R R M J E E V
P A C I F I C R B C Q F J K E
R O B R A H L R A E P W V L I
H T Y U O C D B I B K Z I R P
T F S V S A Q D D O M B U F F
M A W Z H R E A R A O O L K F
E R Q M E R G E R M S U B L N
M C U I L I A M Y S G W E Q O
O R A G L E O A I N V E Z S I
R I B H S R M M A U T X C J S
I A A T K A U I Z G A C N V A
A I T Y B E S O K I N A W A V
L T T A D R E V I E T N A M N
M N L O E D U N E D M A C L I
W A E P Z F M L E B A N O N H
```

Alabama	Carrier	Memorial	Pacific
Antiaircraft	Fleet	Mighty A	Pearl Harbor
Armor	Guns	Missouri	Persian Gulf
Battle	Invasion	Mobile	Shells
Bombard	Korea	Museum	Surrender
Camden	Lebanon	Okinawa	Vietnam

THE TOMB OF THE UNKNOWN SOLDIER

★ ★ ★ ★ ★ ★ ★ ★ ★ ★ ★ ★ ★

*One of the most iconic memorials in Arlington National Cemetery—
if not the nation—is the Tomb of the Unknown Soldier. Learn more about this memorial
dedicated to American servicemen "known but to God."*

Up through the first two years of the Civil War, most of America's war dead were buried quickly in mass graves near the site of the battles in which they fell. Despite the introduction of the national cemetery system in 1862 meant to ensure proper burial, it's estimated that nearly half the servicemen killed in the Civil War were never identified.

When the U.S. entered World War I, servicemembers were issued aluminum discs with identifying information (the precursor to today's dog tags). Despite this, by war's end, large numbers of unidentified Americans lay buried in overseas military cemeteries. In 1921, inspired by France and England, the United Sates decided to repatriate and honor an unknown service member. That October, four unidentified U.S. troops were exhumed from four different American military cemeteries in France; the caskets were gathered together and one was selected at random. The Unknown's casket was then transported to Washington, D.C., where it arrived on November 9, 1921; it was interred in the Tomb of the Unknown Soldier at Arlington National Cemetery on November 11. In addition to receiving a state funeral and a nationwide moment of silence, the Unknown was also presented with the Medal of Honor by President Warren G. Harding.

Following the end of the Korean War, President Dwight D. Eisenhower approved interment of Unknowns from Korea and World War II. In 1958, the Army exhumed the bodies of 18 fallen World War II vets from American military cemeteries in North Africa, Europe, the Philippines, and Hawaii; four unidentified Korean War veterans were also exhumed from Hawaii's National Memorial Cemetery of the Pacific. A final selection was made from each group. Both Unknowns arrived in Washington, D.C., on May 28, 1958, and were interred in their crypts beside the World War I Unknown.

Before the end of the Vietnam War, Arlington began preparing to add an additional crypt. Thankfully, scientific and technological advances meant that the fallen from that war could eventually be identified. By May 1984, only a single set of recovered American remains were still unidentified, and that individual was officially designated the Vietnam War Unknown at a ceremony in Pearl Harbor before the casket was sent to Washington, D.C. The Unknown was interred on Memorial Day 1984 in a ceremony presided over by President Ronald Reagan.

As the Department of Defense and civilian organizations continued in their quest to recover and identify American remains from Vietnam, they discovered compelling evidence to suggest the Vietnam Unknown was Air Force pilot 1st Lieutenant Michael Joseph Blassie, who had gone missing in 1972. Blassie's family requested that the remains be exhumed; after DNA testing confirmed his identity, Lieutenant Blassie was reinterred at Jefferson Barracks National Cemetery in St. Louis. The Vietnam Unknown crypt lies empty to this day but was rededicated to honor all remaining missing American military personnel from Vietnam.

THE TOMB OF THE UNKNOWN SOLDIER

```
F V Y K D T R O P S N A R T D
R I W O E V M T O M B Y E N T
A E R R R I R I B L P G I N H
N T P E R U S O S I B O D K P
D N H A E A R S N S K L L S J
O A B N T C R E A O I O O N S
M M Z W N R S L C L H N S I N
I N Y A I Y I E I O B H G A W
N D E R Z P G A L N V C Q M O
Y V E L G T C O T E G E C E N
A N D N L S C Z E E C T R R K
P R D E T A C I D E D T O H N
W R Q D E I F I T N E D I N U
Q G X Z B I F X L F S F I O N
C A S K E T S Y U R Q X W D N
```

Arlington   Fallen   Random   Technology
Blassie   Honor   Recover   Tomb
Caskets   Identify   Remains   Transport
Crypts   Interred   Repatriate   Unidentified
Dedicated   Korean War   Selection   Unknown
DNA   Missing   Soldier   Vietnam

DORIS MILLER

★ ★ ★ ★ ★ ★ ★ ★ ★ ★ ★ ★

He served breakfast, then became one of the first heroes of World War II. Learn about the remarkable actions of the first Black recipient of the Navy Cross.

Doris "Dorie" Miller was born in Texas in 1919, the third of four boys. He dropped out of school at age 17. At age 20, he enlisted in the Navy as a mess attendant, one of the few ratings available to Black Sailors at the time. He was stationed on the battleship *West Virginia* (BB-48) at Pearl Harbor on December 7, 1941, when the Japanese attacked the naval base.

Early that morning, Miller served breakfast, then was in the process of collecting laundry when the first of seven torpedoes hit the *West Virginia* just before 8:00 a.m. Miller headed to his battle station, an anti-aircraft battery magazine, only to find it had been destroyed. So he headed for a central location on deck to report available for other duties, and his meritorious actions began. He was first commanded to help move wounded Sailors to safety; due to his physical prowess (he was a former football player and the ship's heavyweight boxing champion), he was quickly flagged down to assist in moving the ship's captain, Mervyn Bennion, who had been mortally wounded in the abdomen by shrapnel. Miller and another Sailor attempted to remove Captain Bennion from his exposed position on the bridge, but Bennion refused to leave his post, concerned only with the safe removal of his men from the burning ship. Miller was then instructed to assist with manning two Browning anti-aircraft machine guns. Despite never having received any training on the weapon, Miller successfully manned his gun and was credited with downing at least two Japanese planes. When he ran out of ammunition, he again assisted with moving injured Sailors to the quarterdeck and out of harm's way.

On January 1, 1942, the Navy released a list of commendations for actions taken at Pearl Harbor on December 7. Among them was a commendation for a Black man who was unnamed. Black journalists and the Department of the Navy were able to identify Doris Miller as the man in question, and Miller was awarded the Navy Cross. A campaign to award him the Medal of Honor failed, but Miller was quickly recognized as one of the first heroes of the war and was personally recognized by Admiral Chester Nimitz on May 27, 1942.

Miller spent some time in 1942 and 1943 back in the United States on a war bond tour—and was featured in a Navy recruiting poster—before returning to duty in May 1943. The 24-year-old was killed in action that November when his ship, USS *Liscome Bay* (CVE-56) was sunk by a torpedo from a Japanese submarine during the Battle of Makin.

Among the posthumous honors bestowed on Messman Second Class Miller were the naming of the destroyer escort USS *Miller* (FF-1091) in 1973, and the future USS *Doris Miller* (CVN-81) aircraft carrier, scheduled to be commissioned in 2032. The latter will be both the first aircraft carrier named for an African American and for an enlisted Sailor.

DORIS MILLER

```
E P S S O R C Y V A N L D E P
N D A I N I G R I V T S E W P
A S N O I N N E B L U Q F F L
L S L T F A R C R I A I T N A
P E Q S R M A C H I N E G U N
Q M Q N D T O R P E D O H O B
L S E O P O S T E R X Y I E R
O C W C A M P A I G N T Q N E
Y N I M I T Z W J C I E T L A
B R O W N I N G O N Q F R I K
C O D M G U O M U U R A O S F
S R O N O H M M H L N S C T A
V G R T U E M Y H M L D S E S
L V W I N A M I L L E R E D T
P I B D N Z L W A R B O N D N
```

Ammunition Commend   Machine gun Poster
Anti-aircraft Down   Mess   Safety
Bennion   Enlisted Miller   Torpedo
Breakfast   Escort   Navy Cross   War bond
Browning   Honors   Nimitz   West Virginia
Campaign   Laundry   Plane   Wounded

ORIGINS OF VETERANS DAY

★ ★ ★ ★ ★ ★ ★ ★ ★ ★ ★ ★ ★

*Every November 11, America honors all the men and women
who have served in its Armed Forces.
Learn about how Veterans Day came to be.*

"The Great War," as World War I was known at the time, officially ended with the signing of the Treaty of Versailles on June 28, 1919. However, an armistice agreement had been reached seven months earlier: at the eleventh hour of the eleventh day of the eleventh month of 1918, a ceasefire began between Germany and Allied nations.

In 1919, President Woodrow Wilson proclaimed November 11 to be a holiday commemorating Armistice Day. His intention was for the day to be observed with parades and a brief suspension of business activity at 11:00 a.m. In 1926, Congress officially recognized the end of World War I with a resolution recommending the president declare November 11 a legal holiday. An Act of Congress passed in May 1938 made "Armistice Day" a national holiday set aside for honoring the veterans of the Great War.

In 1954, at the urging of Veterans service organizations, the holiday on November 11 was renamed Veterans Day. World War II had required the largest mobilization of Armed Forces service members in the nation's history, and the Korean War had also sent a number of American military troops to the front lines. With the change in name, November 11 became a day to honor United States military veterans from all wars.

The Uniform Holiday Bill, signed in June 1968, moved the Veterans Day observance to a floating Monday each November so that federal employees could celebrate it (along with Washington's Birthday, Memorial Day, and Columbus Day) with a three-day weekend. But when the law went into effect in 1971, many states continued to celebrate the day on its original date, resulting in confusion. It also became clear how important the historic date was to so many citizens, both military and non-military. In 1975, President Gerald Ford signed another law returning Veterans Day to November 11 every year regardless of the day of the week on which it falls.

ORIGINS OF VETERANS DAY

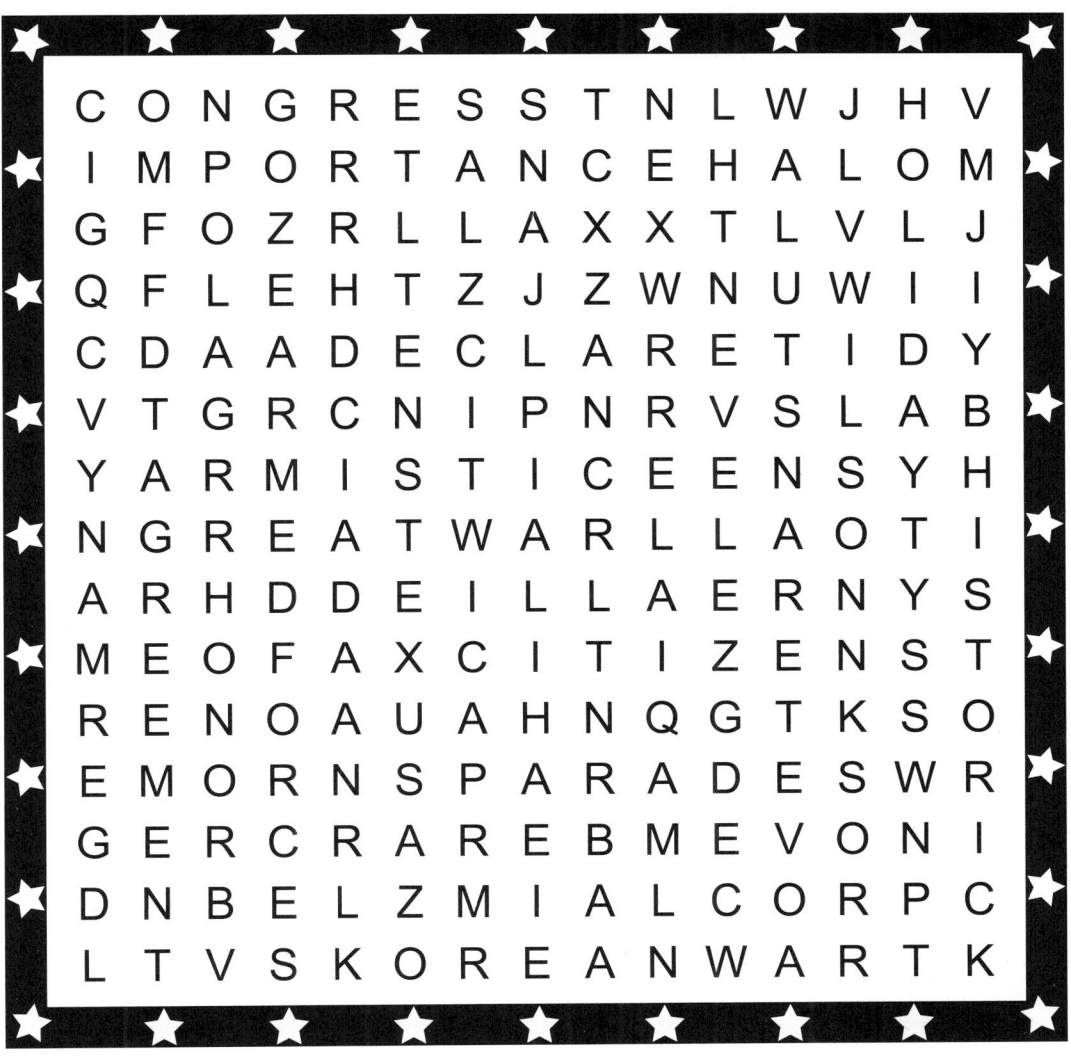

Agreement	Declare	Honor	Parades
Allied	Eleventh	Importance	Proclaim
Armed Forces	Germany	Korean War	Treaty
Armistice	Great War	Law	Versailles
Citizens	Historic	Name	Veterans
Congress	Holiday	November	Wilson

SOLUTIONS

SOLUTIONS

3
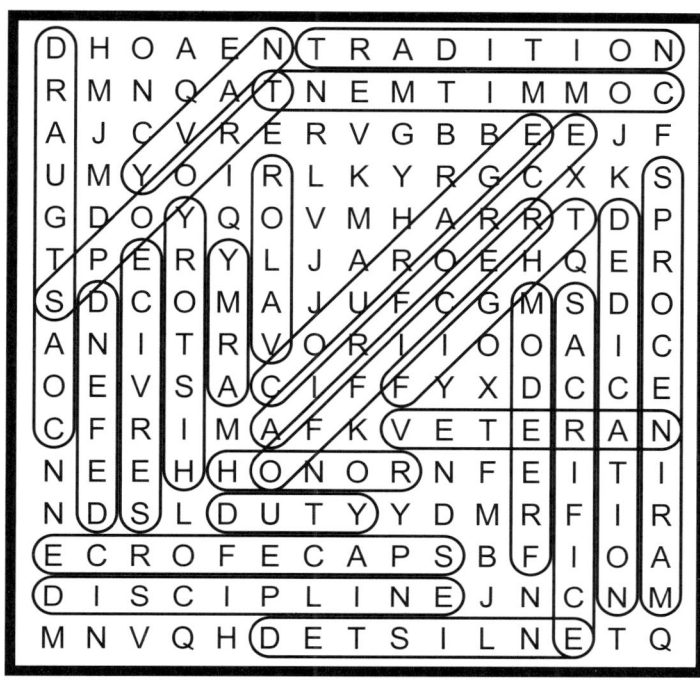

5
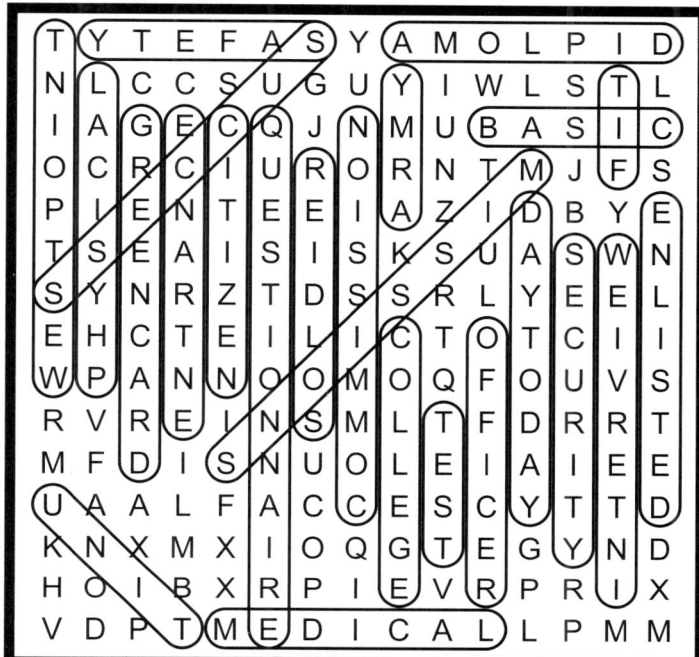

7
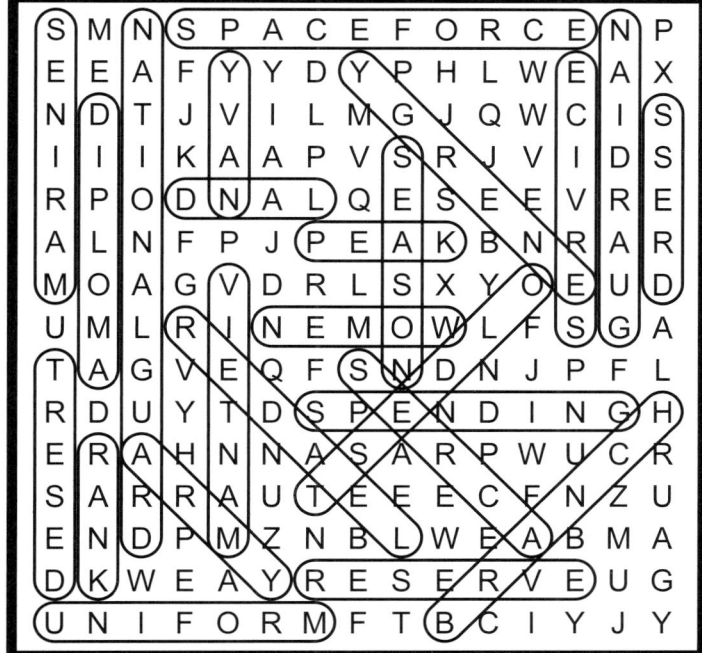

9
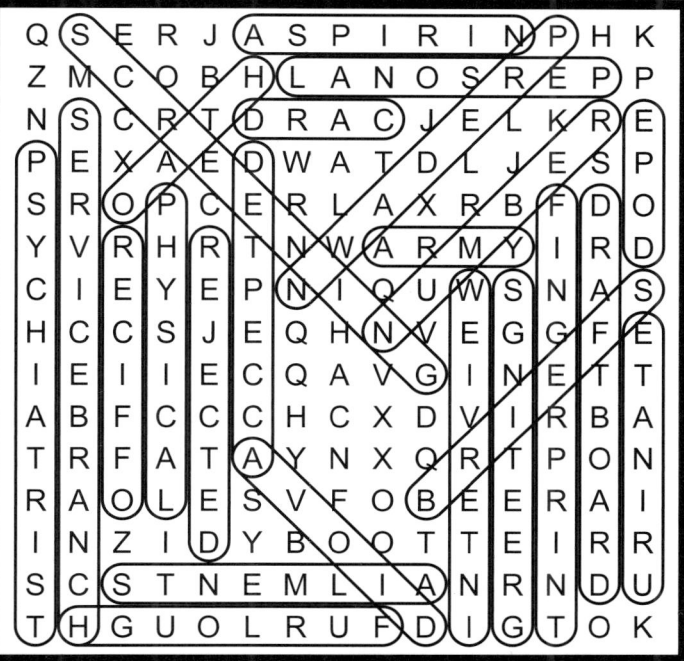

SOLUTIONS

11

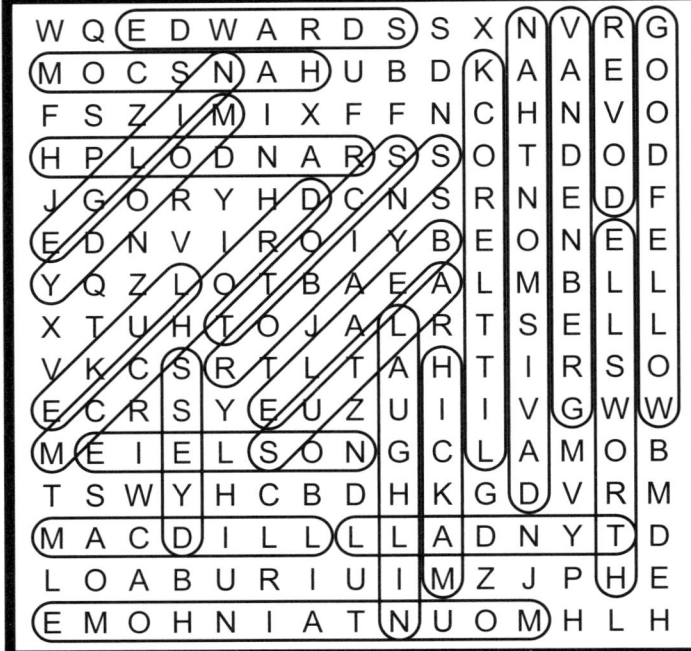

13

15

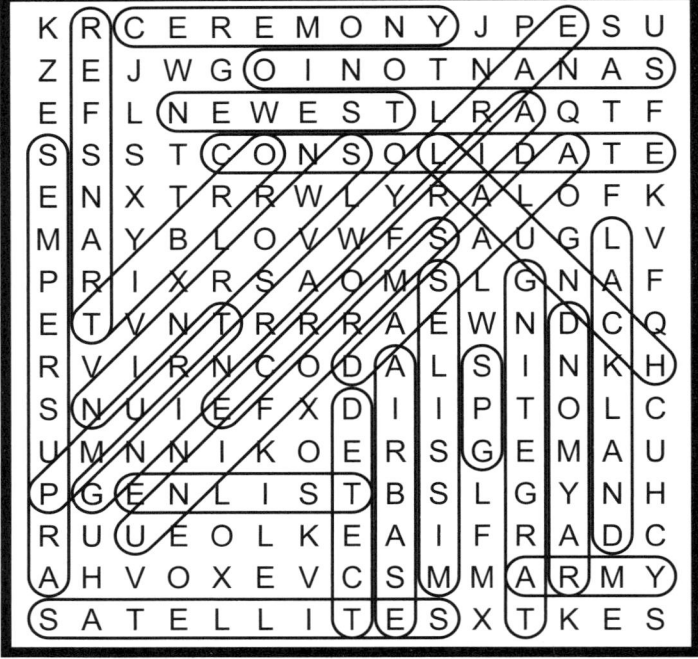

17

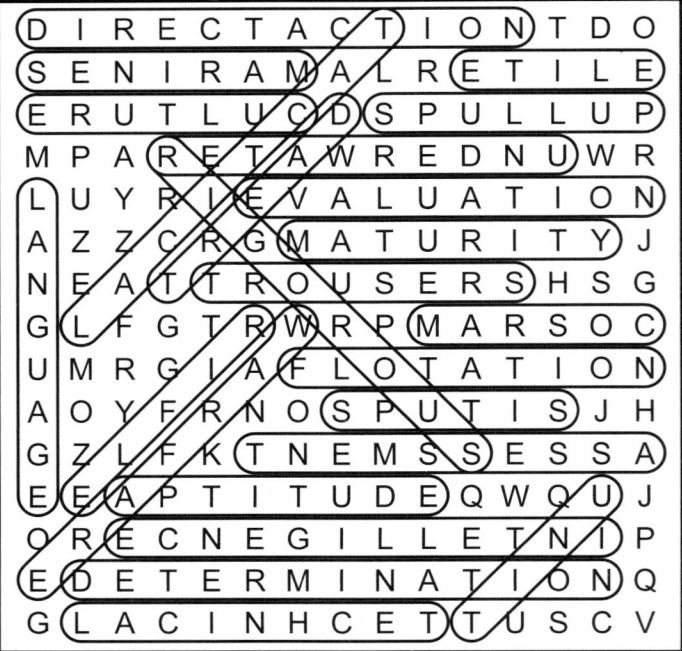

SOLUTIONS

19

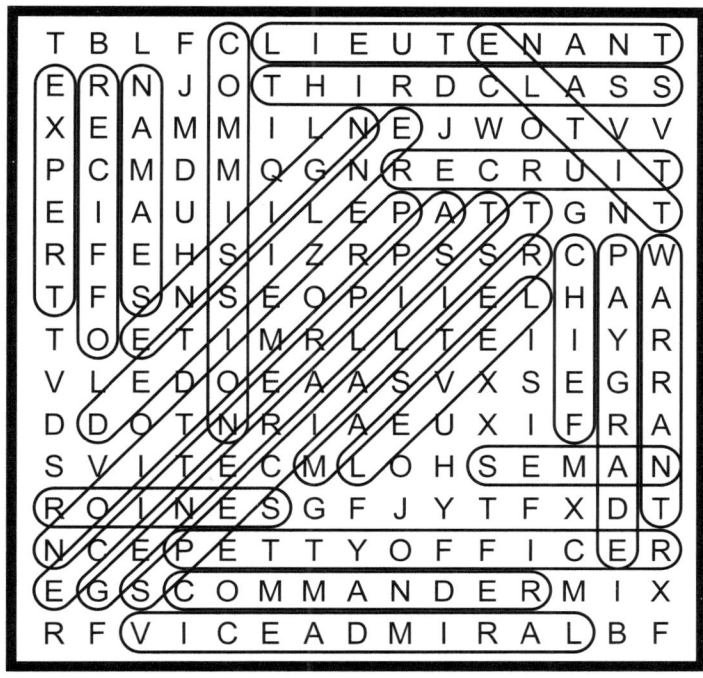

21

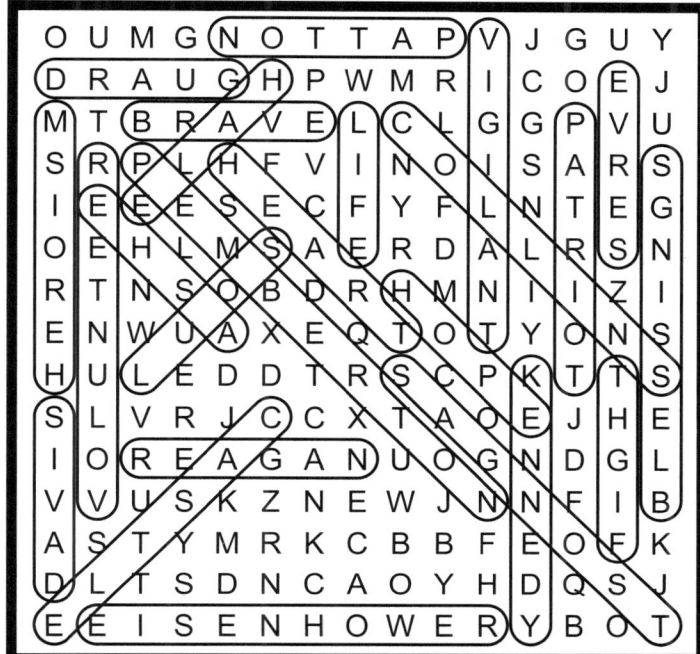

23

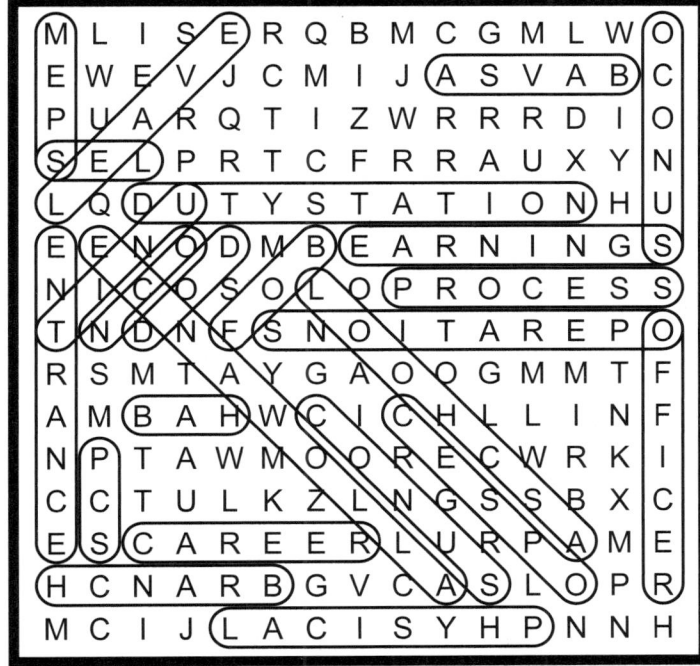

25

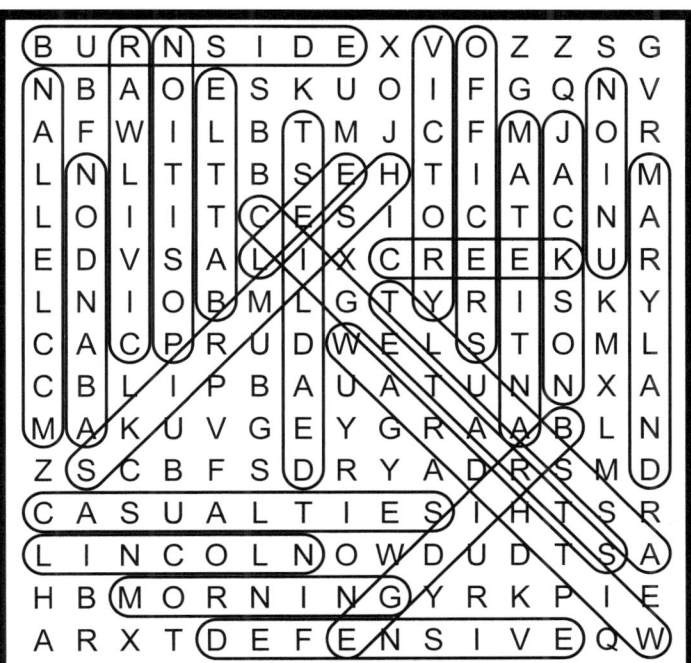

SOLUTIONS

27

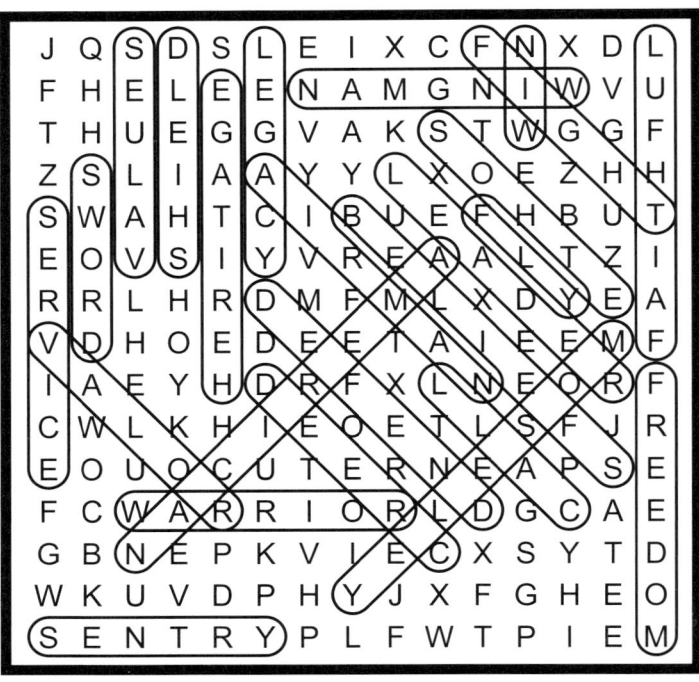

29

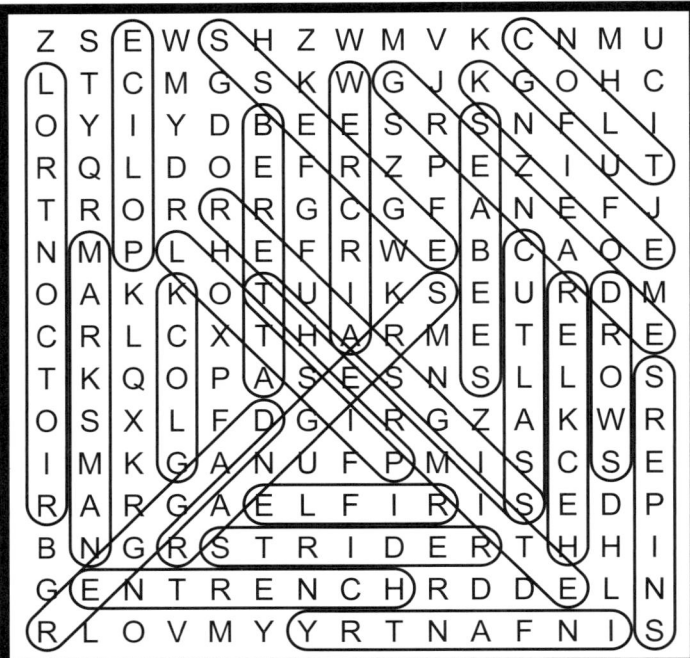

31

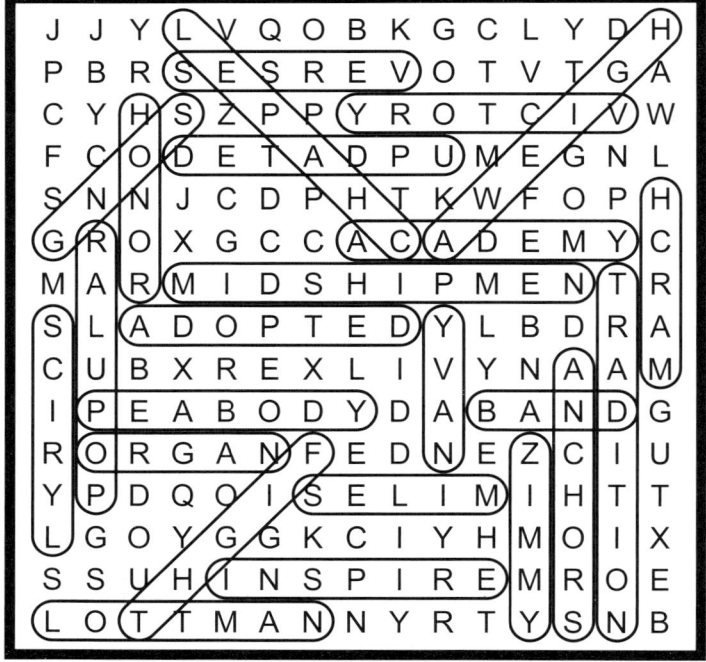

33

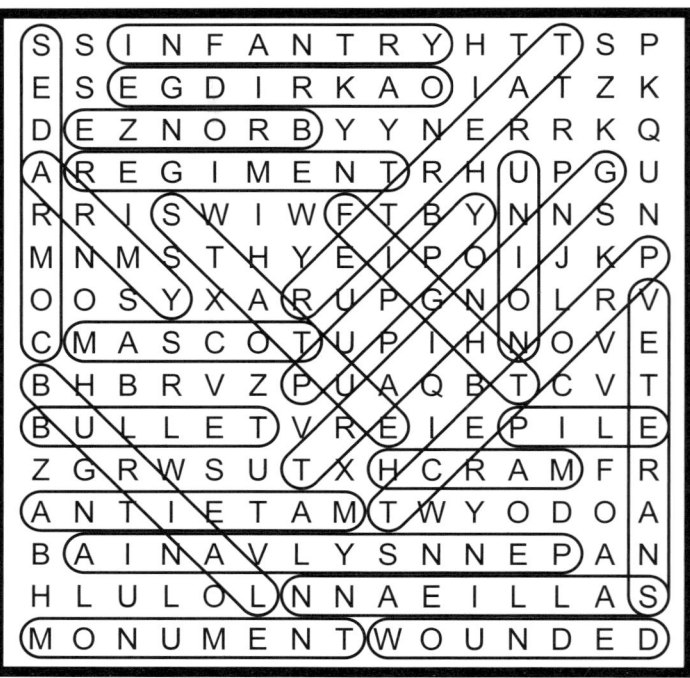

SOLUTIONS

35

37

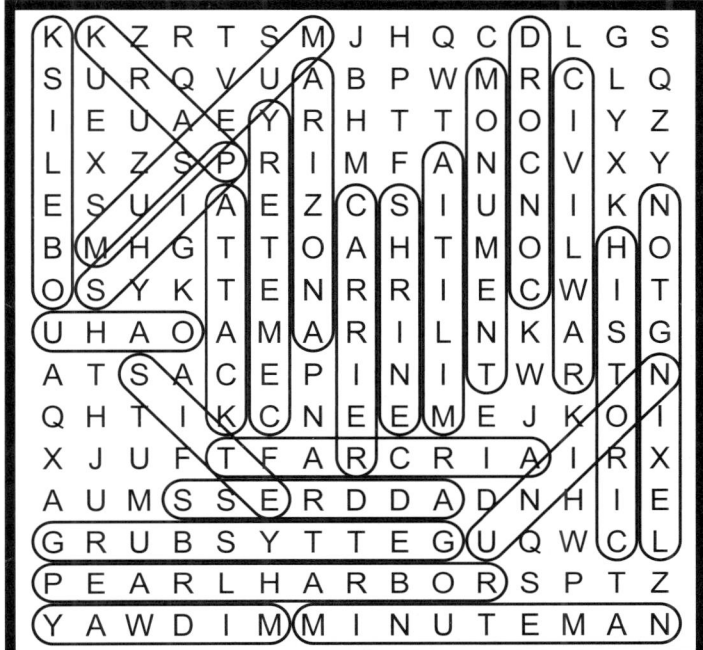

39

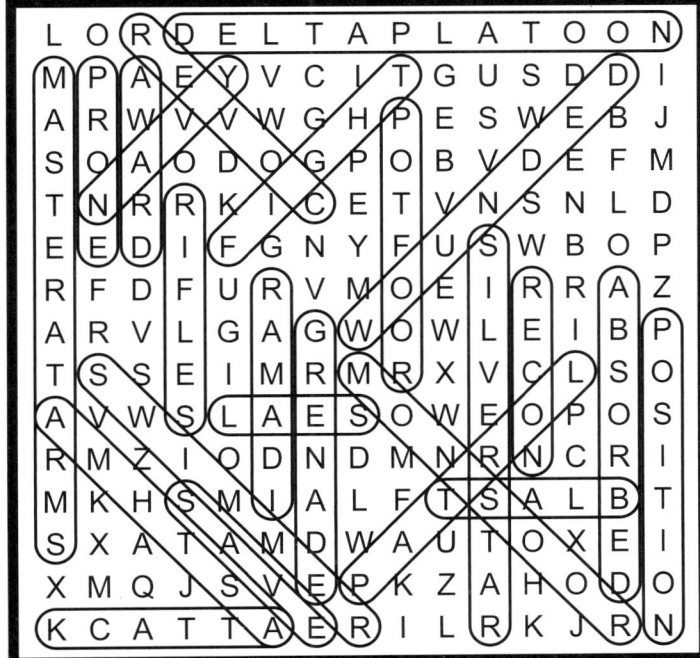

41

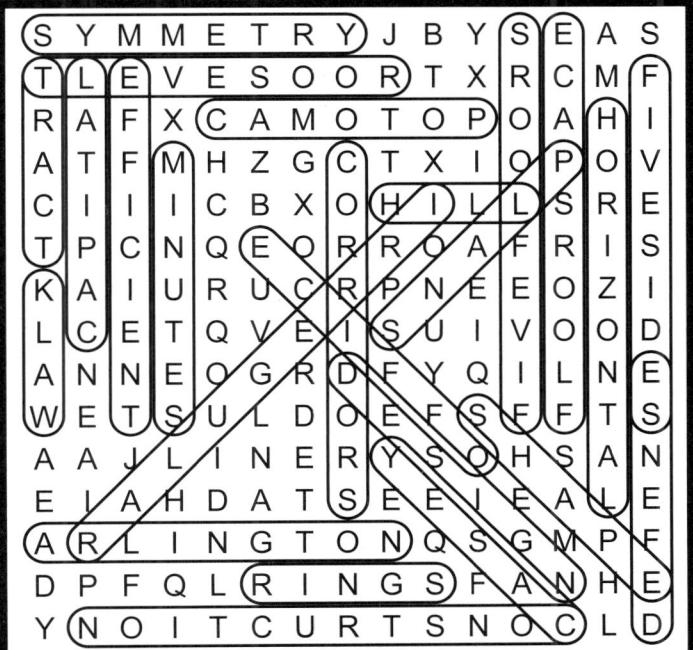

SOLUTIONS

43

45

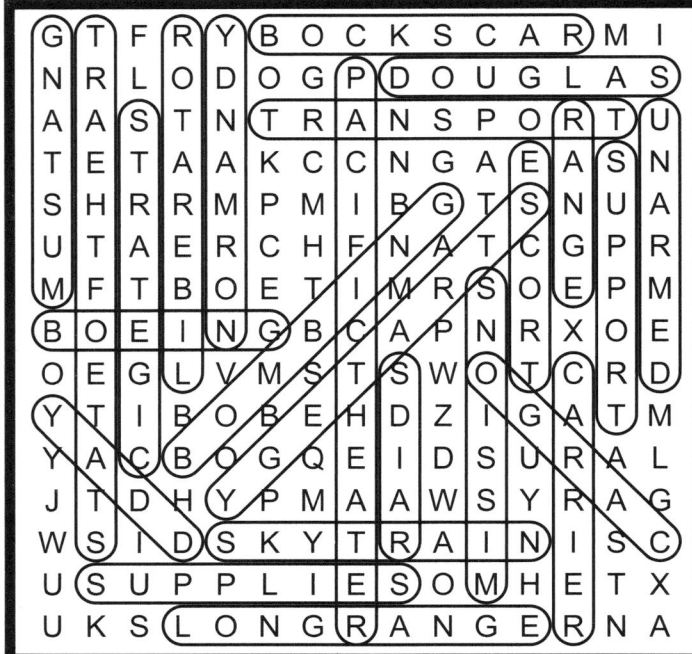

47

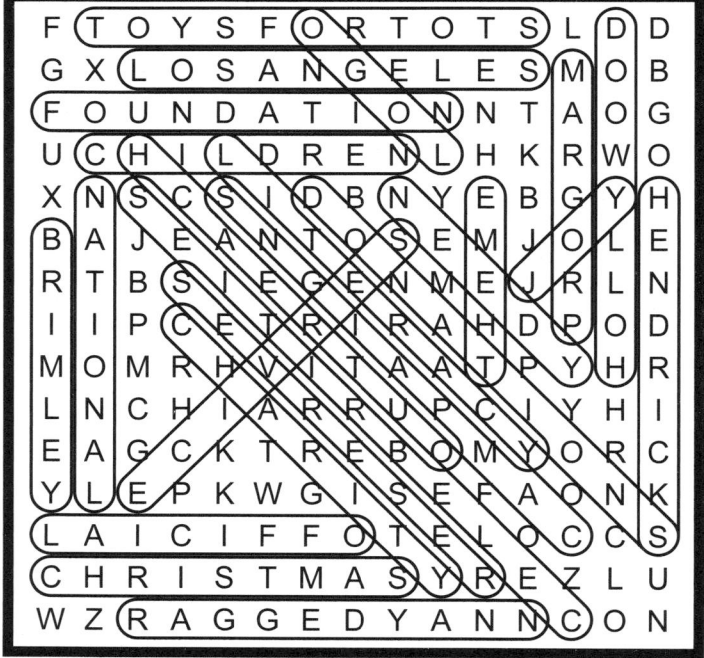

49

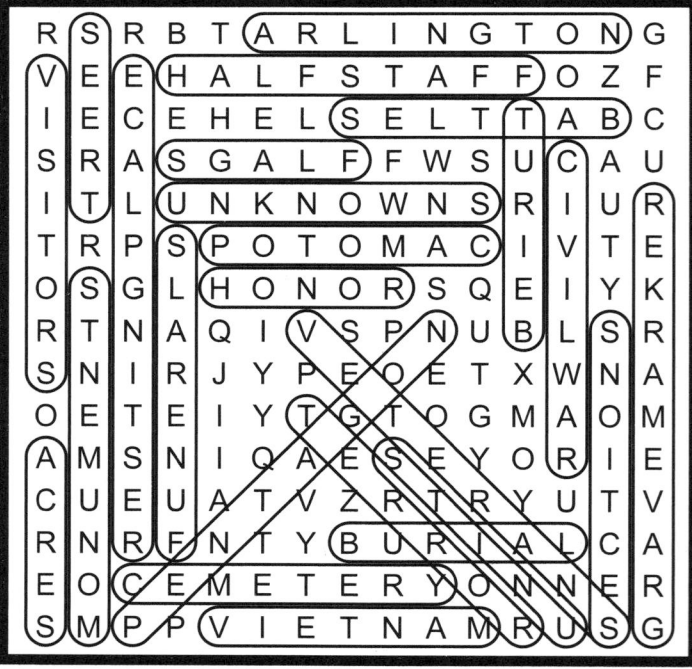

SOLUTIONS

51
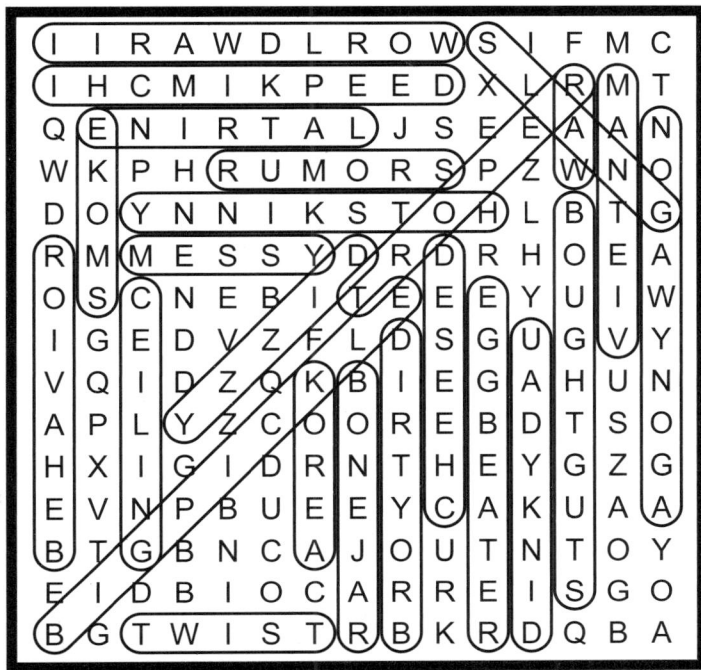

53
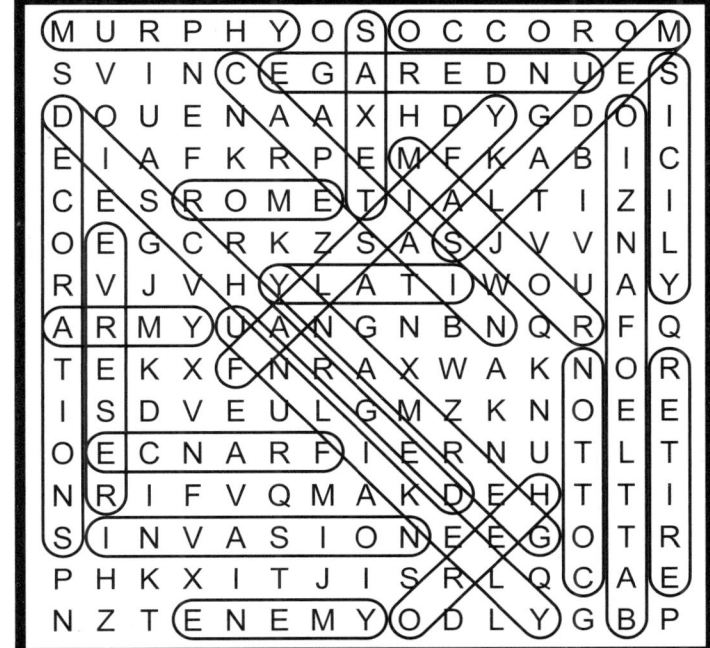

55
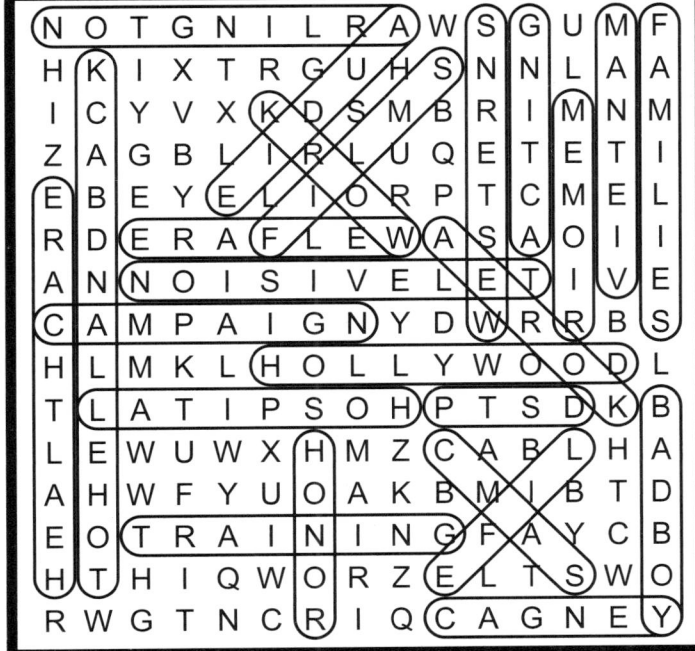

57
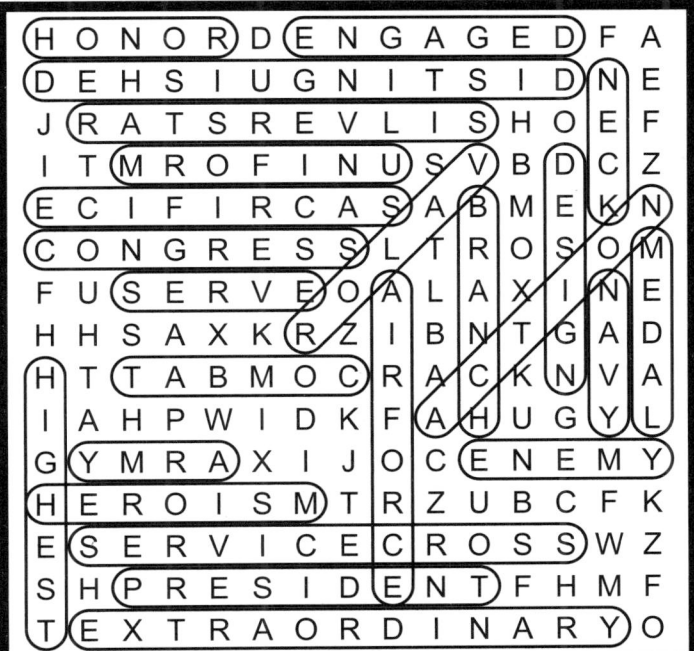

SOLUTIONS

59

61

63

65

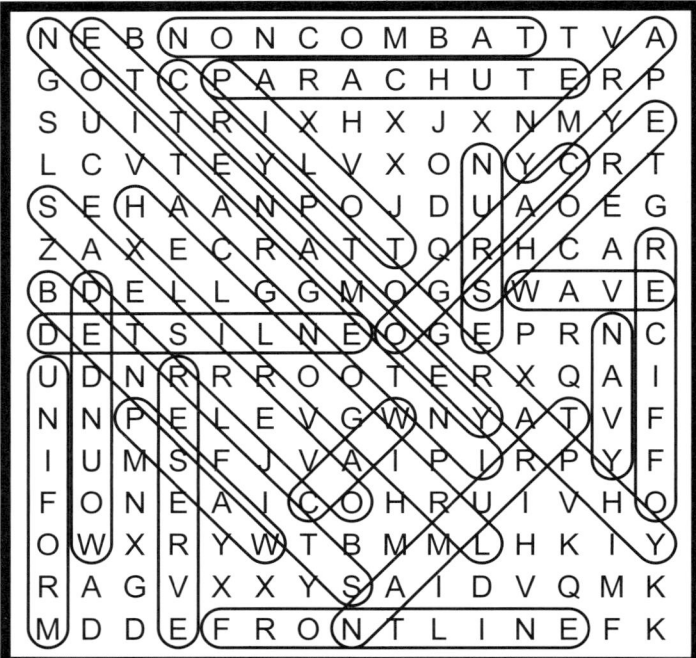
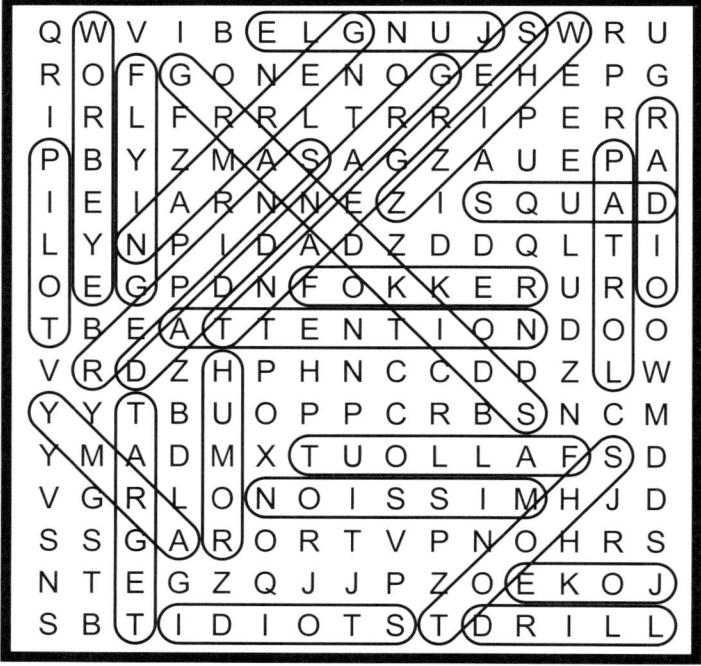
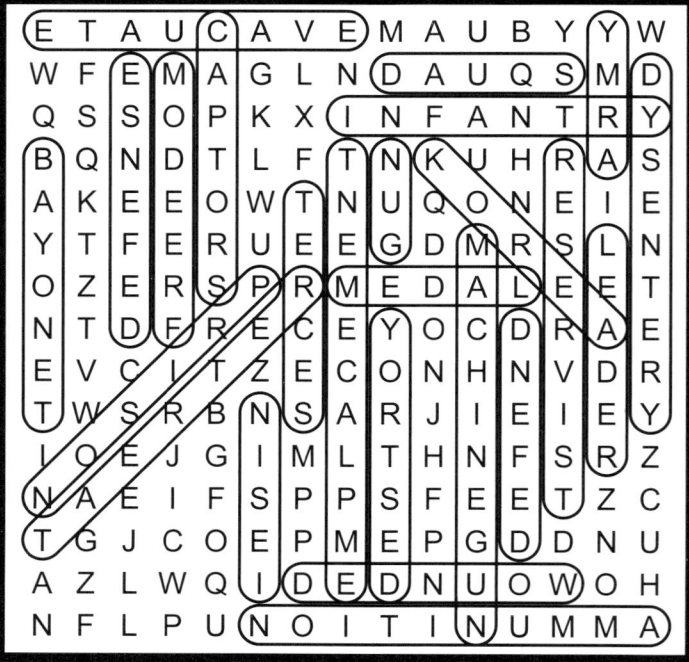

SOLUTIONS

67

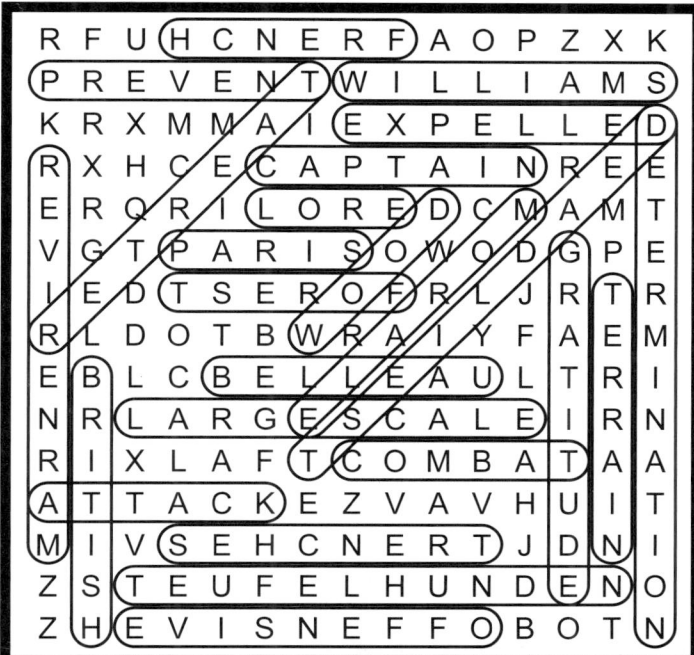

69

71

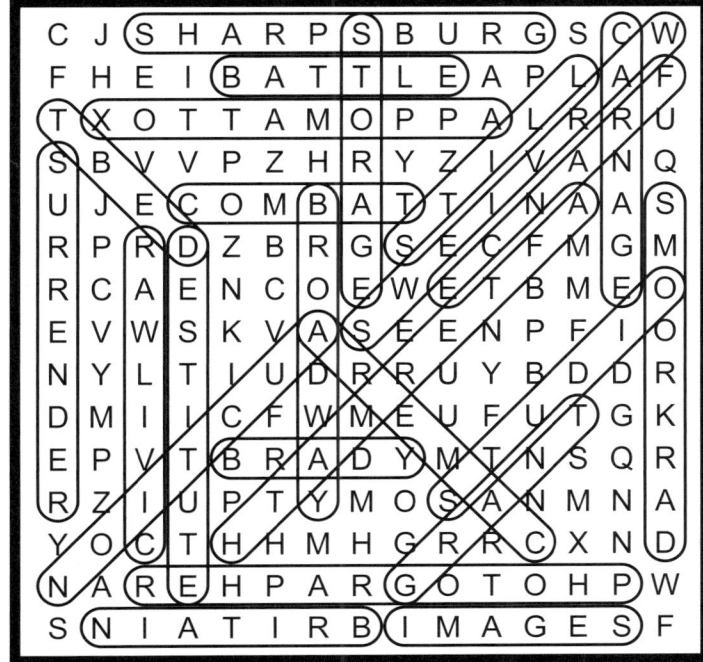

73

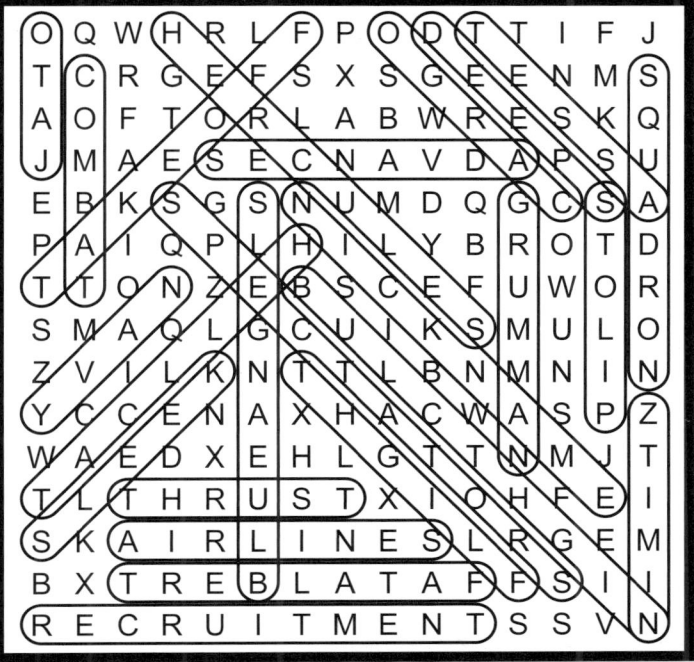

SOLUTIONS

75

77

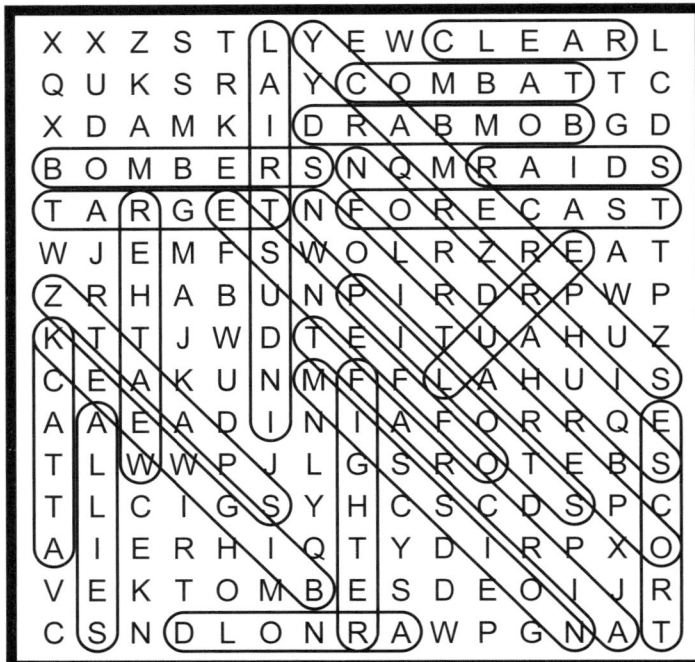

79

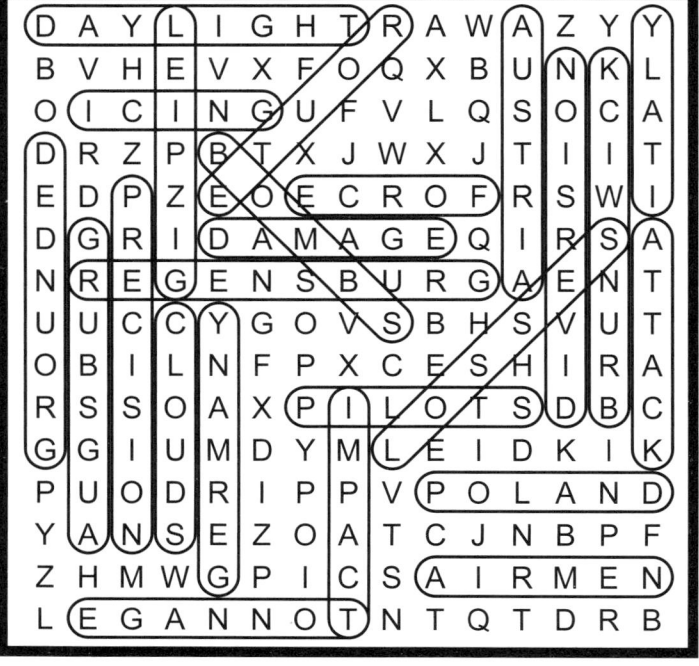

81

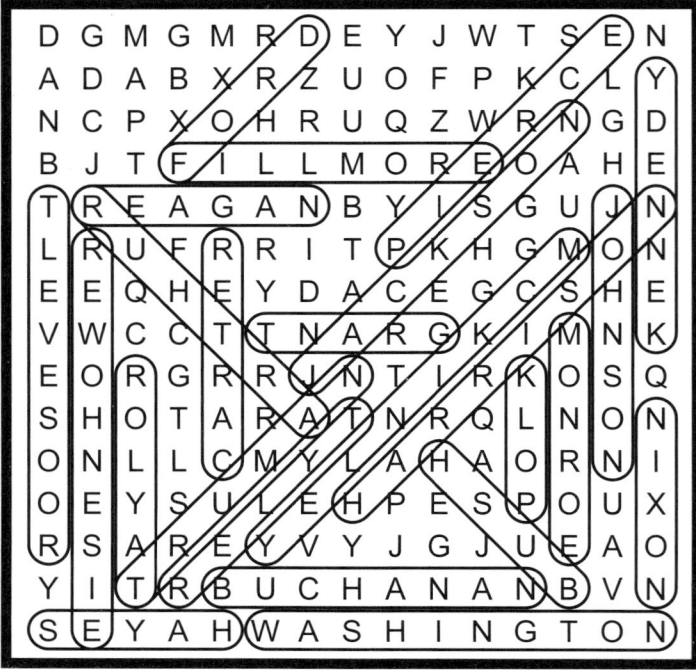

SOLUTIONS

83

85

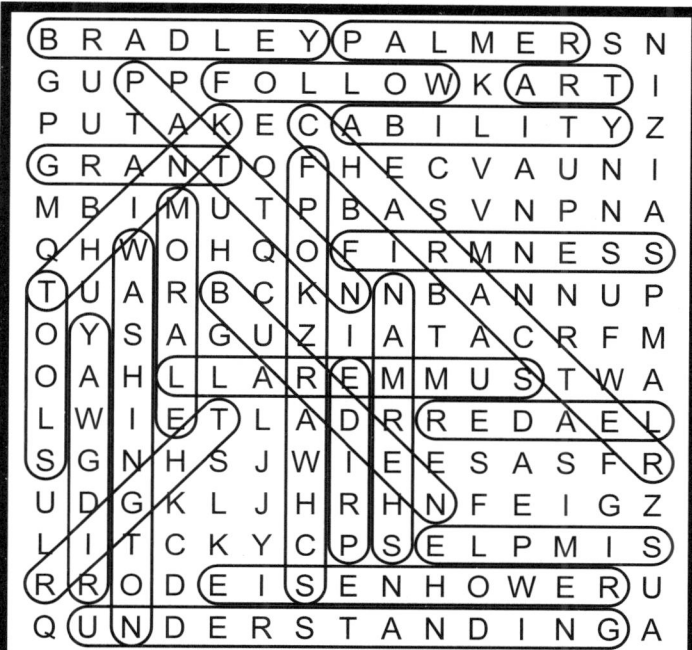

87

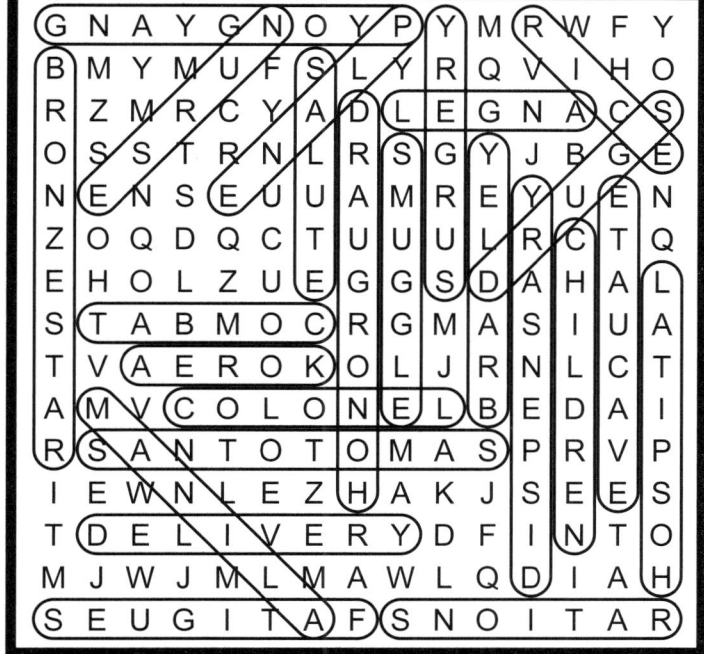

89

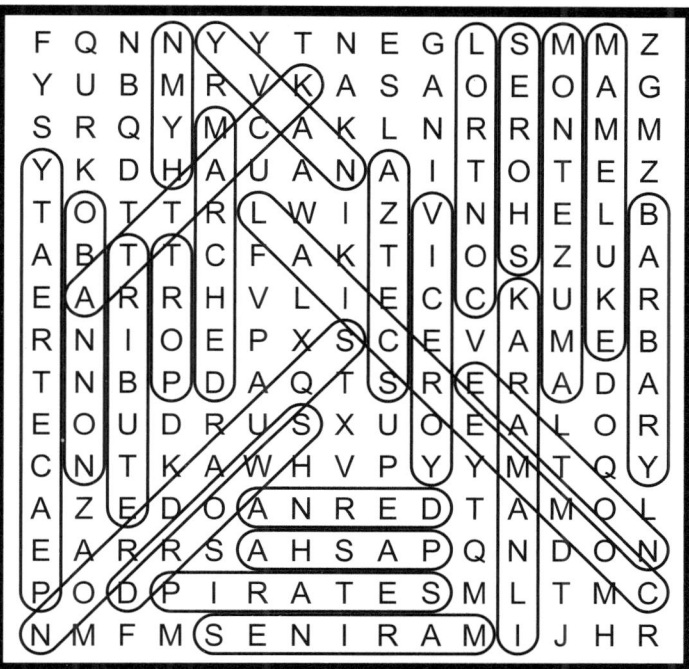

SOLUTIONS

91

93

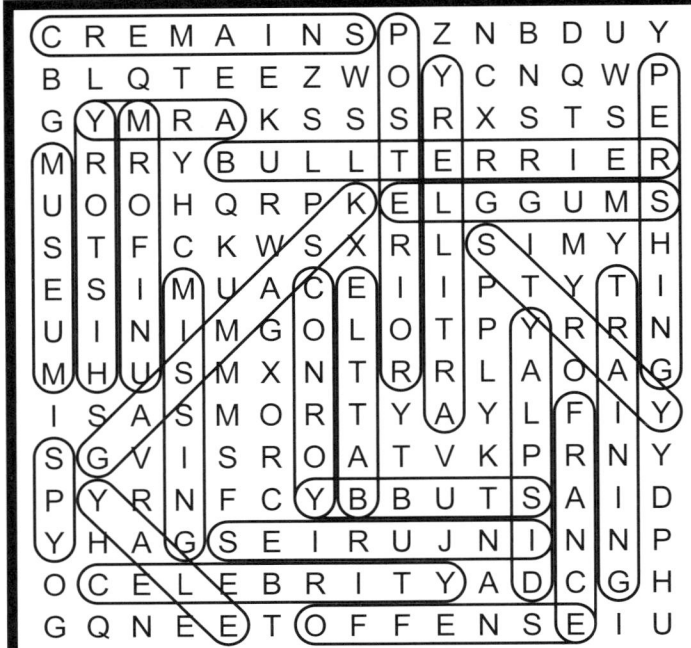

95

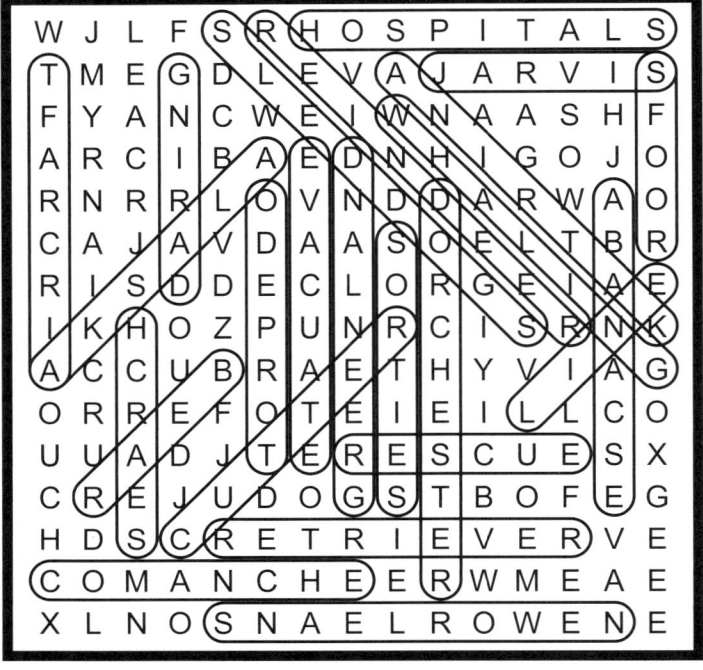

97

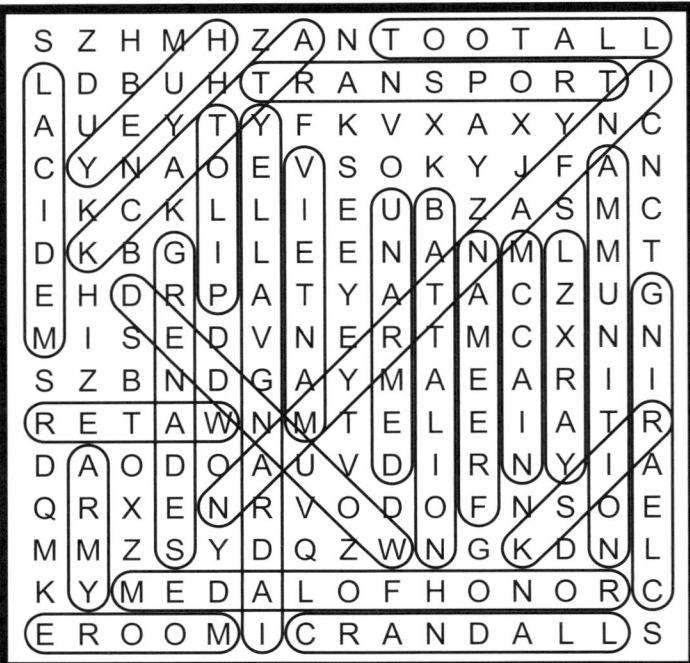

SOLUTIONS

99

101

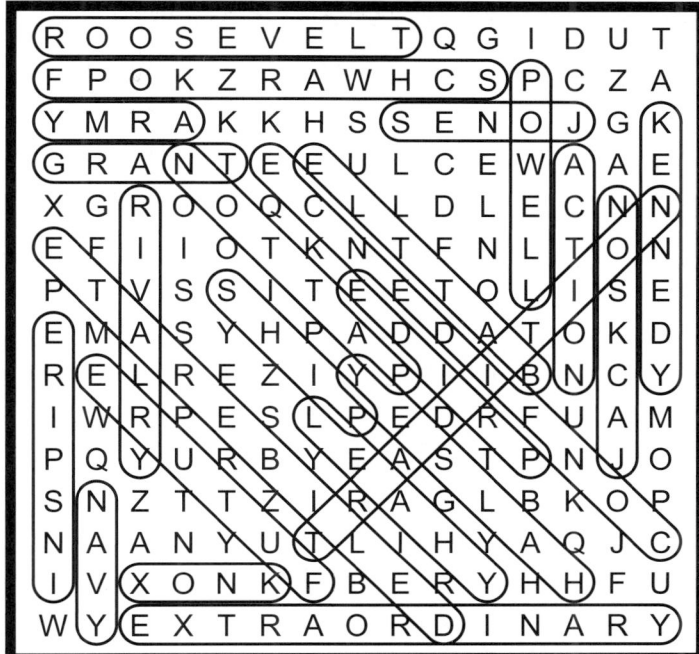

103

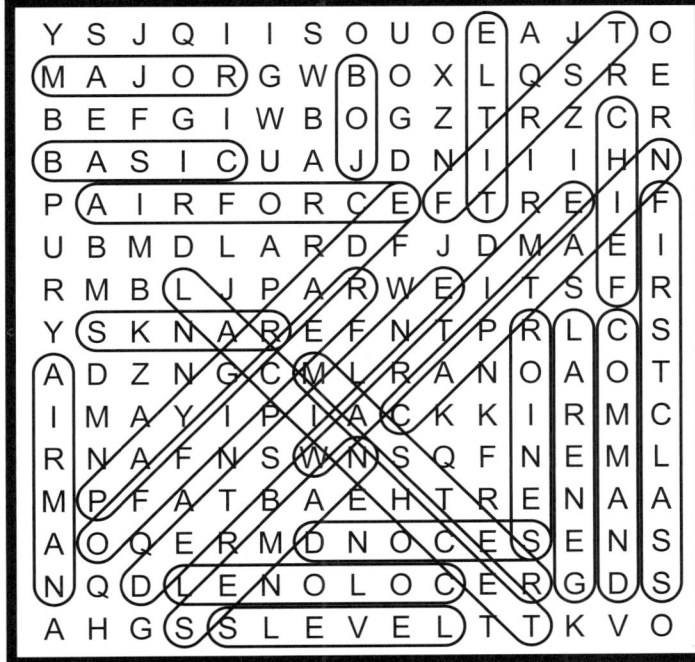

105

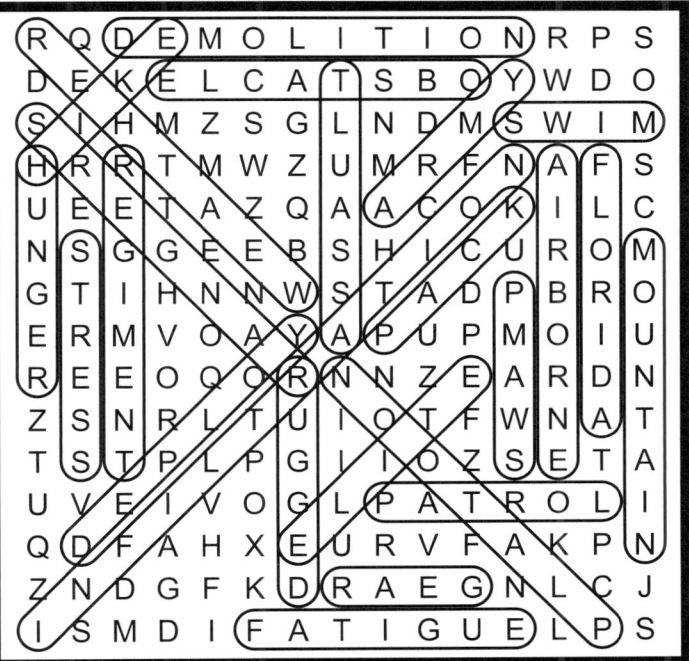

SOLUTIONS

107
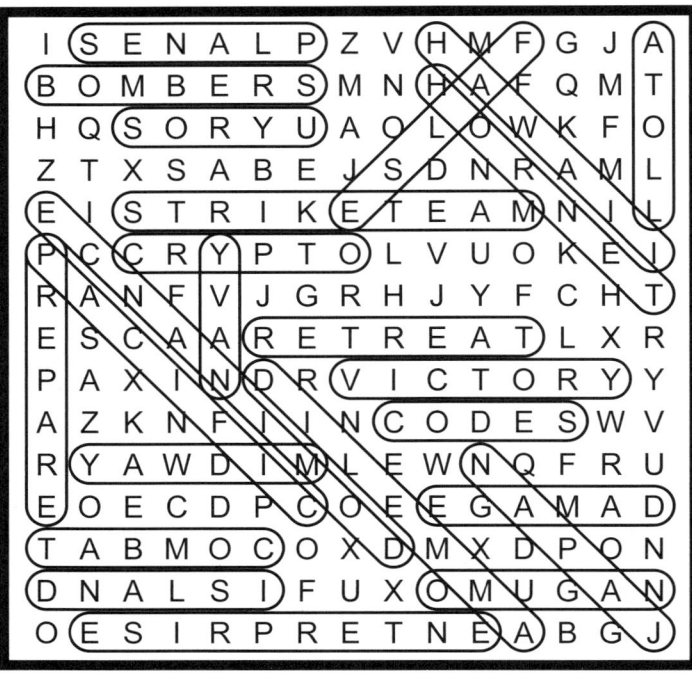

109
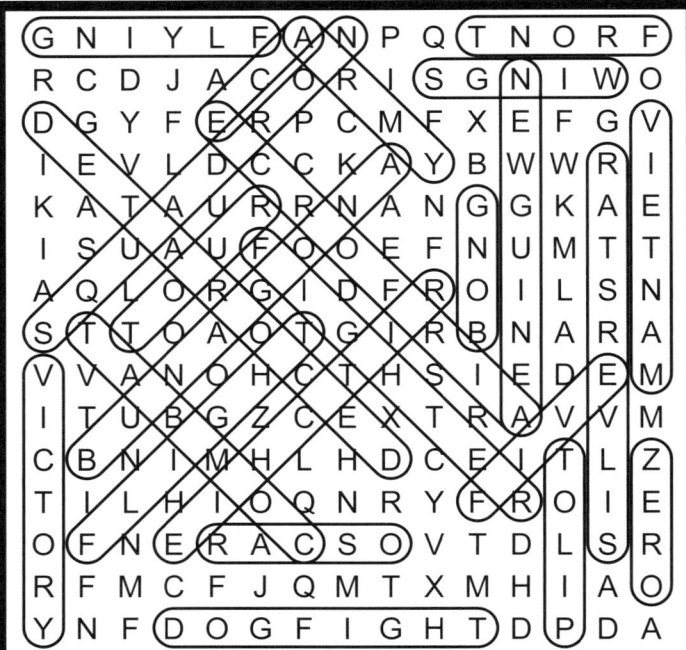

111
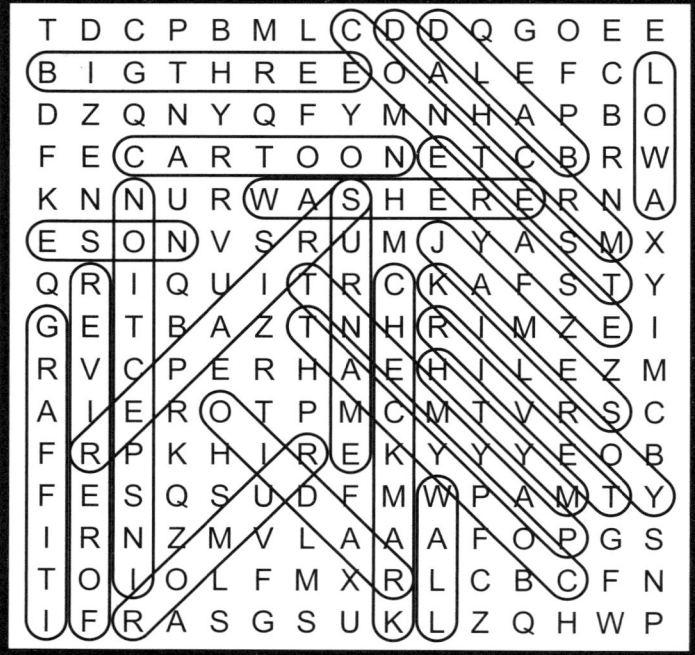

113
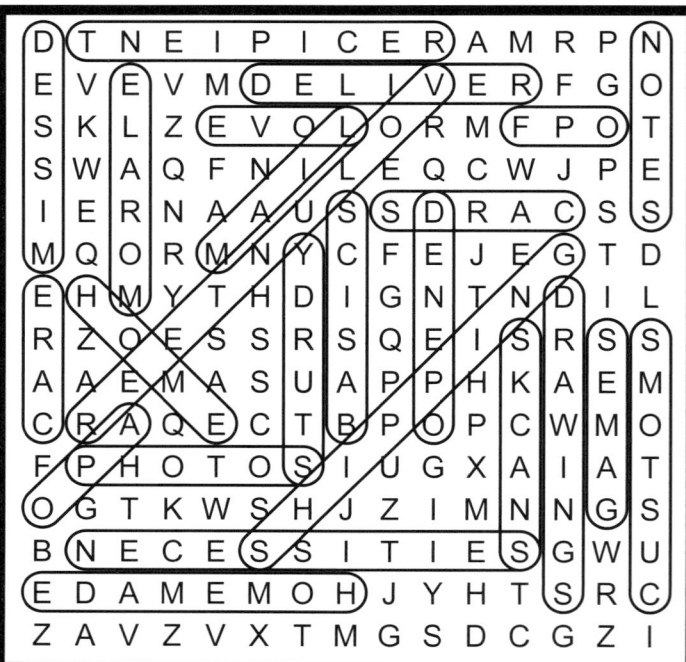

SOLUTIONS

115

117

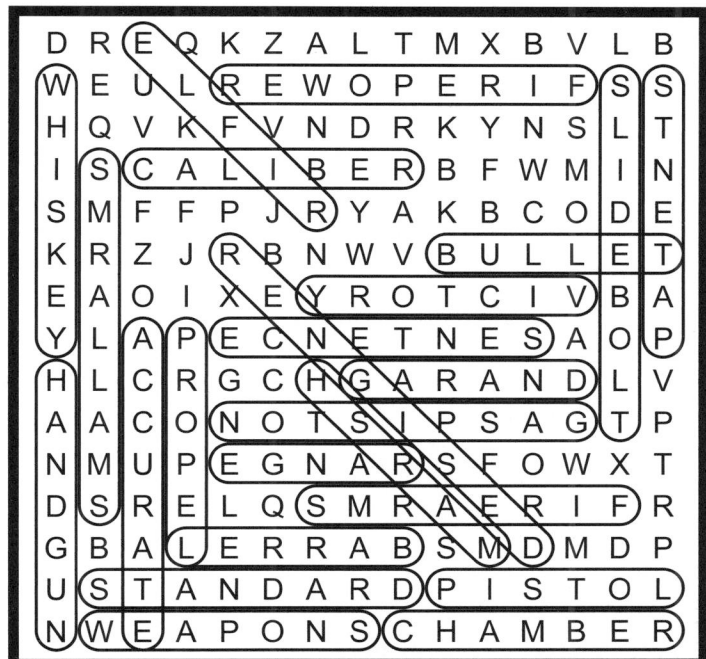

119

121

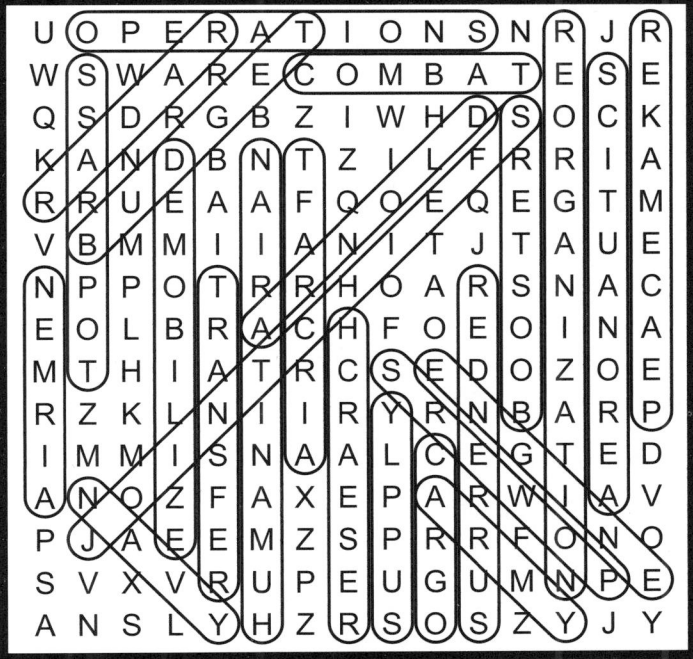

SOLUTIONS

123

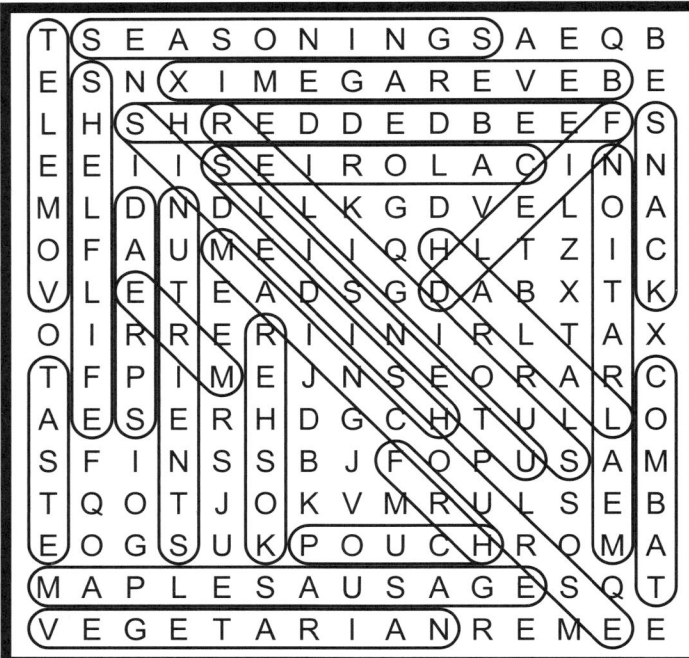

125

127

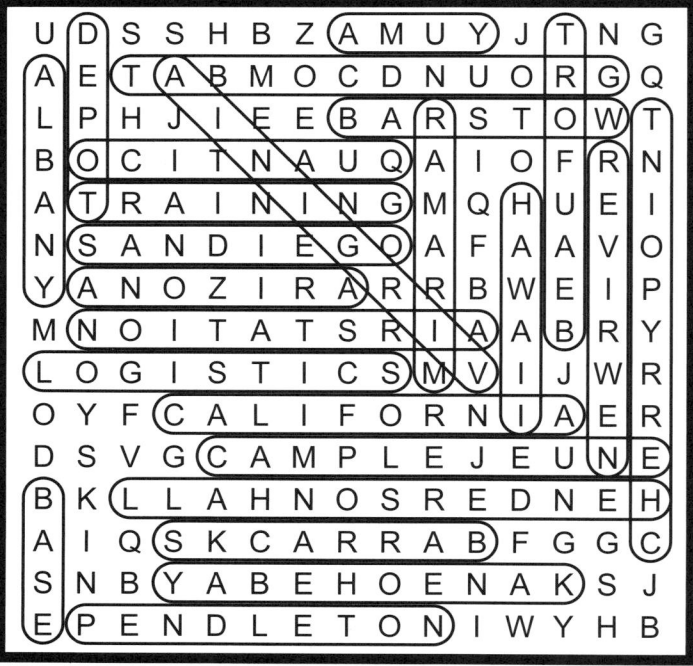

129

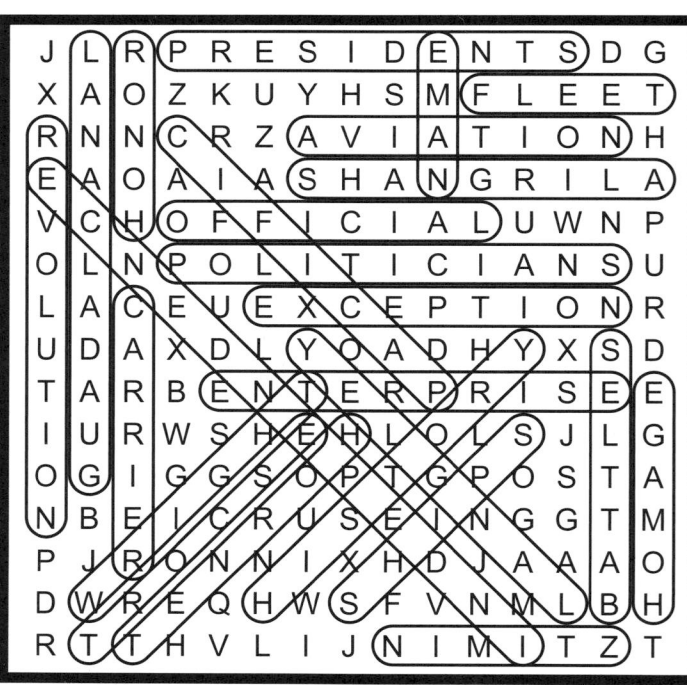

SOLUTIONS

131

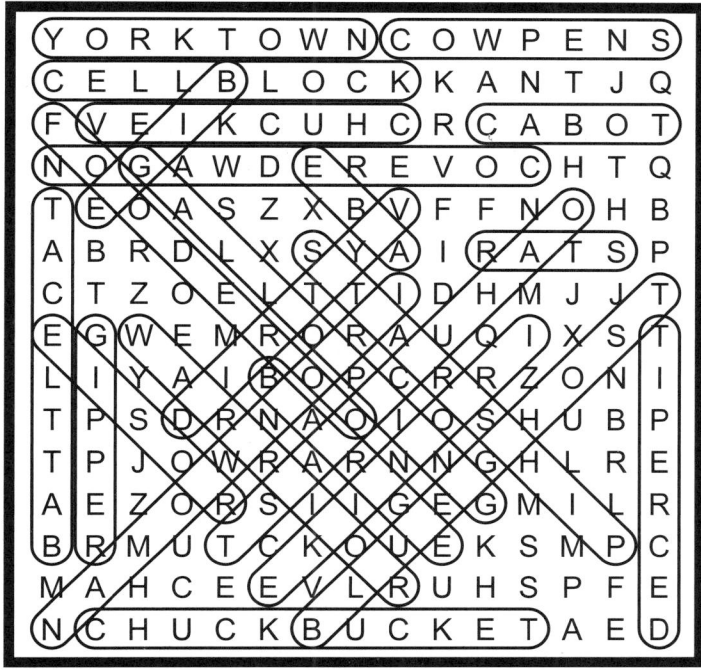

133

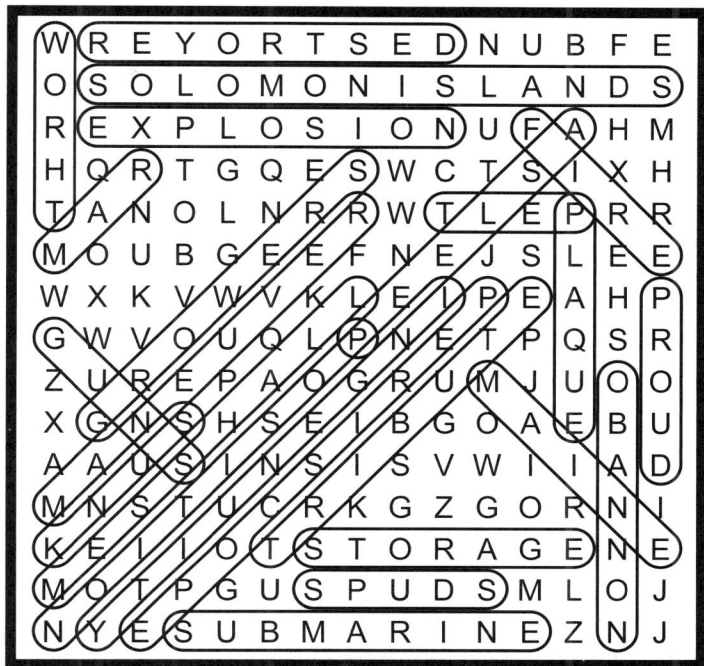

135

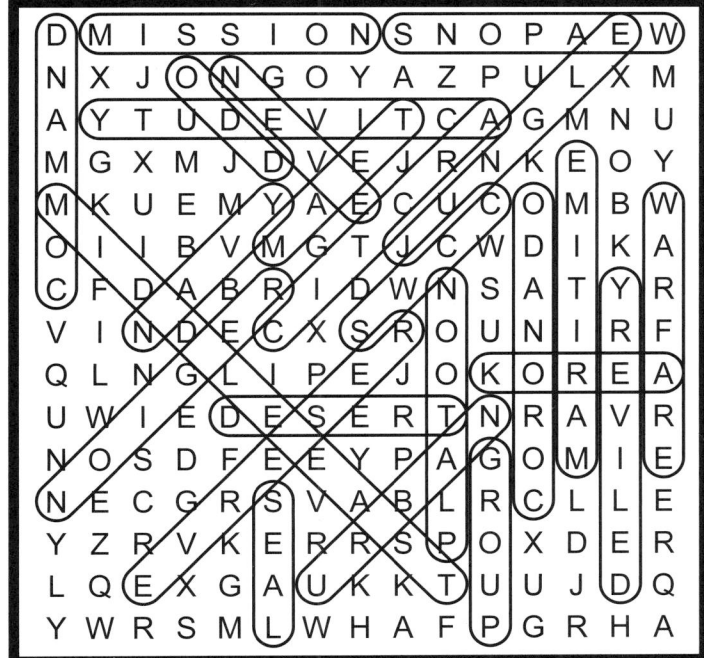

137

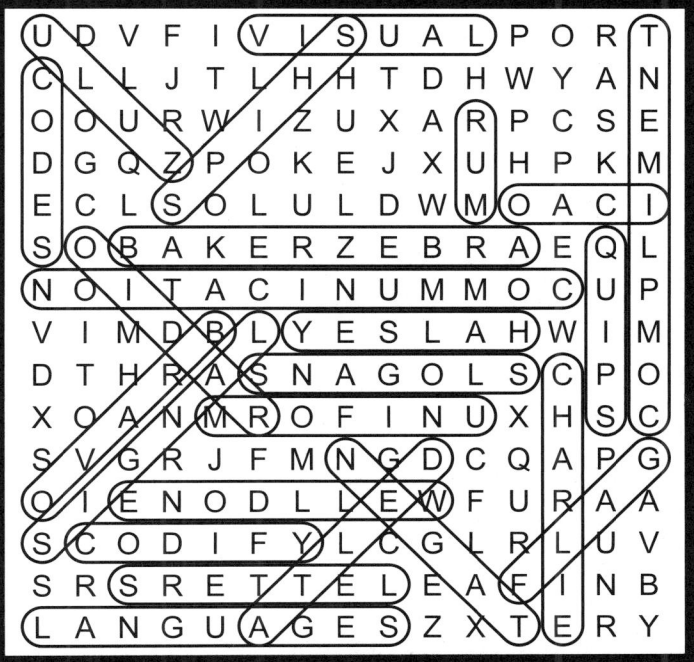

SOLUTIONS

139

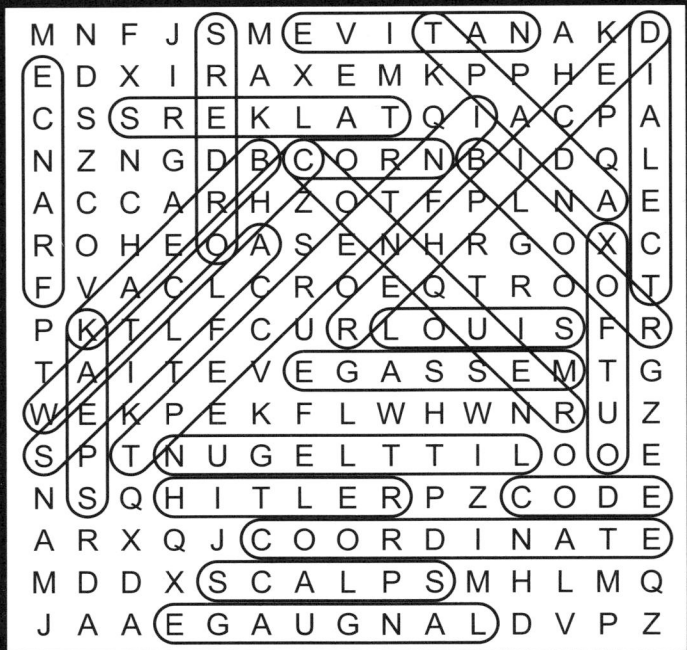

141

143

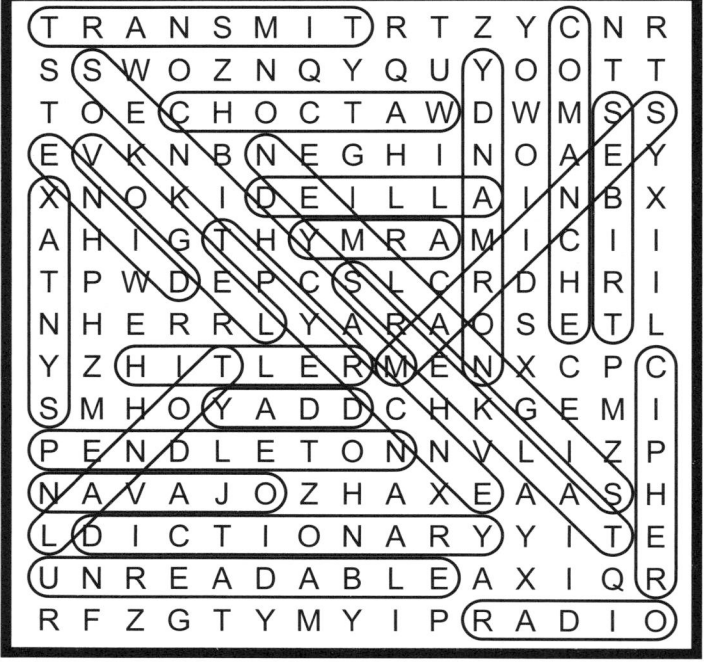

145

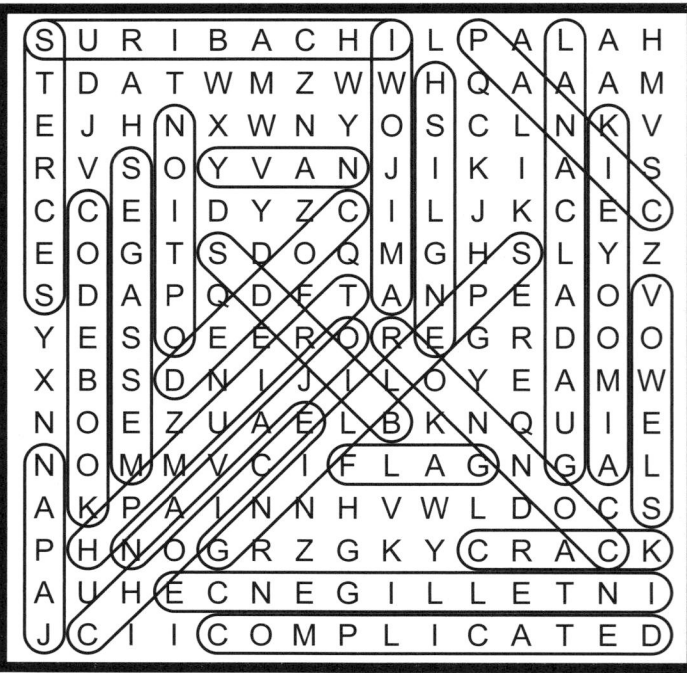

SOLUTIONS

147

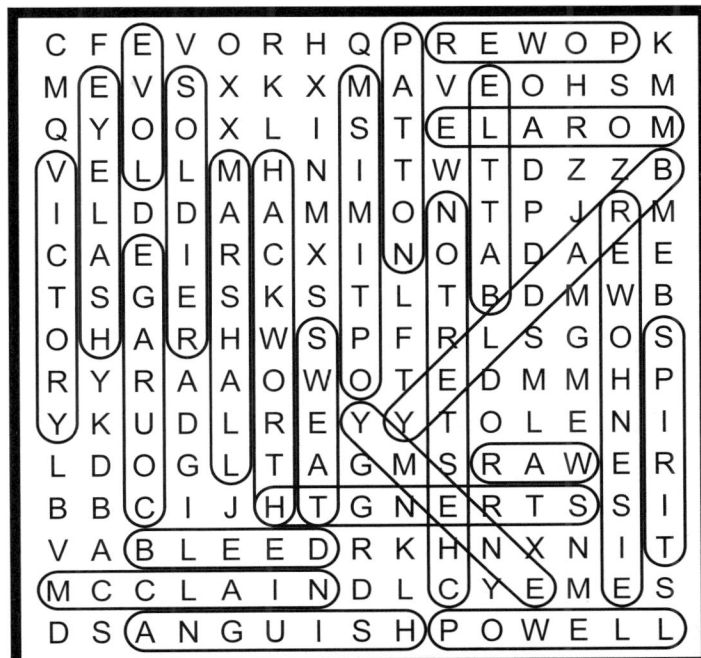

149

151

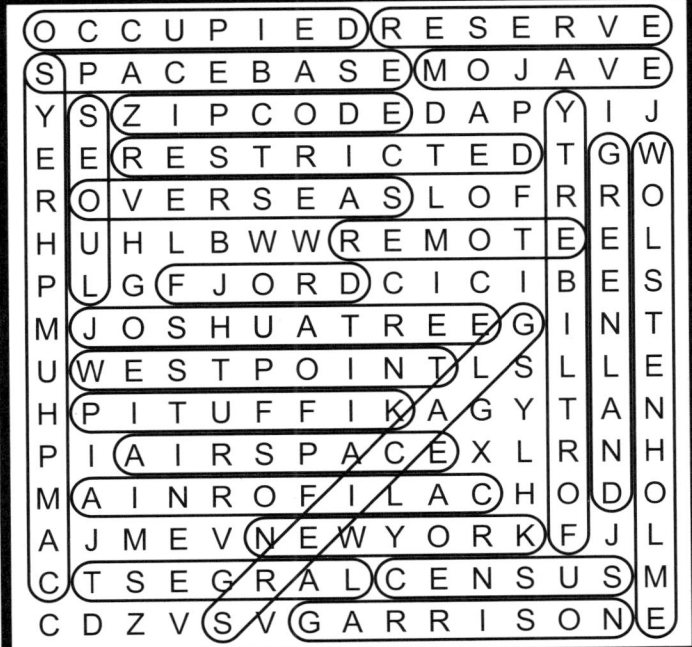

153

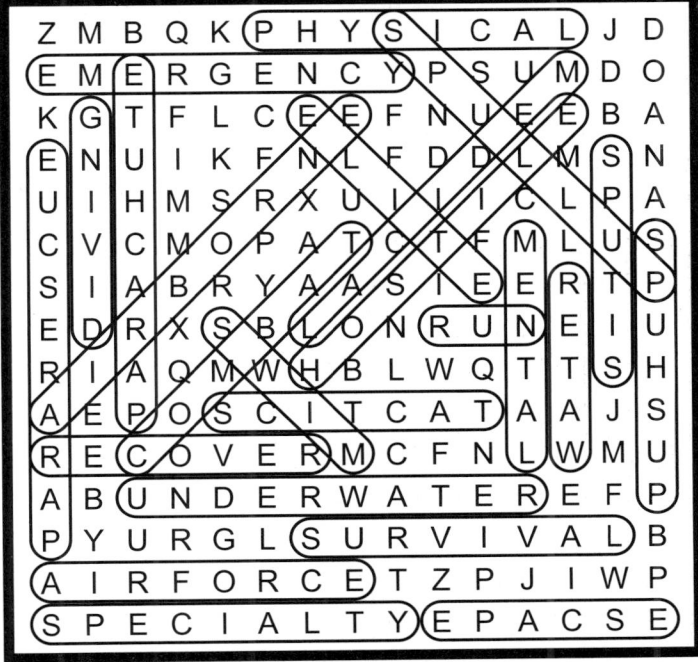

SOLUTIONS

155
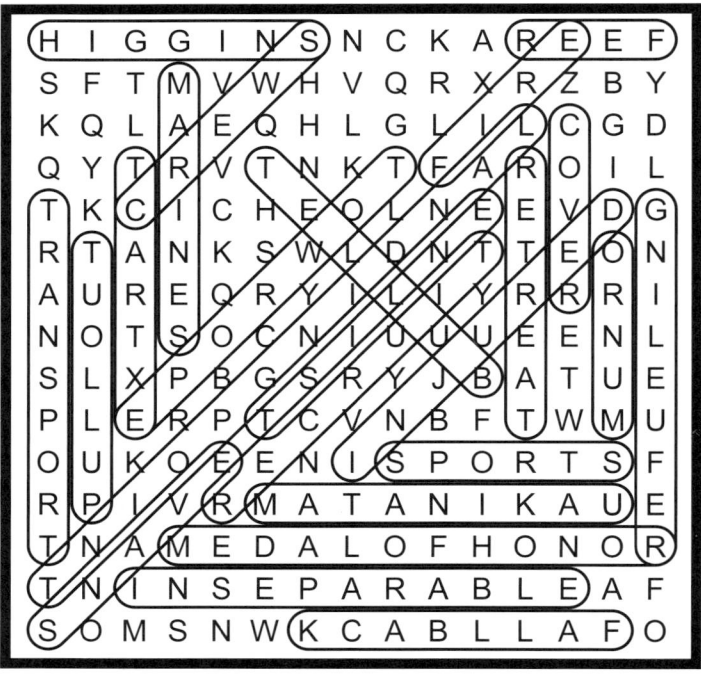

157
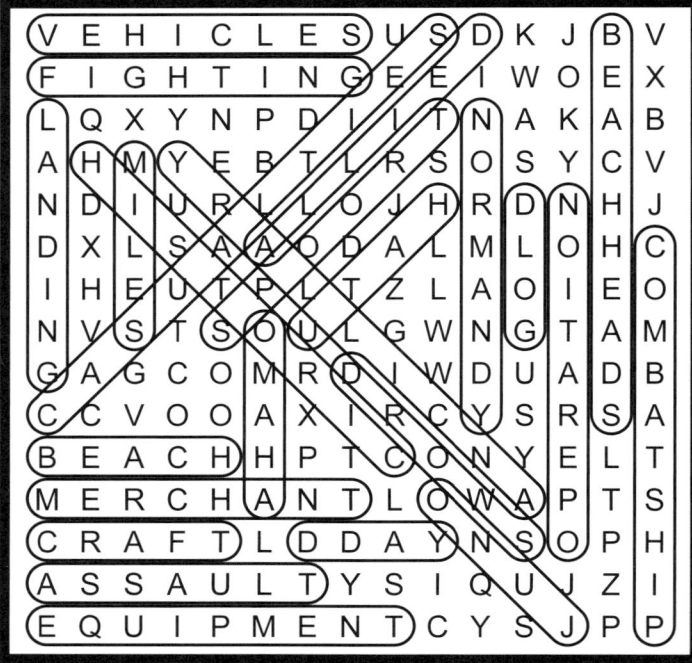

159
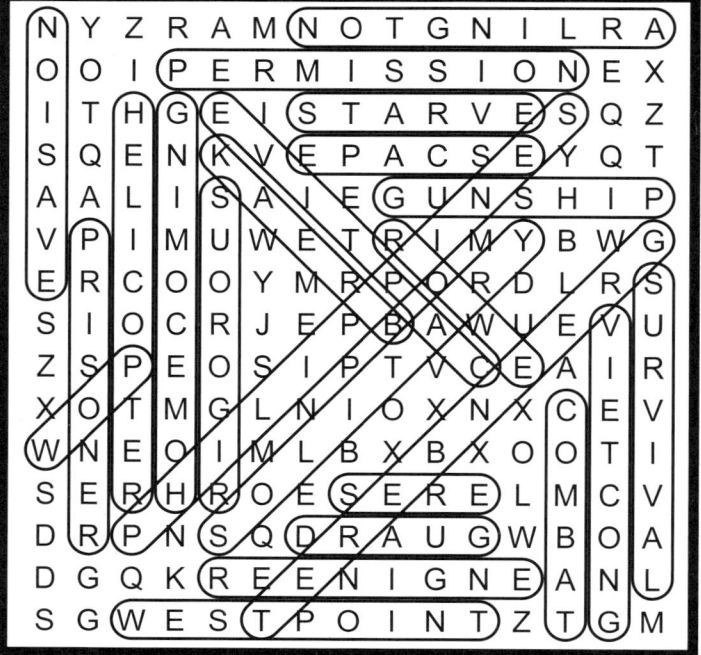

161
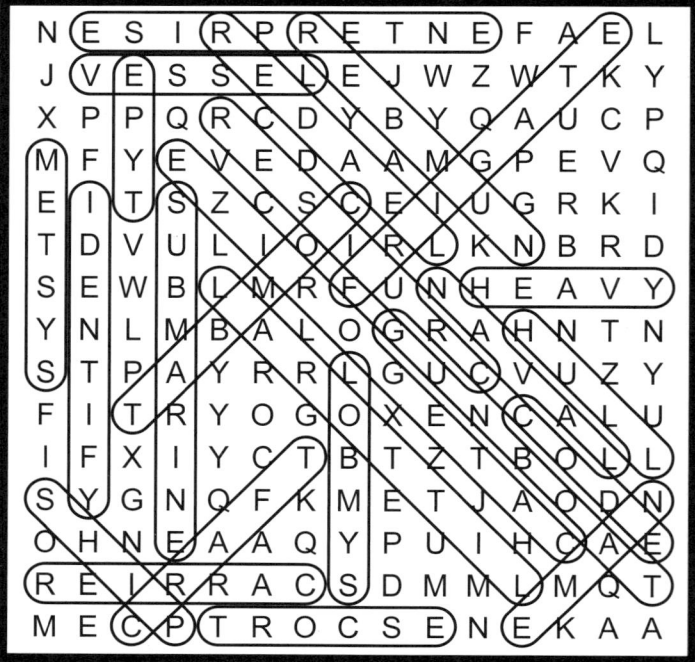

SOLUTIONS

163

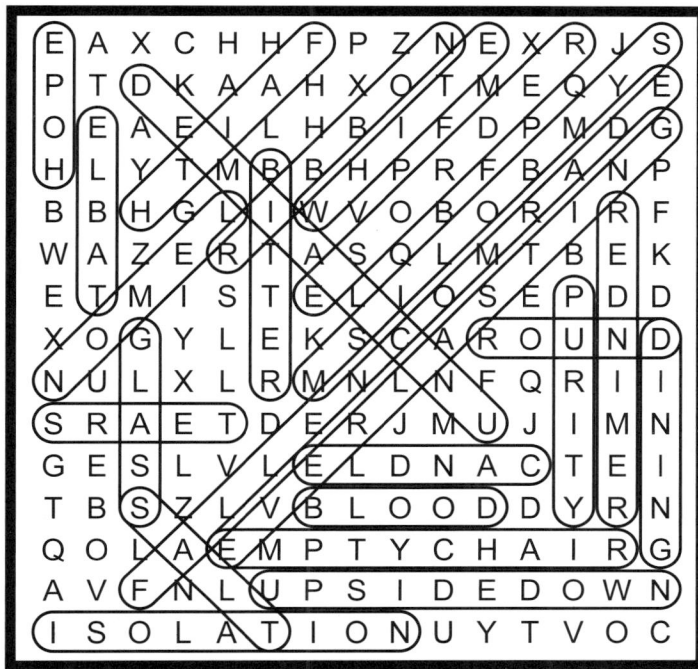

165

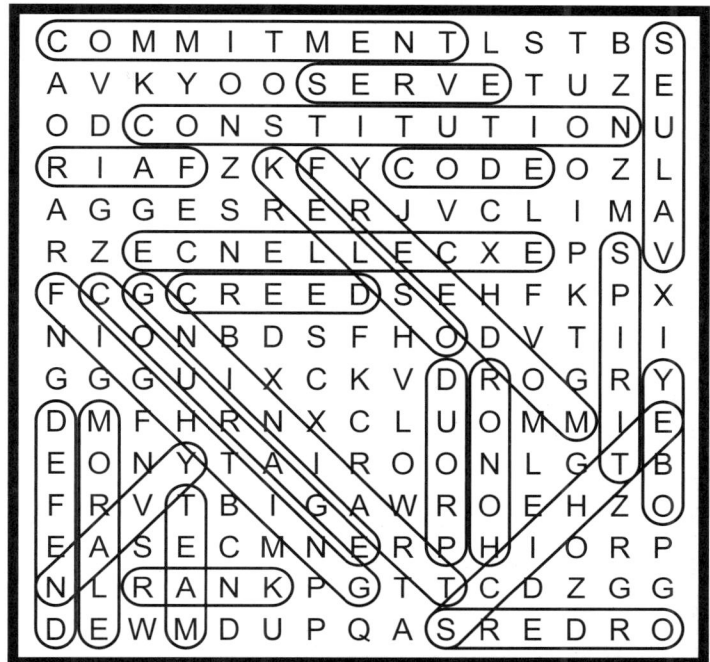

167

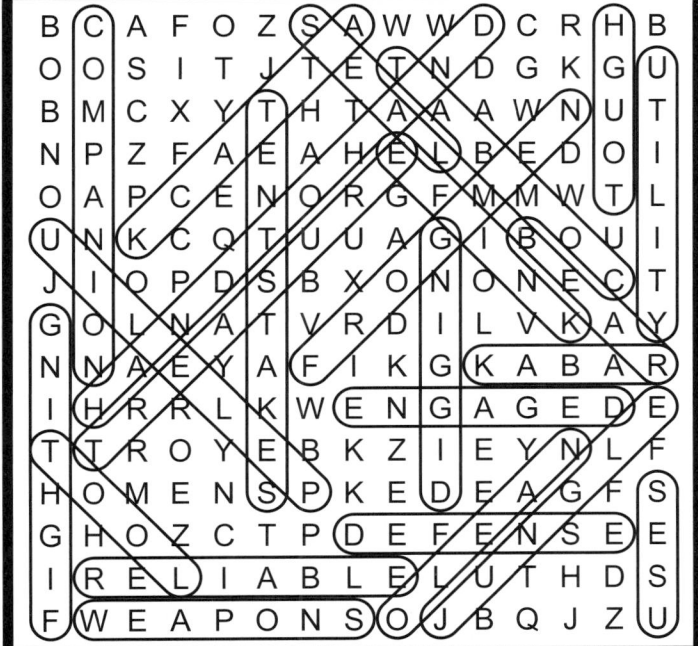

169

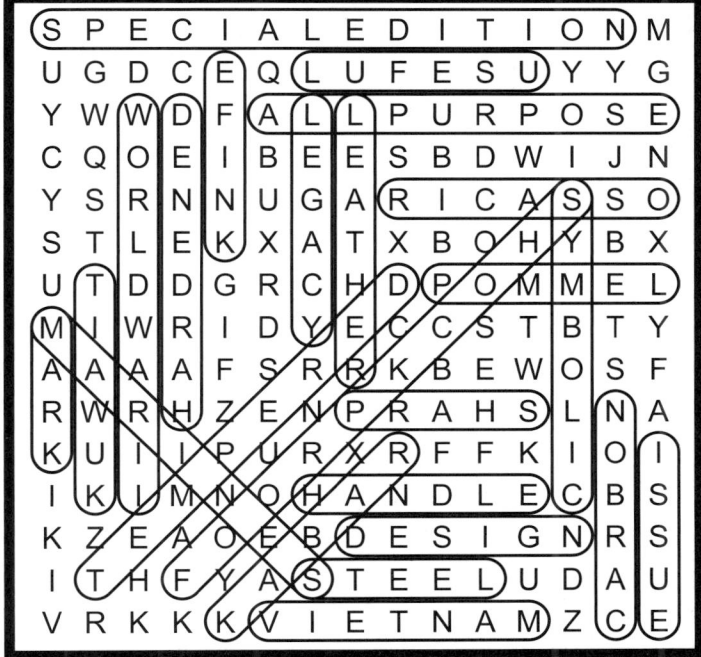

SOLUTIONS

171
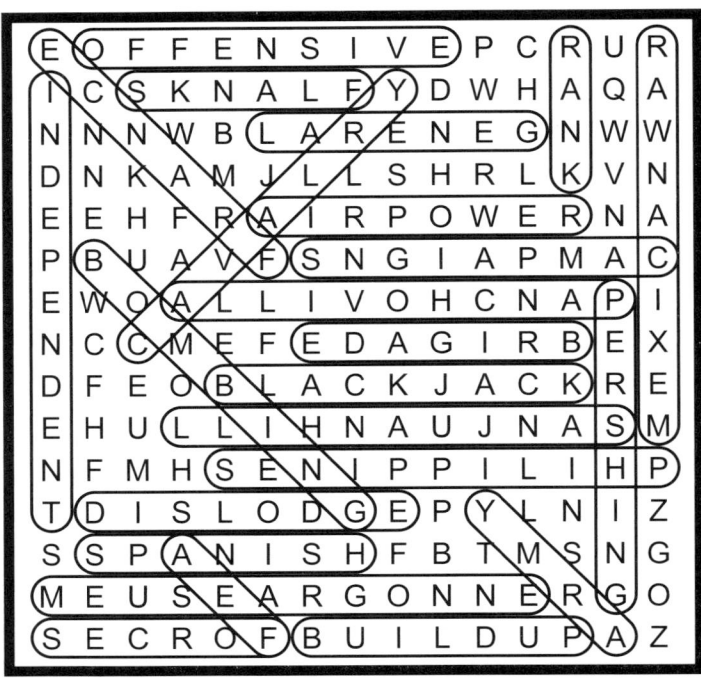

173
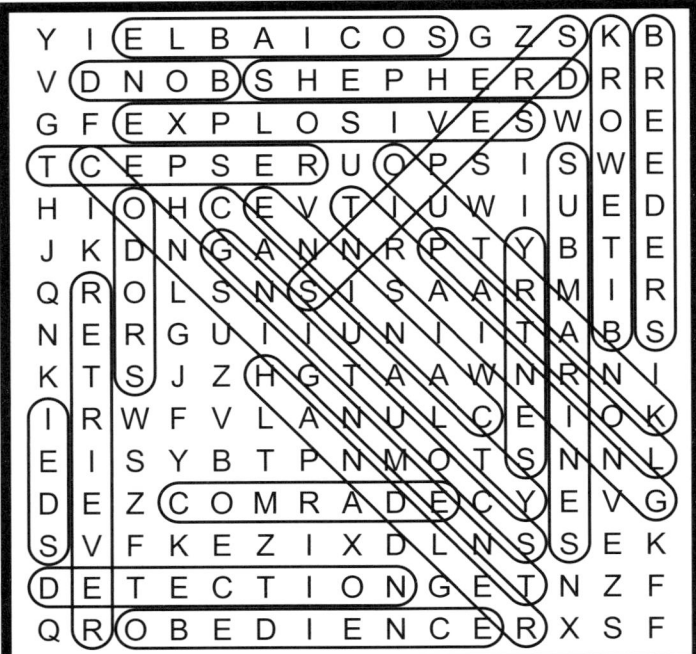

175
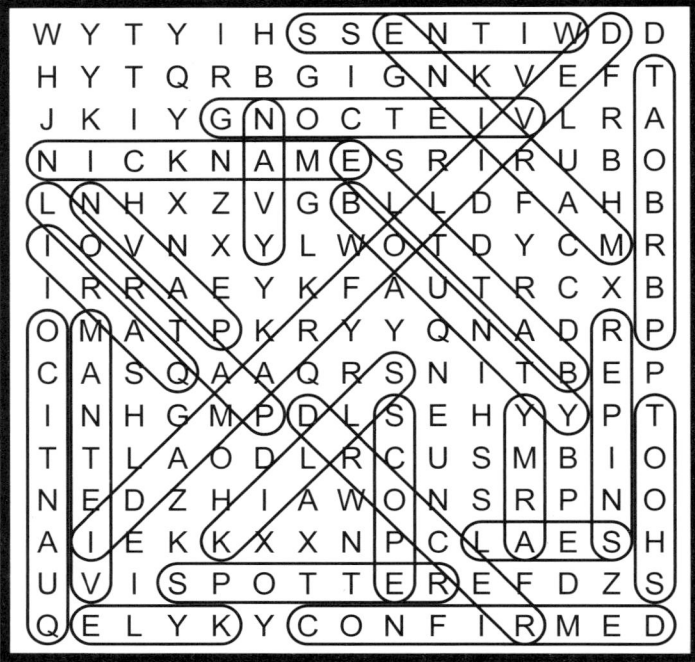

177
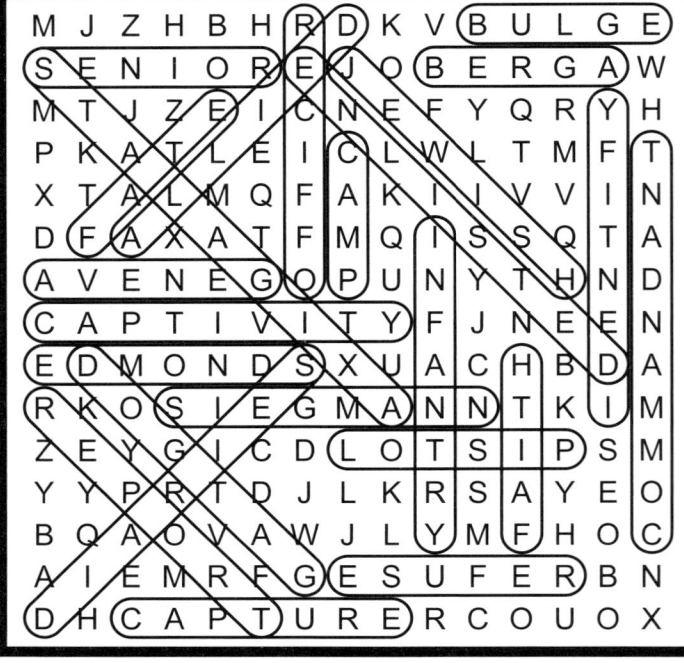

SOLUTIONS

179
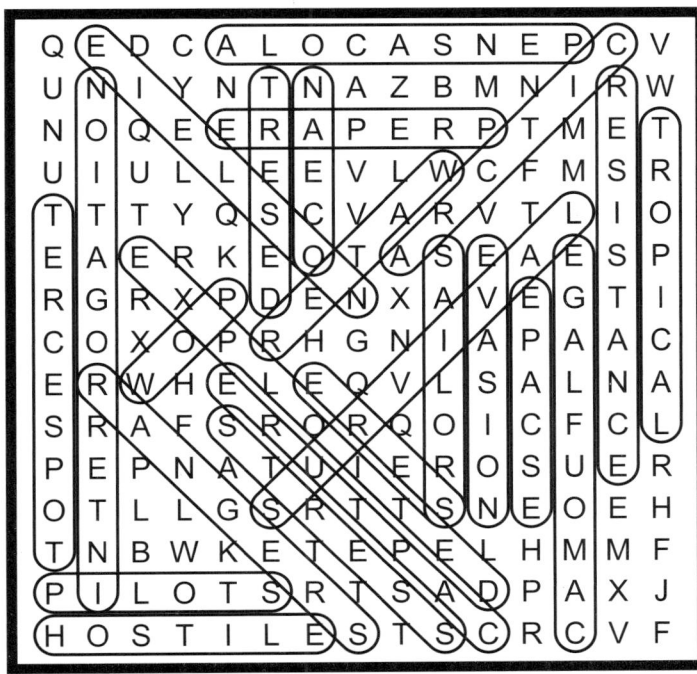

181
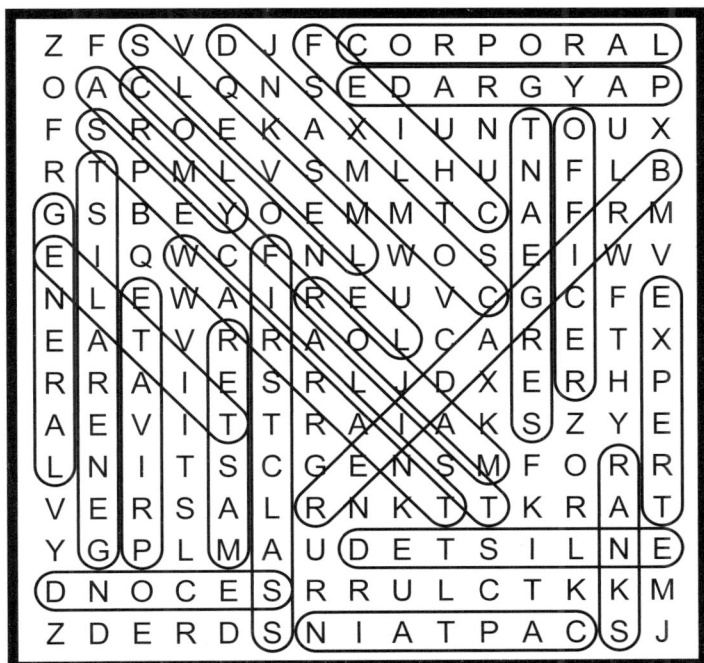

183
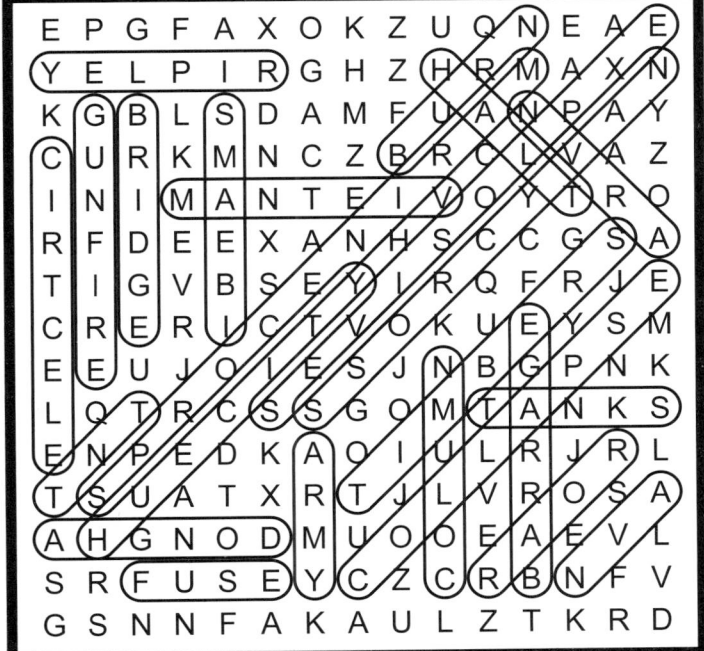

185
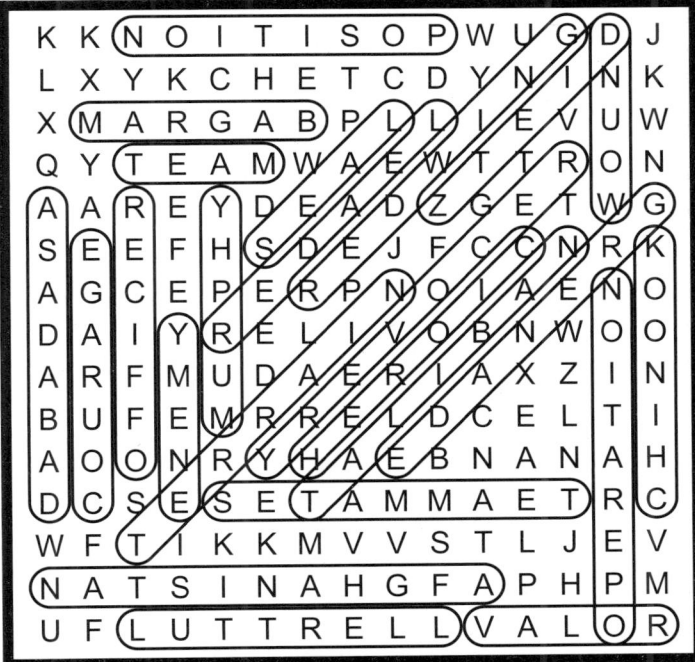

SOLUTIONS

187
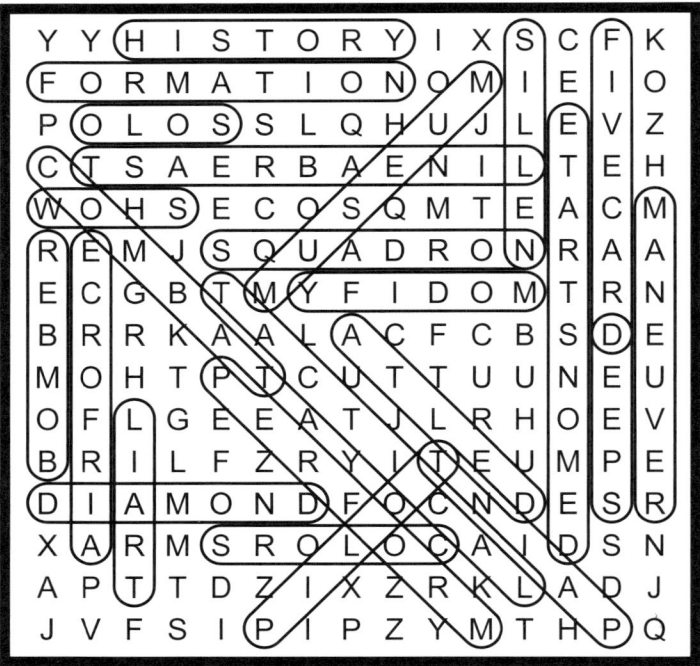

189
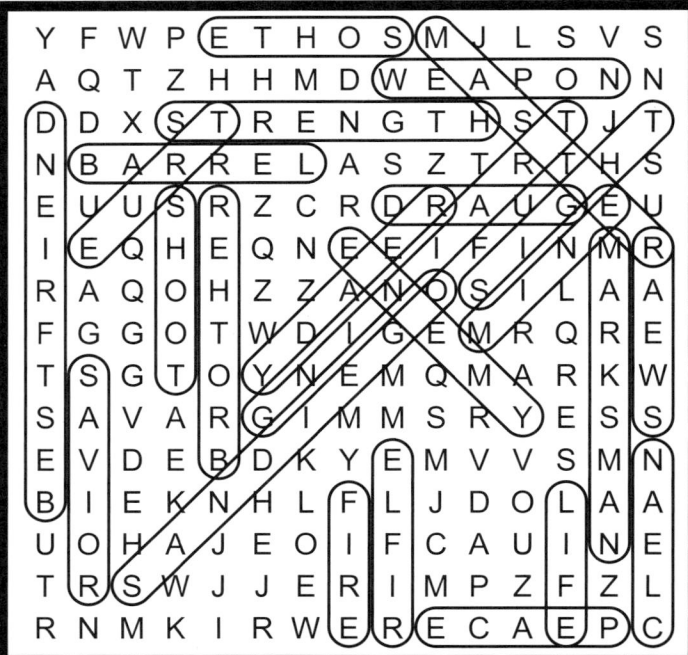

191
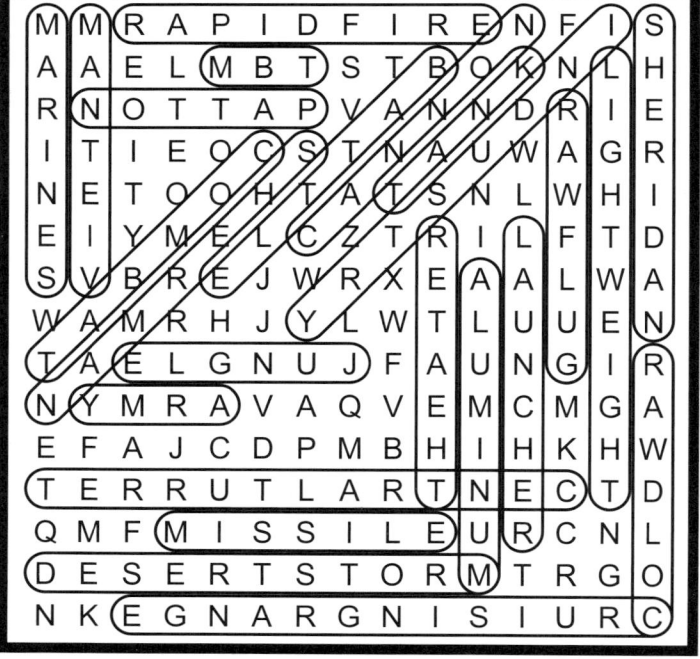

193
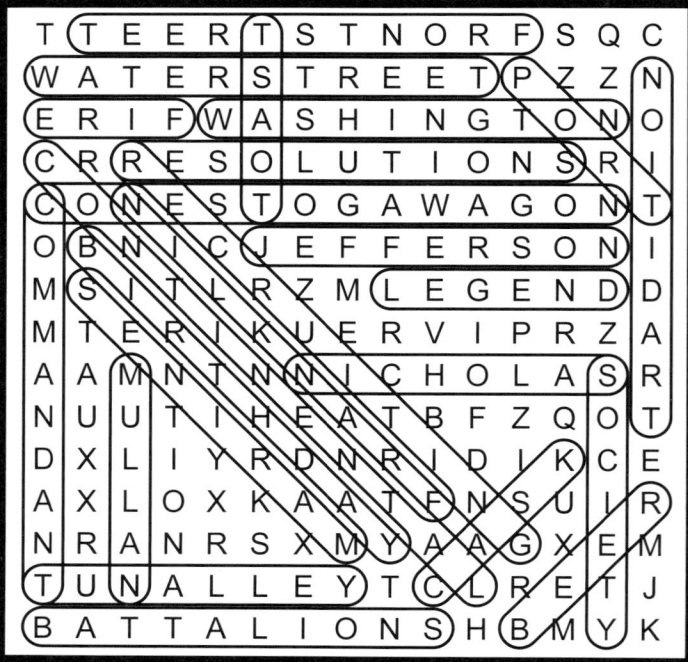

SOLUTIONS

195

197

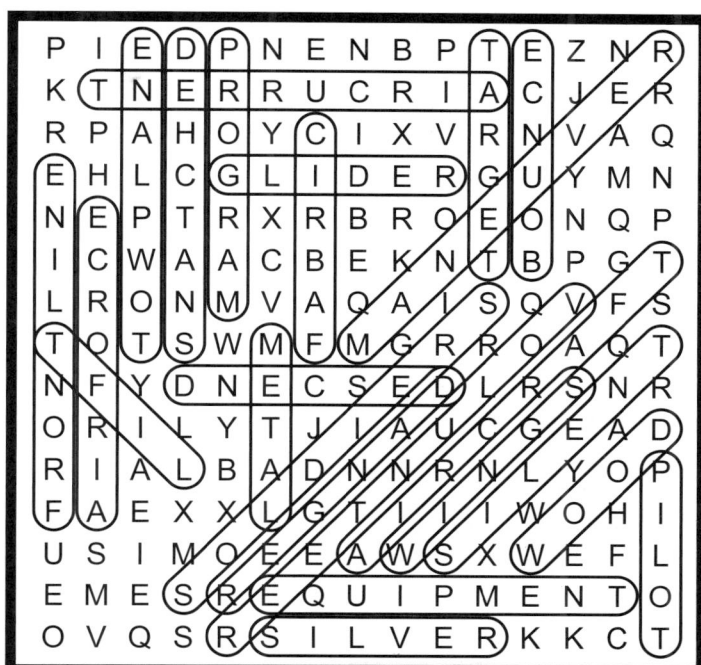

199

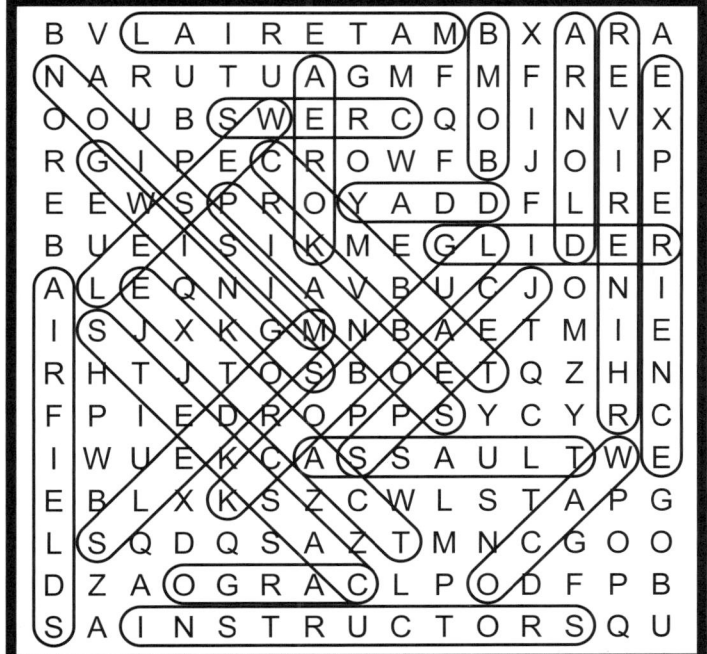

201

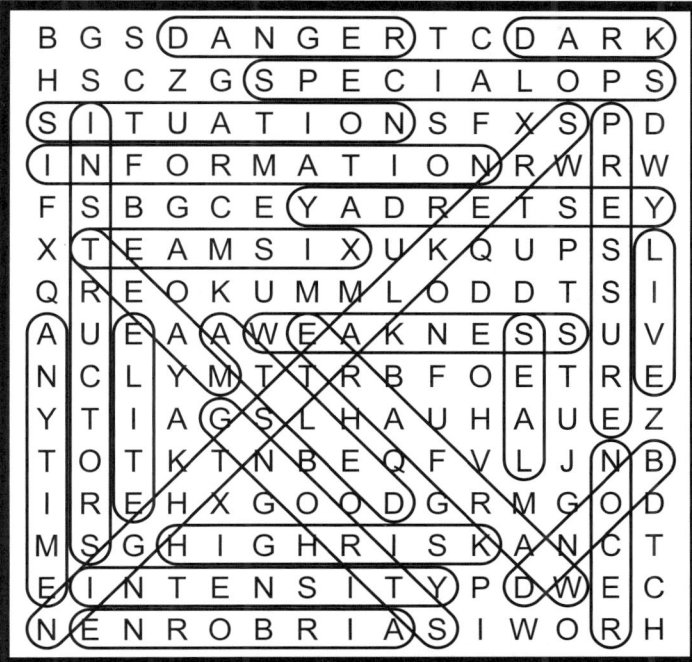

SOLUTIONS

203

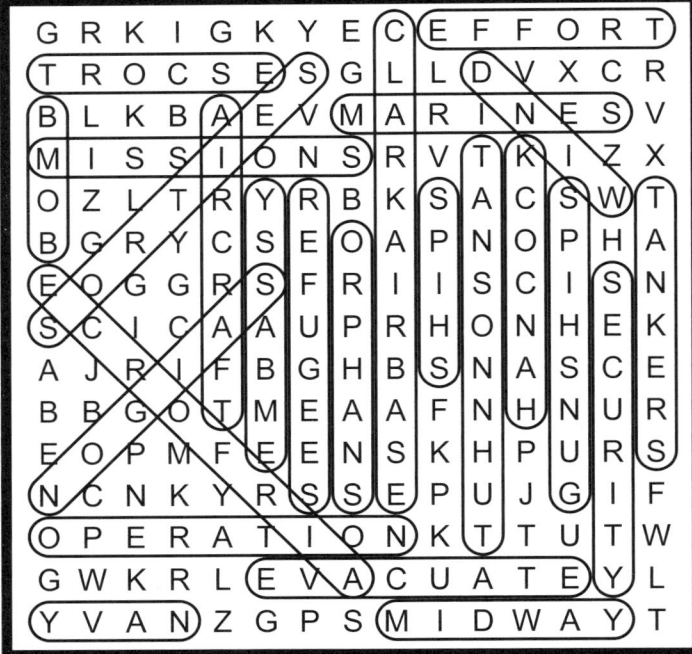

205

207

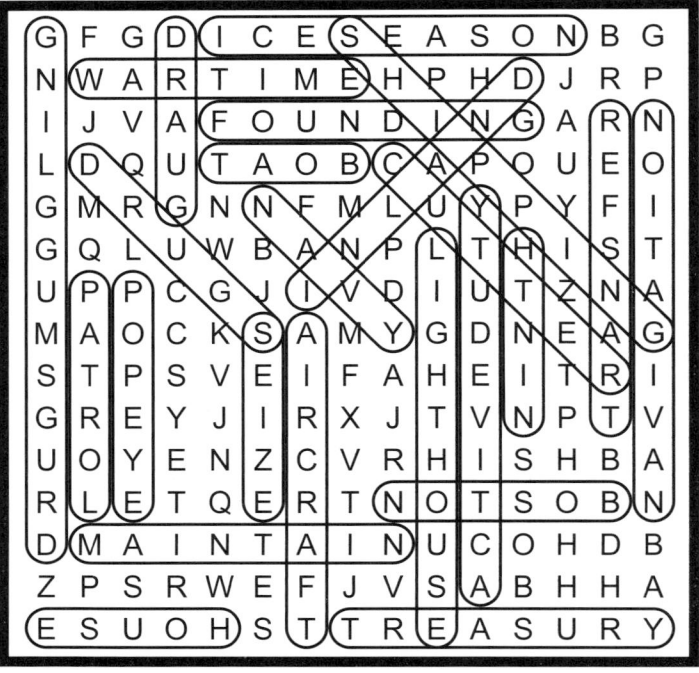

209

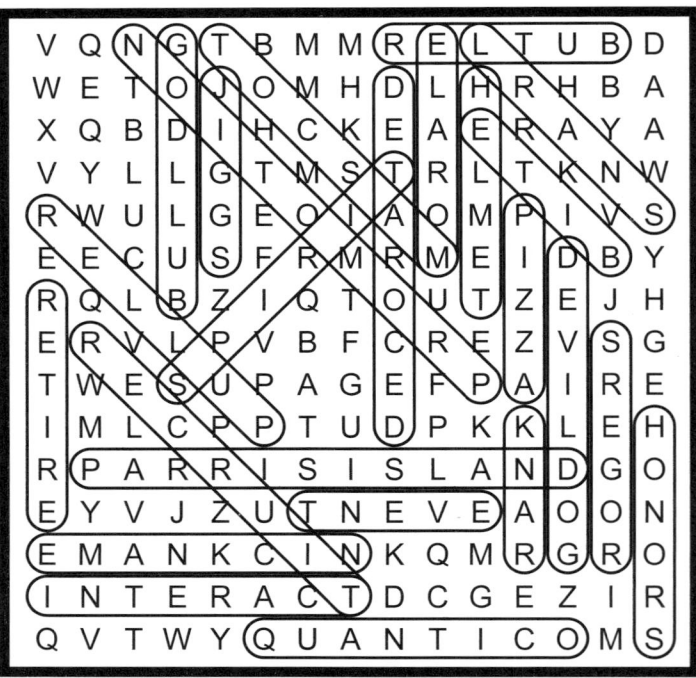

SOLUTIONS

211

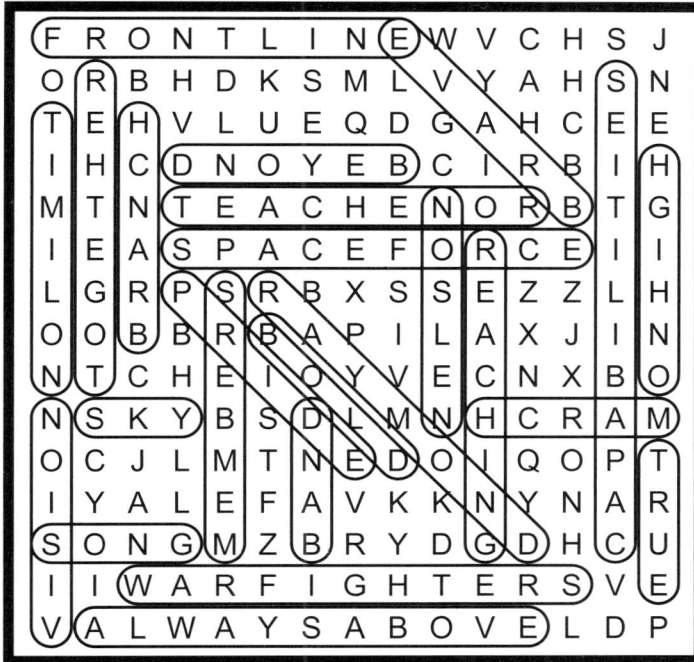

213

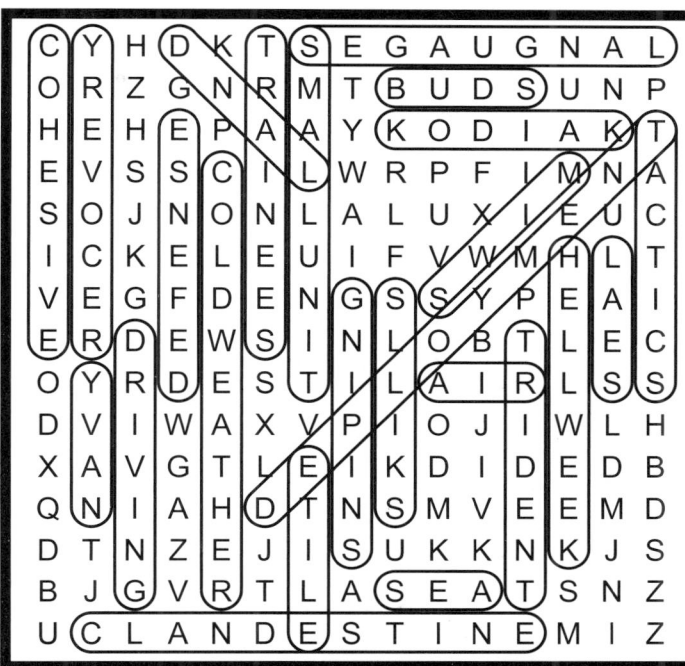

215

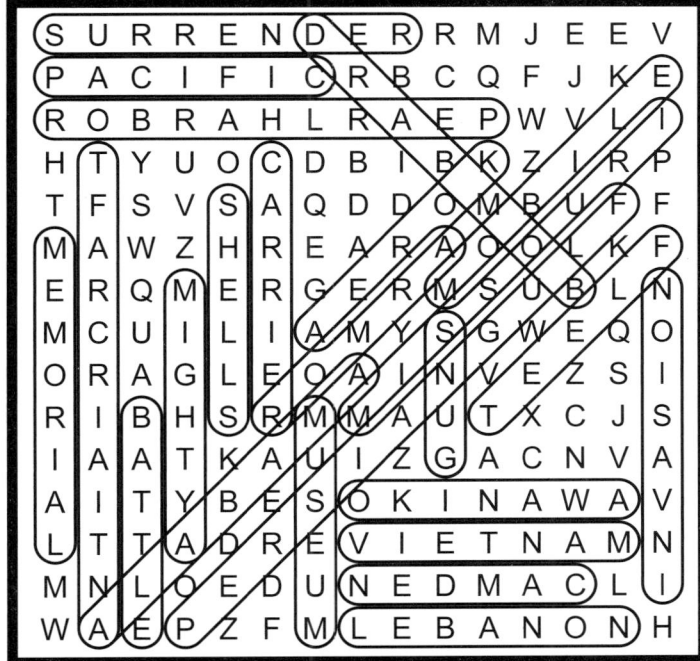

217

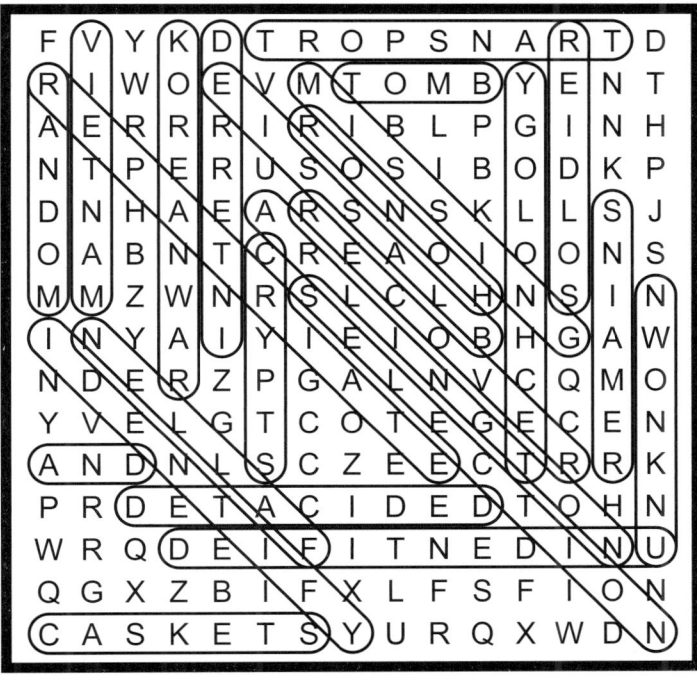

SOLUTIONS

219

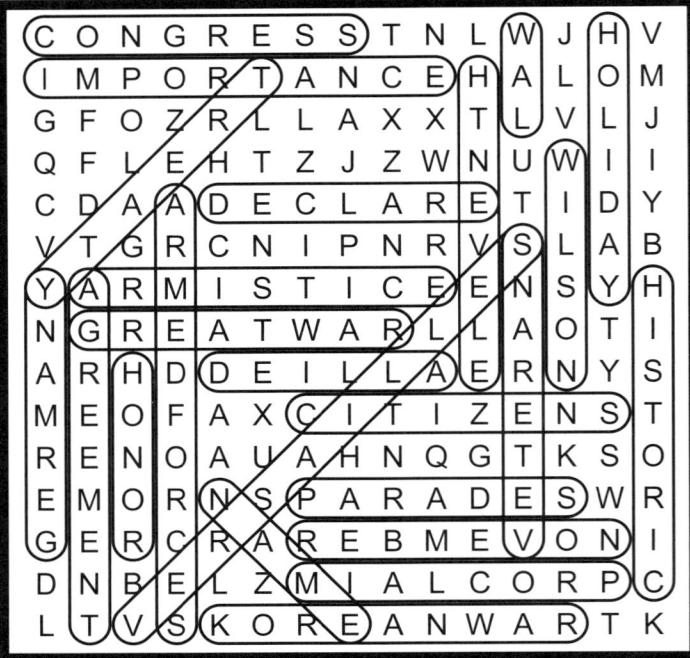

221